MW01125600

ALWAYS WITH US?

PROPHETIC CHRISTIANITY

Series Editors

Bruce Ellis Benson
Malinda Elizabeth Berry
Peter Goodwin Heltzel

The PROPHETIC CHRISTIANITY series explores the complex relationship between Christian doctrine and contemporary life. Deeply rooted in the Christian tradition yet taking postmodern and postcolonial perspectives seriously, series authors navigate difference and dialogue constructively about divisive and urgent issues of the early twenty-first century. The books in the series are sensitive to historical contexts, marked by philosophical precision, and relevant to contemporary problems. Embracing shalom justice, series authors seek to bear witness to God's gracious activity of building beloved community.

PUBLISHED

Bruce Ellis Benson, Malinda Elizabeth Berry, and Peter Goodwin Heltzel, eds., *Prophetic Evangelicals: Envisioning a Just and Peaceable Kingdom* (2012)

Jennifer Harvey, *Dear White Christians: For Those Still Longing for Racial Reconciliation* (2014)

Peter Goodwin Heltzel, *Resurrection City: A Theology of Improvisation* (2012)

Johnny Bernard Hill, *Prophetic Rage: A Postcolonial Theology of Liberation* (2013)

Liz Theoharis, *Always with Us? What Jesus Really Said about the Poor* (2017)

Randy S. Woodley, *Shalom and the Community of Creation: An Indigenous Vision* (2012)

Always with Us?

*What Jesus Really Said
about the Poor*

Liz Theoharis

WILLIAM B. EERDMANS PUBLISHING COMPANY
GRAND RAPIDS, MICHIGAN

Wm. B. Eerdmans Publishing Co.
2140 Oak Industrial Drive N.E., Grand Rapids, Michigan 49505
www.eerdmans.com

© 2017 Liz Theoharis
All rights reserved
Published 2017
Printed in the United States of America

26 25 24 23 22   9 10 11 12

ISBN 978-0-8028-7502-0

Library of Congress Cataloging-in-Publication Data

Names: Theoharis, Liz, author.
Title: Always with us? : what Jesus really said about the poor / Liz
   Theoharis.
Description: Grand Rapids : Eerdmans Publishing Co., 2017. | Series:
   Prophetic Christianity | Includes bibliographical references and index.
Identifiers: LCCN 2016059245 | ISBN 9780802875020 (pbk. : alk. paper)
Subjects: LCSH: Poverty—Religious aspects—Christianity. | Church work with
   the poor.
Classification: LCC BV4647.P6 T44 2017 | DDC 261.8/325—dc23
   LC record available at https://lccn.loc.gov/2016059245

All biblical translations follow the New International Version unless otherwise noted.

To the millions of God's children, those known and unknown, who are buried in potter's fields, to those on whose shoulders we stand, and to those who refuse to rest until all poverty is ended for everyone.

Contents

Foreword

This past year Dr. Theoharis and I traveled to twenty-two states on a Moral Revival Tour, alongside Sister Simone Campbell from Nuns on the Bus, the Rev. Dr. Traci Blackmon from Ferguson, Missouri, and the Rev. Dr. James Forbes, pastor emeritus of Riverside Church in New York. We connected with clergy and impacted people who have been denied Medicaid, lack adequate education, earn too little and work too much, and struggle for their and their family's survival on a daily basis. We met some of the over 15 million children who live in poverty[1] and 64 million people who are living at less than a living wage, including 54% of African Americans.[2] On the tour, we talked about a study that came out in 2011 from the Mailman School for Public Health at Columbia University, which said that 250,000 people die each year from poverty-related causes.[3] And we preached too often about the church's deafening silence on poverty.

Poverty is a scandal, says Pope Francis, in a world of so much wealth. I come from an area of the United States where the scandal is not a reality show but reality itself. I'm from the South—North Carolina, to be exact. This is a part of the country some call the "Bible Belt." Specifically, I'm

1. Yang Jiang, Mercedes Ekono, Curtis Skinner, "Basic Facts about Low-Income Children under 18 Years, 2014," National Center for Children in Poverty, February, 2016, http://www.nccp.org/publications/pub_1145.html.

2. Irene Tung, Yannet Lathrop, and Paul Sonn, "The Growing Movement for $15," National Employment Law Project, November, 2015, http://www.nelp.org/content/uploads/Growing-Movement-for-15-Dollars.pdf.

3. Sandro Galea, Melissa Tracy, Katherine J. Hoggatt, Charles DiMaggio, and Adam Karpati, "Estimated Deaths Attributable to Social Factors in the United States," *American Journal of Public Health* 101.8 (August 2011): 1456-65.

from the first congressional district, one of the poorest districts in the country, that is also the home to the "Black Belt," an area of the American South that has rich black soil ideal for growing cotton and has become known for the large concentration of African Americans living in the area. This district includes the largest number of counties in North Carolina in which the population is more than half African American. Here, poor blacks and whites live together, but very few think biblically and theologically together.

In my state alone, more than 1.9 million people are poor, including 700,000 children. One out of five North Carolinians live below the poverty line. North Carolina is one of the 12 poorest states in the country; 10 of which are in the south. Politico says 95 of the 100 poorest districts are in so-called red political states, where the politicians most averse to policies that flow out of the war on poverty are routinely elected into office. These same areas claim great allegiance to Christianity. So here is the question: What theology is being preached in these highly religious sections of the country that allows persons to claim such loyalty to the gospel of Christ but then elect persons so averse to policies that would help the poor? As a preacher, I believe we must ask this question, holding the Bible and cross in one hand and the newspaper and history book in the other.

It is within the complicated framework of this question that I think Dr. Theoharis's book and willingness to give attention to the subject of poverty is so important and relevant. In 2016, we saw an election where more than 80% of so-called white evangelicals (though I have deep theological problems with the phrase "white evangelicals") voted for a presidential candidate super-billionaire who openly attacked immigrants and said the minimum wage was too high (even though economists note the minimum wage would be $22 an hour rather than $7.25 if it had kept pace with inflation). He was their choice for a president who would be a champion for the destitute and working poor.

This represents to many a strange theology and confusing political ethic, which is why Dr. Theoharis's book is so needed now. In my travels with Dr. Theoharis across the country, she has taught that there is a biblical mandate to end poverty. But it seems that some believe in a twofold commandment. First, "the poor you will always have with you" is a static reality sanctioned by God. The second is like unto the first—if you want to help the poor a little bit, empower the rich.

Dr. Theoharis focuses this book on Jesus's statement that "the poor you will always have with you" (Matt 26:11). I want to examine briefly another key biblical text on poverty. In his first sermon in Luke 4, Jesus said,

> The Spirit of the Lord is on me, because he has anointed me to proclaim good news to the poor. He has sent me to proclaim freedom for the prisoners and recovery of sight for the blind, to set the oppressed free, to proclaim the year of the Lord's favor. (Luke 4:18-19)

This statement, from the beginning of Jesus's ministry, places the poor at center stage. Jesus quotes from the Old Testament prophets (here Isaiah), who centuries before rose to the forefront of the spiritual life as they spoke out against injustice in ancient Israel. Luke identifies Jesus as God's anointed one whose vocation it is to engage in the work of liberation of the poor, blind, captive, and oppressed.

The Greek word for "poor" in Luke 4:18 is *ptochos*, the same word that appears in Matt 26:11. The poor are all those who have to endure acts of violence and acts of injustice without being able to defend themselves. In light of this meaning, Jesus's inaugural message in Luke's Gospel is a major affront to Roman society. Philip Esler comments helpfully, "In light of the stratification which characterized Hellenistic society, how extraordinary it must have sounded to an audience in a Greco-Roman city for the Lucan Jesus to begin his public ministry by specifying beggars and a number of other groups at the very bottom of the social register as the primary recipients of the gospel. Such a perspective entailed a radical upheaval in the prevailing realities."[4]

The church cannot be seduced into considering people like the world considers people. Salvation in Luke 4:18 is God's initiative to bring wholeness back into the created order. It is meant to save humanity from its inhumanity. God desires to save us from anything that oppresses us—including economic injustice and anything that works against the solidarity of the human community. The contemporary church has become so accommodative to capitalism that its theology is often viewed as a justification of economic injustice. Dr. Theoharis's work stands as a challenge to such theology and asserts that poverty is an affront to God. The church must be a prophetic witness and actor in the world.

---

4. Philip Esler, *Community and Gospel in Luke-Acts: The Social and Political Motivation of Lucan Theology*, Society for New Testament Studies Monograph 57 (Cambridge: Cambridge University Press, 1987), 173.

The atmosphere in which Jesus was born and lived was one of oppression caused by the rule of Rome. It was not a social situation Jesus
could ignore and still give meaning to life. There was a demand upon Jesus
to respond to the political, social, and economic issues of his day. In *Jesus
and the Disinherited*, Howard Thurman declares, "This is the position of the
disinherited in every age. What must be the attitude toward the rulers, the
controllers of political, social, and economic life?"[5] Indeed, Dr. Theoharis
grounds her book in the lived reality of the poor of both the Roman Empire
and our times and asserts that you cannot preach good news apart from
the work of doing justice.

Jim Wallis notes that the anointing of the Holy Spirit is the impetus
for a "prophetic spirituality."[6] One purpose of the power of the Holy Spirit
is to produce a new prophetic vision and renewal under which the church
can point to a new way of community. The Spirit challenges the church to
ask, "Who are poor in our midst?" "What are the conditions that create
these realities?" "What are we doing?" This is the call of the Spirit that fuels
Dr. Theoharis's work. The ministry of the church is incomplete unless we
develop a mature awareness of what Christ, through the Spirit, calls us to
do in his name among the least of these. And we must declare that if we
change our ways and follow the ways of God, we can defeat poverty. We
will not always have the poor with us.

WILLIAM J. BARBER II
President, North Carolina NAACP
Architect, Forward Together/Moral Mondays
President and Senior Lecturer, Repairers of the Breach
Senior Pastor, Greenleaf Christian Church

5. Howard Thurman, *Jesus and the Disinherited* (Boston: Beacon, 1996), 120.
6. Jim Wallis, *The Soul of Politics: Beyond "Religious Right" and "Secular Left"* (San
Diego: Harcourt Brace, 1995), 40.

Preface

And what does the Lord require of you? To act justly and to love mercy and to walk humbly with your God.

—Micah 6:8

It seems that since I was a child, I have heard every week or so that "the poor you will always have with you" (Matt 26:11 NIV; parallels in Mark 14:7; John 12:8) means that poverty is inevitable, that it can never be ended, and that my work and vision for ending poverty is futile. I have known in my heart that this inevitability-of-poverty argument is incorrect. It took me many years as a scholar to understand just why and how it is incorrect—which is much of the focus of this book.

The issue of poverty has been my focus for my entire adult life. I have spent days, weeks, months, years, and now decades organizing alongside poor people who are building a social movement to end poverty in the United States and across the globe. I was raised to understand that faith must be linked to practicing social justice. I started teaching Sunday school at age 13, helped plan "Beyond Racism" Day Camp at 14, and began visiting shut-ins as a deacon at 16. When I was 18, I moved from my hometown of Milwaukee, Wisconsin, to Philadelphia to attend college. The following summer, I began visiting Tent City, an encampment of homeless families set up by the Kensington Welfare Rights Union, trying to survive one of Philadelphia's hottest summers. It was there that I was propelled into theology and deeper biblical studies.

Beginning in 2002, I helped found the Poverty Initiative at Union Theological Seminary to raise up generations of religious and community leaders dedicated to building a social movement to end poverty, and I have served as its coordinator since then. I am also the codirector of the Kairos Center for Religions, Rights, and Social Justice, launched in 2013, which now houses the Poverty Initiative. The genealogy of the Poverty Initiative and Kairos Center can be traced back through decades of poor people working to organize themselves across racial and other dividing lines into a broad social movement,[1] including the Kensington Welfare Rights Union, the National Union of the Homeless, the National Welfare Rights Organization, Martin Luther King Jr.'s Poor People's Campaign, and the Southern Tenant Farmers' Union. We have exchanged lessons with social movements of the poor globally, including the Landless Workers' Movement of Brazil, the Assembly of the Poor in Thailand, the Indian Farmers' Movement, and the South African Shackdwellers' Movement. Through three national poverty truth commissions; two leadership schools; twelve poverty immersion courses; thirteen faculty-sponsored, semester-long courses; sixteen one-day seminars; six books and numerous religious and theological resources; twelve strategic dialogues; six intensive study programs; and numerous events, symposia, and exchanges with global grassroots and religious leaders, we have established a wide and deep network of community and religious leaders spanning over thirty states and seventeen countries.

Along with my scholarly and political work, I am an ordained minister in the Presbyterian Church (USA) with the Poverty Initiative/Kairos Center as my validated ministry. I administer the sacraments, preach and teach the gospel, and comfort and prod members of our growing network

1. Much of this genealogy and the lessons and influences from this work are documented in a series of articles written by leaders of the Kensington Welfare Rights Union and Poor People's Economic Human Rights Campaign, including Willie Baptist and Noelle Damico, "Building the New Freedom Church of the Poor," *Cross Currents* 55 (2005): 352–63; Willie (William) Baptist and Mary Bricker Jenkins, "The Movement to End Poverty in the United States," in *Economic Rights in Canada and the United States*, ed. Rhoda E. Howard-Hassmann and Claude E. Welch Jr. (Philadelphia: University of Pennsylvania Press, 2006), 103–20; Willie (William) Baptist, Mary Bricker-Jenkins, and Monica Dillon, "Taking the Struggle on the Road: The New Freedom Bus—Freedom from Unemployment, Hunger and Homelessness," *Journal of Progressive Human Services* 10, no. 2 (1999): 7–29; Willie Baptist and Cheri Honkala, "A New and Unsettling Force," *The Other Side Magazine* (Winter 2003): 38–39; David Wagner, *What's Love Got to Do with It? A Critical Look at American Charity* (New York: New Press, 2000); Guida West, *The National Welfare Rights Movement: The Social Protest of Poor Women* (Westport, CT: Praeger, 1981); David Zucchino, *Myth of the Welfare Queen* (New York: Scribner, 1997).

of leaders who are building this new social movement for these times. I am also the mother of two children, raising them within this growing social movement of the poor and our liberationist interpretations of the Bible and religious tradition. This book is dedicated to the unsung saints in our growing movement to end poverty and to all of God's children, including my beautiful Sophia and Luke, who deserve to thrive, not just barely survive.

My work is guided by the desire to understand and share poor people's biblical and theological interpretations, and to shine light on models of organized poor people partnering with religious communities to abolish poverty. I believe that the Bible provides guidance on how Christians should live their lives; the New Testament documents a movement of poor people who gathered around the person and teachings of Jesus to right the wrongs of their day. In this book, I seek to document the stories, lessons, and biblical interpretations of poor people today building a similar movement. I do so to add my particular energy to these efforts, to illuminate implications for our churches, and to chart the development of a liberation theology for the United States in the twenty-first century.

Ever since encountering the Kensington Welfare Rights Union and National Union of the Homeless in my first year of college, I have tried to define Micah 6:8 in my own life. Justice is the poor leading a movement to end poverty once and for all. Mercy is moving beyond charity to taking action and sharing fellowship alongside poor people in order to bring about shalom-justice and lasting social transformation. Discipleship is speaking and praying to God through the collective actions and reflections of the poor and oppressed of our society, rather than only through an individual relationship with Jesus Christ. These ideas are my compass and it is as both a committed activist in this movement and a trained interpreter of biblical texts that I offer this book.

My current movement project is the revival of Martin Luther King Jr.'s Poor People's Campaign (poorpeoplescampaign.org). On December 4th, 1967, Rev. King gave one of his last major speeches. In it he called for poor people of every race to unite in order to end what he called "the three evils of society"—poverty, racism, and militarism. Just months later, he was assassinated and his vision for the Poor People's Campaign was never fully realized. On the upcoming occasion of the fiftieth anniversary of that speech, we will revive and relaunch that campaign. We expect to struggle for many years to achieve the vision—and we invite you to join us.

*   *   *

In this book I seek to rethink the role of the church in the world and to challenge some of the most widely held misinterpretations of the Bible and poor people. I assert that the poor constitute some of the least-recognized theologians in the twenty-first century. Using many of the sources that theologians of the past have used to develop their theology, including Christian tradition and the Bible, many of these grassroots organizations led by the poor have developed theology based on a direct, collective relationship with God, their experience as poor people, and—most importantly—their conscious and collective actions to secure housing, health care, and food for all. Just like theologians of the past, these Poverty Scholars grapple with issues of sin and salvation, asserting that "poverty is a sin; being poor isn't." The individuals and families building this movement know that poverty is not an individual problem but a systemic problem—a systemic sin. We know and proclaim that God loves all people, and salvation, therefore, is for everyone. We assert that God hates poverty and wills it upon no one. We understand that it is not enough to affirm that God loves the poor, but it is the collective responsibility of Christians and all people of faith and conscience to eliminate poverty. What is "good news for the poor" if it is not ending the poverty and suffering in this life? What do we mean when we pray, "on earth as it is in heaven"?

In the introduction I describe the homeless takeover of St. Edward's Church in Philadelphia in 1995, using this episode as an entrée to the discussion of poverty in general and an opening to a new interpretation of "the poor you will always have with you."

The rest of this book will return us to the biblical text itself, to the lived reality of the poor during Jesus's time and during contemporary times, to show how Matt 26:11 is taken out of context, distorted, and cynically politicized to justify theories about the inevitability of poverty and to provide religious sanction for the dispossession of the majority for the benefit of the few. It will explore what Jim Wallis calls "the most famous biblical text on the poor" by offering a different interpretation of "the poor you will always have with you" and by suggesting that there is a moral imperative to work to end poverty. In Chapter 1, I discuss various popular and academic treatments of the biblical response to poverty, centered on Jesus's statement that "the poor you will always have with you."

Chapter 2 begins with a contextual Bible study in which leaders of poor people's organizations (re)examine the passage surrounding "the poor you will always have with you" as it appears in Matt 26:6–13 (and Mark 14:3–9; John 12:1–10). The chapter continues by offering tools and practices that will enable Christians to lead and participate in contextual Bible studies and to practice the method of "Reading the Bible with the Poor" in their own settings. Techniques described in this chapter include drawing parallels between biblical stories and contemporary stories of poor people surviving and organizing; engaging in historical and contemporary storytelling and biblical and ethical reimagination; and investigating important social issues, both contemporary and historical, such as taxation, debt, infrastructure and development, charity and patronage, and wealth and political power. By gathering and analyzing the perspectives of grassroots antipoverty organizers and leaders who are working to build a social movement to end poverty, led by the poor, this book offers these interpretations as theologically revealing and politically legitimate.

Chapter 3 establishes that the phrase "the poor you will always have with you" and the larger story of the anointing at Bethany actually mean the opposite of their traditional interpretations. The chapter begins by looking at some of the prophetic commandments and teachings from Hebrew Scriptures that state that the existence of poverty is against the will of God. In particular, this chapter demonstrates that "the poor you will always have with you" in Matt 26:11 echoes Deut 15:4–11, one of the most liberating "Jubilee" passages in the Old Testament, which comes from the second giving of God's law to the people and states that there will be no needy people if the children of God follow the commandments that God has given them. In Chapter 3 I argue that, through this reference to Deuteronomy 15, Jesus is demonstrating that poverty need not exist and, therefore, that the poor will not need loans or charity if people follow God's laws and commandments, especially by putting into practice the "sabbatical year" and "Jubilee." Jesus is criticizing the disciples with this echo of Deut 15:11, which establishes that poverty is the result of society's disobedience to God and of following the laws and commandments of empire instead.

Chapter 4 presents the social, economic, and political position of Jesus as being poor and shows that his disciples were also poor. It argues that Jesus's statement "the poor you will always have with you, but you will not always have me" is not about pitting the poor against Jesus or even about pitting the poor Jesus against other poor individuals. Instead, Jesus suggests that the significance of his role and that of the disciples is in its contribution to the ending of poverty through the epistemological, political, and moral agency and leadership of the poor. The chapter posits that the poor are a stand-in for Jesus (as he established in Matt 25:31–46, the Last Judgment): the foundation of the movement to materialize God's reign on earth is not the rich, not the usual philanthropists or "change-makers," but the poor. God is not only aligned with the poor but is, in fact, present in (and of) the poor.

Chapter 5 examines Jesus's response to the disciples' critique of the woman who anoints Jesus and their proposal to sell the ointment and give the proceeds to the poor. It shows how Jesus's response is actually a condemnation of charity, philanthropy, buying and selling, and the larger economic system. Exploring translation and other details related to the biblical passage—beginning with the fact that Bethany means the "house of the poor" in Hebrew—I argue that Jesus is suggesting that if the disciples and other concerned people continue to offer charity-based solutions, Band-Aid help, and superficial solace instead of social transformation with the poor at the helm, poverty will not cease (in disregard of and disobedience to God). I offer a four-pronged critique of charity from the Scriptures and Jesus's teachings found in Matthew 26: ideological (challenging the belief that charity demonstrated how much the rich cared about the poor), political (showing how patronage actually helped the wealthy to gain a political base and a following), spiritual/moral (exploring how charity and patronage are directly tied to state religion, the imperial cult, and religious expressions that actually justify inequality), and material (explaining how charity, benefaction, and patronage made more money for the wealthy and at the same time did not meet the needs of the poor). Chapter 5 includes attention to the story that directly follows Matthew 26, where the blood money that Judas receives from the chief priests for turning over Jesus ends up creating a potter's field that does not resolve poverty but instead establishes a burial plot where the poor are buried in mass graves with no dignity or liberation.

Chapter 6 argues that Jesus is anointed and made "Christ" only in the anointing at Bethany. This establishes Jesus as playing three main roles: teacher, leader of a popular social movement, and popularly acclaimed ruler/messiah. This profile of Jesus has implications for interpreting both this story and the Bible as a whole, suggesting that Jesus's role as the messiah must be linked to his actions as a social and political leader who promotes economic rights and dignity and calls on his followers and society at large to proclaim good news and jubilee to the poor in the here and now. Chapter 6 also posits that when Jesus says, "Truly I tell you, wherever this gospel is preached throughout the world, what she has done will also be told, in memory of her" (Matt 26:13), he is proposing a communion that is about material conditions, eradicating hunger, and charging more leaders to take part in bringing heaven to earth.

The conclusion returns to the experiences and theological lessons that emerge from the struggles of the poor in the United States. It describes and develops "Reading the Bible with the Poor," a biblical hermeneutic that argues that the poor are epistemological, political, and moral agents of change in our society, and therefore, when the organized poor appropriate the Bible, new historiographies and interpretations are brought into clear view. It asserts that the Bible is a living document that offers inspiration and parallels to the realities and visions of poor people today. The conclusion looks at contemporary ideas of discipleship, faithfulness, sin, and salvation, reframing them as important concepts in Christian efforts to end poverty and transform society to benefit all.

Acknowledgments

I want to thank the many people who have contributed to this book over the past ten years and to the work on which this book stands. Thank you to all the Poverty Scholars who have dedicated their time and talents to not just improving their lives but ending poverty for all. These leaders from Flint, Michigan, Plaquemine Parish, Louisiana, Baltimore, Maryland, Goldsboro, North Carolina, Aberdeen, Washington, El Paso, Texas, Elkhart, Indiana, and so many other towns and cities across the country are the real heroes and heroines of this nation; they embody what Rev. Dr. Martin Luther King Jr. called "a new and unsettling force in our complacent national life" and they are transforming society around the needs of the least of these who are most of us, as they learn and lead, walk and talk, educate and organize. Thank you to the teachers in the streets and classrooms who have insisted that poverty defiles our world and defies our God. Thanks especially to the leaders and participants in Kairos Center/Poverty Initiative activities, including Poverty Scholars Leadership Schools, "Reading the Bible with the Poor," "The Gospel of Matthew," and "The Gospel of Paul: Poverty and Spirituality" semester-long classes, immersion courses, Poverty Scholars Strategic Dialogues, Roman Empire and New Testament Convenings, Moral Revivals, Poor People's Campaign Planning meetings, and the many other undertakings referenced throughout that greatly contributed to this book.

Thank you to my dissertation advisor, Brigitte Kahl, and the rest of my dissertation committee: Hal Taussig, Aliou Niang, and Richard Horsley. And thank you to the administration of Union Theological Seminary for supporting my work and the work of the Kairos Center/Poverty Initiative since our founding in 2003. Thank you to Rev. Barber for writing the foreword to this book and for reminding our nation that we need moral defibrillators to revive the heart of our democracy. Thank you to the Prophetic Christianity Series editors, Peter Heltzel, Malinda Berry, and Bruce Benson, as well as to Bill Eerdmans, who helped bring the series to fruition on the publisher's side, and to my editors at Eerdmans, Beverly McCoy and Andrew Knapp. I deeply appreciate all the people who edited various drafts of this book and the dissertation on which it is based over the years, including Willie Baptist, Adam Barnes, Chris Caruso, Larry Cox, Shailly Gupta Barnes, Dan Jones, Charon Hribar, Emily McNeil, Amy Miller, Thia Reggio, Aaron Scott, Joe Strife, Jeanne Theoharis, Colleen Wessel-McCoy, John Wessel-McCoy, and Atticus Zavaletta. Thanks to everyone, especially my sister, Jeanne, for combing through this book and the dissertation before it, helping me to find my voice as a biblical scholar and social theorist as well as activist. Many thanks to Colleen Wessel-McCoy, Amy Miller, and Chris Caruso, who stepped in at the last minute to read and reread drafts as the book was going to print.

I thank my family and community of friends who labor for justice beside me and who have supported me, prodded me to achieve more, and watched my kids so I could work (on this book and building a movement to end poverty) including my parents, Athan and Nancy Theoharis; my siblings, Jeanne and George Theoharis; my niece and nephew, Ella and Sam Theoharis; my in-laws, George, Joanne, and Greg Caruso; our band of Kairos Center kids, Indi, Jack, and Michael Barnes, Skye and JJ Bingham, Esperanza Carmín Cardinale Hernandez, Hardy and Eirene Eville, Carolina Lugo-Feliz, Josiah Maskell, Elijah and Jude Plummer Polson, Sophia and Luke Theoharis Caruso, Kenji Vasquez, and Myles and Josephine Wessel-McCoy; and my friends and colleagues in this work of doing justice, loving kindness, and walking humbly with God—especially those who have passed on their responsibilities to the rest of us and now rest in power: General Baker, Ron Casanova, Veronica Dorsey, Larry Gibson, Dottie Stevens, Kathleen Sullivan, and so many others.

I particularly appreciate the love, support, and mentorship I have received from Willie Baptist over the past two decades, who embodies what it is to be a Poverty Scholar. I am deeply honored to codirect the Kairos Center with Larry Cox, who supports me and the rest of us to keep up with Rev. Dr. King and to reignite a new Poor People's Campaign. I cannot thank Chris Caruso, my partner in struggle and life, enough; his clarity on what is wrong in our society, commitment and faith that another world is possible, competency in absolutely everything, and connection and deep love for humanity inspires me (and our whole network). Thanks, Chris, for everything, especially for raising such amazing kids! I want to include a special acknowledgment of our children, Sophia and Luke, who have taught me about justice, grace, mercy, and why ending poverty is so urgent and necessary.

*   *   *

Portions of the Introduction, Chapter 1, and Chapter 6 reuse material from my "Reading the Bible with the Poor," with Willie Baptist, in *Reading the Bible in an Age of Crisis: Political Exegesis for a New Day*, ed. Bruce Worthington (Minneapolis: Fortress, 2014), 21-52. Used with permission.

Introduction

Why do we worship a homeless man on Sunday
and ignore one on Monday?

In the winter of 1995, I was working with a group of homeless families with the Kensington Welfare Rights Union (KWRU) who broke the locks and moved into St. Edward's Catholic Church at 8th and York Streets in North Philadelphia. The church had been closed that year because its members were poor and the expansive, beautiful, old building was expensive to heat. We broke the locks, moved in, and posted passages from the Bible on the walls, including Matthew 25, Luke 4, and Acts 4. We hung posters asking, "Why do we worship a homeless man on Sunday and ignore one on Monday?" When asked by nine Catholic priests from the archdiocese to leave, we refused, stating, "We talked to God, and God doesn't want any more homeless families. All are welcome to stay in God's house." And when we were threatened with eviction, we urged supporters to come witness with us at the church, declaring, "Jesus is being evicted from a church in North Philadelphia!"

Black, white, and Latino families arranged the pews for their living and sleeping quarters. Confessionals became closets. The altar held basic necessities for the residents. The youngest resident was 4 months old, the oldest in his 90s. While it was about 40 homeless men, women, and children who moved into St. Edward's Church, those numbers doubled and tripled in the ensuing weeks. Neighbors from nearby blocks and distant suburbs showed up with donations of food, clothing, toys, and space heaters. From the sanctuary of St. Edward's each day, children left to attend

1

school, many adults went to work, and others continued to organize in the community. Every Sunday we held interfaith prayer services. Although the majority of the people living in St. Ed's were Christian, the church takeover also had Muslim, Jewish, Hindu, Buddhist, and other residents and supporters.

The church takeover was an embodiment of what Rev. Dr. Martin Luther King Jr. called a "Freedom Church of the Poor"—a place of sanctuary and community for the poor as well as a base of operations for a budding movement to end poverty, led by the poor. It was a proactive response to the failure of organized religion to take poverty seriously either theologically or practically. Indeed, the church was one of nine that the Archdiocese of Philadelphia had closed in poor neighborhoods that year, and former parishioners still prayed outside the closed church each week. When KWRU entered the church, these parishioners entered with them. The takeover sparked a debate in the city of Philadelphia over the religious response to poverty. Some nuns who allied themselves with the church takeover started a newsletter raising these important moral issues of poverty and the abandonment of the church. They titled it "The Substandard," riffing off the name of the official publication of the diocese, called "The Standard." As a result of the St. Edward's Church takeover and the response it elicited, the Catholic archdiocese moved its offices from downtown to a poor area in North Philadelphia, and new evangelical Christian, mainline Christian, and interfaith groups began to partner with poor people to end poverty.

The Community of Goods[1]

Many of the people who moved into St. Edward's had been living at Tent City, where over forty homeless families inhabited tents, shacks, and cardboard boxes the previous summer. Tent City was located at 4th Street and Lehigh Avenue on an abandoned lot where the Quaker Lace Factory used to stand. Tent City was also a KWRU project—a temporary encampment about the size of a football field with over thirty tents, shacks, and other makeshift structures where the poor lived together in community. There was a central meeting area that we called "the Living Room." We gathered

1. The term used to describe the communal living arrangements in the early Christian communities as discussed in Act 2 and Acts 4.

in the Living Room to meet, socialize, and worship together. Common meals were prepared in a temporary kitchen with charcoal grills. Fire hydrants became the showers. Local businesses allowed the residents to use their bathrooms.

Tent City became a community and church much like the first Christian communities. There, homeless families of various races lived together, sharing donated toys, clothing, food, and toiletries. One disabled veteran was dropped off at the lot by an ambulance from the VA hospital because he had nowhere else to call home. A sixteen-month-old boy took his first steps among the rocks, rubble, and garbage left when the Quaker Lace Factory burned. Just as in Deut 15:4 and Acts 4:34, there was no needy person there. When families were evicted and moved to Tent City, they would present their food stamps to the community. When someone needed to go to an appointment, families would volunteer to do childcare and pool their money to pay for bus fare. When it was hot, people in the surrounding neighborhood would drop off water, juice, and sometimes popsicles for the kids.

Government and religious institutions were largely skeptical. They said (and continue to say) that there is not enough to go around. They told us, "the poor you will always have with you." But in the United States, we throw away 46 million tons of food each year when it only takes 4 million tons to feed everyone. Policy makers say that we cannot end homelessness, but there are more than 12 million *empty* luxury housing units in the country—more than the estimated 10 million homeless people. In fact, in Philadelphia in the mid-1990s when Tent City and the St. Edward's Church takeover were happening, there were 39,000 abandoned houses in the city and only about 27,000 homeless people. But families moved to Tent City because the homeless shelters were closed, affordable housing programs were cut, and the City of Philadelphia was saying that there was simply too much need.

A miracle took place at Tent City—a miracle, that is, if we believe that feeding everyone is impossible without a miracle. Perhaps it was the sharing of what the families brought with them; perhaps it was the donations from those who had more than enough—including local religious congregations—in the surrounding city and suburbs; and perhaps it was God's work of creating something out of nothing. While the families who moved there had very little, somehow food and other necessities were abundant at Tent City and during the St. Ed's takeover. In fact, not only was everyone fed (and housed, for that matter)—there were often too many donated clothes, too much food, and plenty of all the basic necessities.

KWRU began distributing the extra food, clothing, and toys to the surrounding neighborhood. Families went out each day with secondhand baby strollers full of donations and distributed them because people in the neighborhood were also poor. Not only were we able to feed the KWRU families who were living at Tent City and the church, but hundreds of families in the poorest neighborhood in Philadelphia were fed with the surplus. As the months went on, many religious congregations came to witness, pray, worship, help out, and share what they had. People heard the good news that there was a place where everyone was fed—and more poor families came, and more church people came, and they came, and they came. All were amazed at the abundance.

The move from Tent City to the church was planned very quickly when the weather turned cold and the rats started to move in. Our decision was informed by a study of history as well as an analysis of the current crisis of poverty and the neighborhood. Indeed, the St. Ed's takeover was part of a project that KWRU called "the New Underground Railroad." The homeless families living at Tent City got together to strategize—reaching back into history to inform our next steps. Together we learned and remembered that slaves had had to break the law in order to escape from slavery and survive—and we affirmed that a similar nonviolent civil disobedience survival movement was necessary today in the midst of growing poverty, homelessness, and misery. We thought about Harriet "Moses" Tubman who led her people out of slavery, being inspired by her own experience, the cries of the people, and her belief in a God of freedom and justice. We decided that as poor leaders, we had the responsibility to follow in the footsteps of Harriet Tubman and other abolitionists. We set the abolition of poverty as our goal and north star.

"Jesus Was Homeless"

By hanging a sign that read "Why do we worship a homeless man on Sundays and ignore one on Mondays?" homeless members of the KWRU made a bold statement that Jesus was a poor and oppressed person. They asserted that Christianity had to go beyond "pie in the sky when you die" and be relevant to the material reality of poverty and want of so many of God's children. The identification with Jesus as poor went farther than simply the social and economic context of Galilee in Jesus's day. These homeless families demonstrated that Christianity, the Jesus movement, was a social, political, economic, and spiritual movement led by the poor to transform all of society.

Many people (including some visitors to St. Edward's Church) deny that Jesus was homeless, choosing to ignore his economic situation and painting him as an educated, almost-middle-class, white man. Others explain his poverty and homelessness by asserting that he was a Cynic philosopher and an itinerant preacher—that Jesus chose a "homeless lifestyle." They assert that Jesus wasn't homeless like today's homeless—setting up a dichotomy of the deserving poor versus the undeserving poor or voluntary homelessness versus pathological homelessness. But in Matthew and Luke, Jesus's parents do not have sufficient stature or resources to find a place to stay for his birth. Through all the New Testament, including the Sermon on the Mount and the teachings of the parables in the Gospels, the community of goods in Acts, the collection for the poor of Jerusalem in Paul's letters, the denunciation of rich oppressors in the Pastoral Epistles, and the dire situation of exploitation and conquest in Revelation, Jesus and the Jesus movement center the poor and disenfranchised. The social base of the Jesus movement is the poor and dispossessed and the program that Jesus brings to Galilee and across the Roman Empire is about forgiving debts, releasing slaves and prisoners, and bringing good news to the poor.

Luke 9:58 reads, "Foxes have dens and birds have nests, but the Son of Man has no place to lay his head." In this passage we learn that animals all have homes but Jesus has none. It suggests that human beings are the only group in God's creation that becomes homeless. Additionally, the use of "the Son of Man," a reference in the apocalyptic tradition to the coming messiah, helps to highlight Jesus's humanity in his homelessness. The Kensington families challenged surrounding churches to interpret Matthew 25 literally: "For I was hungry and you gave me something to eat, I was thirsty and you gave me something to drink.... Whatever you did for one of the least of these brothers and sisters of mine, you did for me." This church takeover in Kensington was a living testimony to Jesus, who was poor and homeless like us. And it was here that I heard my call to the ministry. I had grown up in a religious family but it was in these actions of the poor, Tent City and the St. Ed's Church takeover, where I saw my church—where the call of the gospel was made real to me in the world. Once I joined this political, economic, spiritual movement of the poor, I never left.

"We Talked to God"

The police arrived within hours of the families breaking the locks and moving in to the church. Moments after the police, nine priests arrived, wearing their clerical collars and dressed in their robes, intimidating the fifty homeless men, women, and children attempting to find sanctuary and shelter in the church. The priests gave KWRU 48 hours to find somewhere else to live (not wanting the church to look bad by immediately evicting this group of homeless people). One KWRU member quickly scrawled a sign on a big white sheet and hung it at the entrance asking, "48 hours— Where next, God?"

When the priests returned two days later, they noticed that the number of homeless families living in the church had doubled, a "kitchen" with donated food had been arranged, an area for donated clothing and toiletries had been set aside near the entrance, and it was clear that the families were not going anywhere. The priests approached the director of KWRU, Cheri Honkala, a formerly homeless mother herself, and asked, "Cheri, you gave us your word; why haven't you left this church?" She responded with a smile. "We talked to God too," she said, "and God doesn't want any more families to be homeless. We are welcome here."

It was not easy for the families to defy religious leaders. Many were terrified—of both civil and spiritual authorities—but together they were brave, and their assertion that these poor people talked directly to God had a powerful effect. It challenged the idea that only clergy have access to God, that you need a seminary degree or the right clothes or a proper theological background to discern what God needs us to do in this hurting world. It shattered the notion that people are poor because we are not right with God—and affirmed that God's preferential option for the poor is alive and well in these yet to be United States. Without disrespecting the priests' stature as leaders in the church, these homeless people insisted that, through prayer and action, we all relate directly to God. Indeed, all are welcome in God's house. God is in the struggle, in the movement. God is in and of the poor.

"Jesus Is Being Evicted"

When the KWRU families moved into St. Edward's, we saw no other choice for housing everyone. Philadelphia's homeless shelters were full.

The weather had turned cold and rats had started to move into the tents at Tent City where the families were living. We did not want to split up our community—we needed space for many—and we knew that we were stronger and safer together. When the families were told to leave, we again discussed our options but had nowhere else to go.

Supporters from across the city responded to the St. Edward's take-over. A group of students from Eastern College, a small Christian college in the suburbs of Philadelphia, saw the homeless families on TV and began bringing student volunteers to the church to help with setup and child care. One afternoon, the police came back to St. Edward's and said that they would be returning to evict the families because of fire codes. We later learned that the warning was actually a gift from individual police officers, giving us time to call a "phone tree" of supporters to help prevent our eviction. Within two hours, hundreds of people from all over the city— including two off-duty firemen who knew the codes and brought smoke alarms and fire extinguishers—joined the families in the church. The Eastern College students who had gotten the call ran around the school dorms alerting their fellow students that "Jesus is being evicted from a church in North Philadelphia!" By that evening, nearly two hundred Eastern College students came to witness, and many spent the night in the church.[2] When the police arrived the next morning, they saw the smoke detectors, the fire extinguishers, and all of those students supporting the homeless families. No one was evicted.

The students and residents of St. Ed's said that *Jesus* was being evicted, which was bold language—some said extreme. We asserted that what was happening in the church was Christ's work even though it was against the will of church authorities. Our actions raised questions about the number of churches being closed down in poor communities—not for lack of members, but because the members were poor. And by making a theological statement about where Jesus is present, we challenged Christians to see the ways in which our congregations and denominations sometimes push Jesus away.

2. For another account on the St. Edward's Church takeover and especially the role of students from Eastern College see Shane Claiborne, *The Irresistible Revolution* (Grand Rapids: Zondervan, 2006).

Introduction

"All Are Welcome to Stay in God's House"

Poor families moving into "God's House" was one of many examples of oppressed people finding shelter and safety in the church. For the homeless families, this shelter and security were found both in the church building itself and in the community of residents and allies that developed inside. Throughout history, church sanctuaries have had multiple uses. As (well as) a place to worship God, church sanctuaries have served as safe places for marginalized and oppressed people. Blacks escaping slavery were housed in churches in the nineteenth century. In the latter part of the twentieth century, political and economic refugees escaping persecution in Central America were protected by US churches in the Sanctuary Movement. Today, some churches have begun inviting undocumented immigrants to seek refuge inside their church so the authorities cannot separate them from their families and deport them.

Ron Casanova, vice president of the National Union of the Homeless, an organization of homeless people with twenty-five chapters across the country (which inspired KWRU), wrote about the sanctuary provided by the collective actions of homeless people in his autobiography *Each One Teach One: Up and Out of Poverty, Memoirs of a Street Activist*. Casanova describes the growth of encampments of homeless people in Tompkins Square Park in New York City in the 1980s and 1990s. These encampments are still popping up in cities and towns across the country more than twenty-five years later.

> People just kept coming. . . . The park became a sanctuary. . . . We were getting a lot of clothes donations, which we hung up on fences for anybody who needed them and could use them. Beside each one of the tents we had campfires, and there was one communal campfire where we fed any people who were hungry. People in the neighborhood would go out and buy or collect food and bring it for our kitchen. People began to get the word that we were feeding the homeless and anybody was welcome.[3]

Casanova described the "sanctuary" of homeless families living together and looking after one another. Just as the community of poor people at

---

3. Ron Casanova and Stephen Blackburn, *Each One Teach One: Up and Out of Poverty, Memoirs of a Street Activist* (New York: Curbstone Press, 1996), 123.

Tompkins Square drew people from all over, the church takeover at St. Ed's attracted poor and homeless people from across Philadelphia. Although the majority of the people living in the closed-down church came from Tent City and the surrounding neighborhood, word got out in Kensington and throughout Philadelphia that there was a place where homeless people were living together, sharing their resources, and challenging city and religious institutions to play a role in resolving problems of poverty and homelessness, living out the Lord's Prayer.

The St. Edward's Church takeover was a parable of the reign of God. In Luke 14:15-23, Jesus tells of a great banquet, where the host invites all the poor and hungry from throughout the area to attend a great feast, after the influential people declined. In this story, the wealthy invitees were too busy getting married and buying property to come to the banquet. The host then invites the poor and the lame to come partake in the feast. It suggests that meals where the poor come together and share are common in the Kingdom of God. Indeed, this tradition of the poor partaking in meals together was being made manifest in a takeover church in the "City of Brotherly Love."

Poverty Is a Sin, Being Poor Isn't

St. Edward's Church was located in the neighborhood of Kensington, which was once Philadelphia's industrial district. Kensington produced Stetson Hats, Quaker Lace, Radio Flyer Wagons, and garments for JCPenney. From the 1960s to the 1990s, however, more than 250,000 jobs left Kensington through a process of deindustrialization. As many jobs were automated, robots replaced thousands of blue-collar workers. Other jobs moved to Latin America and Asia, where workers are paid one-tenth what unionized workers used to be paid to do the same work. This left Kensington with two main sources of income: welfare and drugs. Entire blocks were lined with abandoned houses where the workers used to live. It was 30% white, 30% black, 30% Latino, and the remaining 10% were immigrants from Asia, Eastern Europe, the Middle East, and Africa. With the diversity of people came a mosaic of religions. The majority of the population was less than 25 years old, but people of all ages lived in the neighborhood. Poor health was visible in their faces and bodies. In 1998, a peasant organizer from Haiti visited Kensington and talked with us at KWRU, explaining that the conditions of housing, living, and health she was seeing looked no better than in Haiti, which is the poorest country in the Western Hemisphere.

The Kensington community in the 1990s was a microcosm of our country today—there are multiracial, intergenerational, poor communities engaged in struggles for their very survival much like Tent City and St. Ed's all over this country. You will see it in Lorain, Ohio; Welch, West Virginia; Flint, Michigan; Columbia and Biloxi, Mississippi; San Jose, California; Decatur, Illinois; Grays Harbor, Washington; Minneapolis, Minnesota; and elsewhere. Since my time at Tent City and the St. Edward's Church takeover, I have had the opportunity to partner with poor people's organizations in these diverse towns and cities, helping weave them into a larger network focused on economic human rights and good news for the poor. I have met real heroes and heroines of our time and place—today's saints who are uniting against all odds, affirming that ending poverty is necessary and possible, even as their homeless encampments, churches of the poor, communities of those locked down and pushed out, and very right to survive are threatened and attacked.

Indeed, since 1995 when KWRU established Tent City and took over the church, poverty has grown across our country. Wages have dropped or remained stagnant for the vast majority of workers over the last several decades. US consumer debt has increased rapidly as millions struggle to pay their bills. This is not a story we have tended to hear in recent times. Except for a few moments when US poverty and racism have been displayed for the world to see—like in the aftermath of Hurricane Katrina—poverty remained mostly hidden in the 1990s and early 2000s.

These days we occasionally hear more because since the "Great Recession" began in December 2007, the gulf between rich and poor has deepened. Reports document that 4 in 5 Americans live in or live in danger of falling into joblessness and poverty, and that nearly 1 in 2 Americans is poor or has a low income (family living at less than 200% of the poverty line).[4] In communities across the United States, banks foreclose on an average of 10,000 homes a day. Nearly 40% of Americans between the ages of 25 and 60 will experience at least one year below the official poverty line—in 2016 that means a family of 4 makes less than $24,300. Half of all American children will, at some point during their childhood, reside in a

---

4. Associated Press, "4 in 5 Americans Live in Danger of Falling into Poverty, Joblessness," July 13, 2013, http://usnews.nbcnews.com/_news/2013/07/28/19738595-ap-4-in-5-americans-live-in-danger-of-falling-into-poverty-joblessness.

household that uses food stamps.[5] And poverty, low levels of education, poor social support, and other social factors contribute to as many deaths in the United States as familiar causes like heart attacks, strokes, and lung cancer combined.[6] Poverty disproportionately impacts people of color and women. Nearly 1 in 3 Native Americans (29.2%), over 1 in 4 African Americans (27.2%), 1 in 4 Hispanics/Latinos (23.5%), 1 in 10 Asians (10.5%), and 1 in 10 non-Hispanic whites (9.6%) live below the federal poverty line. More than half of all children below the poverty line live in families headed by women, and women make up two-thirds of all minimum-wage workers.

Over the past twenty-plus years, I have been able to talk and work with many people who put faces on all these statistics. I give you the following examples of what I've witnessed, not to overwhelm or elicit guilt, but to tell the truth and elicit action. There are thousands of families still impacted and displaced in New York, New Jersey, and Connecticut four years after Hurricane Sandy. Hundreds of thousands of Detroit residents have had their water shut off since the year 2000 and many are now having their children taken away from them because they are poor and lack running water. The privatization of water in Detroit and Highland Park, Michigan, is linked to the poisoning of water systems in Flint, Michigan—in fact the entire town of Flint has experienced irreparable harm because the city was trying to save money instead of paying Detroit's higher prices for water. There are families in the Gulf Coast, in Appalachia, in the Navajo Nation, and in other Native American territories whose hope of living healthy and full lives has been stolen, many years after the BP oil spill, Sago Mine disaster, Gold King disaster, and other manifestations of extreme environmental extraction. Indeed, as I write this book, families living in encampments in Standing Rock, North Dakota, are fighting to protect their source of water, which they recognize as their source of life. So many people are struggling to provide for their families while they contend with having their water and land poisoned by multinational corporations that are amassing excessive wealth at their expense.

There are thousands of people without adequate health and health care—who have to share heart medicine in New Jersey, who don't receive

5. Mark Rank, "Poverty Is Mainstream in America," *New York Times*, November 2, 2013.

6. "How Many U.S. Deaths Are Caused by Poverty, Lack of Education, and Other Social Factors?" July 5, 2011, https://www.mailman.columbia.edu/public-health-now/news/how-many-us-deaths-are-caused-poverty-lack-education-and-other-social-factors#sthash.084dF56U.dpuf.

chemotherapy in Vermont, who are denied Medicaid in Mississippi and North Carolina and so cannot afford to get treatment when they get sick—and all this is true even after the passage of the Affordable Care Act. Immigrant and US-born workers who pick tomatoes in Florida for poverty wages are sometimes forced into slave rings—here in the twenty-first-century United States. Philadelphia implemented fire station brownouts (rotating stations closed one day a week) to cut costs and children died in fires. Families in West Virginia lose their homes and family burial grounds because coal companies use mountaintop removal mining processes. Homeless citizens are buried in unidentified mass graves in potter's fields in New York and other states across the country. Millions of workers—people we see every day—are paid too little to be able to feed, house, and clothe their families adequately.[7]

Poverty is a defining issue of our day, even as we largely ignore it. Indeed, the poor have come to represent the social ills of racism, sexism, homophobia, xenophobia, ageism, ecological devastation, violence and war—and are disproportionately impacted by these ills. But throughout the country, poor people are rising to confront it. We often miss this too because we think poor people lack the agency and will, the organizational savvy and resources, to challenge poverty. But I have seen a movement brewing in poor communities across the country—it is small and sometimes scattered—but it is certainly real. The purpose of this book is to argue that we must read the Bible with that perspective—that we are called to join and support a necessary and growing social movement to end poverty, led by the poor. This is what the Bible and our faith demands.

7. There are organizations addressing these issues: people are fighting against slavery and poverty wages for farm work in Florida and the American South with the Coalition of Immokalee Workers (ciw-online.org); for universal health care and people's budgeting in Vermont with the Vermont Workers' Center (workerscenter.org); against foreclosure, eviction, and the privatization of water and other public utilities in Detroit with the Michigan Welfare Rights Organization (mwro.org); to end poverty among low-wage workers in Maryland with the United Workers (unitedworkers.org); against cuts to public services, education, and wages with the Media Mobilizing Project in Philadelphia (mediamobilizing.org); against mountaintop removal and strip-mining in West Virginia with Stop Mountaintop Removal; as well as trying to rebuild communities and livelihoods in the Gulf Coast (bridgethegulfproject.org).

CHAPTER 1

Is Ending Poverty Possible?

While Jesus was in Bethany in the home of Simon the Leper, a woman came to him with an alabaster jar of very expensive perfume, which she poured on his head as he was reclining at the table. When the disciples saw this, they were indignant. "Why this waste?" they asked. "This perfume could have been sold at a high price and the money given to the poor." Aware of this, Jesus said to them, "Why are you bothering this woman? She has done a beautiful thing to me. The poor you will always have with you, but you will not always have me. When she poured this perfume on my body, she did it to prepare me for burial. Truly I tell you, wherever this gospel is preached throughout the world, what she has done will also be told, in memory of her."

—Matt 26:6–13

The Bible—a text replete with calls for economic justice and denunciations of the scourge of indifference to the poor—has been misused and cynically politicized to suggest that poverty is a result of the moral failures of poor people sinning against God, that ending poverty is impossible, and that the poor themselves have no role to play in efforts to respond to their poverty. Biblical texts, especially "the poor you will always have with you," are used to justify the inevitability of inequality and to provide religious sanction for the dispossession of the majority for the benefit of the few. The well-known preacher Jim Wallis[1] regularly conducts a short Bible quiz with American

---

1. Jim Wallis is the founder of *Sojourners Magazine* and community in Washington, DC. He is one of the most vocal evangelical voices on poverty in the United States.

audiences that he speaks to, asking the question: "What is the most famous biblical text about the poor?" Every time, he receives the same answer: "The poor you will always have with you."[2] People quote "the poor you will always have with you" as a way to discredit antipoverty organizing, justify the foreordination of poverty, and support the idea that charity is the best response to poverty. Such assertions are made by people who place a great deal of authority in the Bible as well as people who describe themselves as atheists or agnostics.[3]

Such readings of "the poor you will always have with you" are widespread, pervasive, and damaging. They are used in various arenas, including the mainstream media, popular culture, and the speeches, sermons, and writings of politicians, preachers, and biblical scholars. The passage is used by leading figures in both major political parties in the United States: President Barack Obama opened his remarks with it at Georgetown University's Poverty Summit in May 2015,[4] and Texas governor Rick Perry was quoted saying, "Biblically, the poor are always going to be with us in some form or fashion."[5]

This interpretation of Matt 26:11 has become the common-sense[6] understanding of the whole of Jesus's teachings on poverty. A Bible study guide promoting the Millennium Development Goals, prefaced by Dr. Antonios Kireopoulos, the Associate General Secretary for International Affairs and Peace for the National Council of Churches, states that although

2. Les Fussell, "The Poor Will Be with You Always," https://web.archive.org/ web/20080720063924/ http://www.baptist.org.au/index.php?option=com_content&task =view&id=22&Itemid=8.

3. Gareth Stedman Jones, a self-identified agnostic historian and the author of *An End to Poverty: A Historical Debate* (New York: Columbia University Press, 2008), raised the question of whether ending poverty was impossible, as is stated in the Bible, at a public presentation at Columbia University on November 9, 2005, in response to Jeffrey Sachs. Other panelists included Eric Foner, James Jordan, Emma Rothschild, Amartya Sen, and Joseph Stiglitz.

4. Paul Elie, "The President and Poverty," *The New Yorker*, May 13, 2015, http://www .newyorker.com/news/news-desk/the-president-and-poverty.

5. Luke Brinker, "Rick Perry: The Bible Proves That Poverty Is Inevitable," *Salon Magazine*, December 10, 2014, http://www.salon.com/2014/12/10/rick_perry_the_bible _proves_that_poverty_is_inevitable/.

6. Antonio Gramsci uses the phrase "common sense" in his writings. To Gramsci, common sense is the popular consensus about how the world works: "Many elements in popular common sense contribute to people's subordination by making situations of inequality and oppression appear to them as natural and unchangeable." Antonio Gramsci, *The Antonio Gramsci Reader: Selected Writings 1916–1935*, ed. David Forgacs (New York: New York University Press, 2000), 421.

Jesus admits we can never end poverty, it is nonetheless our duty to care for the poor and work to eradicate "extreme" poverty. In the following, I uncover and analyze the dangerous ideas, ideologies, and assumptions made about poverty and the poor through traditional interpretations of Matt 26:6–13. I will attempt to reinterpret the passage in subsequent chapters to show that "the poor you will always have with you" is actually one of the strongest statements of the biblical mandate to end poverty.

Popular Treatments

It is not news that the Bible is the most widely read, distributed, and translated book in the United States. Always on the top of the bestseller list, it is cited for a boundless range of moral stances and consulted for everyday personal decisions as well as political decisions with major social implications. The issue of poverty appears throughout the Bible—the Old and New Testaments are full of instructions on how we are to respond to poverty and injustice. Jim Wallis surveyed key biblical themes, noting that

> in the Old Testament, the suffering of the poor was the second most prominent theme. . . . In the NT we found that one out of every sixteen verses was about the poor. In the Gospels, it was one out of every ten, in Luke, one of every seven, and in James, one of every five verses.[7]

Common throughout the New and Old Testaments are texts addressing the redistribution of wealth and the abolition of poverty: "Is not this the kind of fasting I have chosen: to loose the chains of injustice and untie the cords of the yoke, to set the oppressed free and break every yoke? Is it not to share your food with the hungry and to provide the poor wanderer with shelter—when you see the naked, to clothe them . . . ?" (Isa 58:6–7); "Speak out, judge righteously, defend the rights of the poor and needy" (Prov 31:9); "[God] has lifted up the humble. He has filled the hungry with good things" (Luke 1:52–53); "For I was hungry and you gave me something to eat, I was thirsty and you gave me something to drink. . . . Truly I tell you, whatever you did for one of the least of these brothers and sisters of mine, you did for me" (Matt 25:35, 40).

---

7. Jim Wallis, *Faith Works: Lessons from the Life of an Activist Preacher* (New York: Random House, 2000), 71.

Yet, while passages like these are common, many people fixate on a small handful of passages: "You will always have the poor among you" (John 12:8); "The one who is unwilling to work shall not eat" (2 Thess 3:10); "For whoever has will be given more, and they will have an abundance. Whoever does not have, even what they have will be taken from them" (Matt 25:29). These verses are regularly cited to assert that poverty cannot be ended and that if God wanted to end poverty, God would do so. They have been used to claim that the only "good news" that poor people will hear will be in heaven, and interpreted to mean that while some lepers and hungry people in Jesus's day deserved compassion, today's poor people are at fault for their own poverty.

To see the omnipresence of this biblical statement, one only needs to do a search for "the poor will always be with you" online. Available are hundreds of thousands of references (728,000 mentions in one of my searches), as well as a debate emerging on the role of Jesus, the Bible, and faith communities in the eradication and amelioration of poverty.[8] Typically, this debate takes the form of a personal assertion, reflection, blog post, or series of questions on whether or not this statement in Matt 26:11, John 12:8, and Mark 14:7 is saying (a) that we can never end poverty; (b) that it is the role of Christians, not the government, to try to care for the poor; or (c) that Jesus rather than the poor should be our concern.

Following are some examples of these contemporary interpretations of Matthew 26, Mark 14, and John 12. I have emphasized (in bold) key assumptions about poverty and poor people in each. When explored together and in the context of hundreds of other similar online entries, these statements reveal some of the most insidious beliefs in contemporary American society about the meaning of the biblical statement "the poor you will always have with you."

> **Poverty will never be eradicated.** As Jesus said, "The poor will be with you always. . . ." There will always be people who are physically unable to work, and people who will never work because they simply will not, and

8. There are various publications that argue that the Internet is becoming a site of research and public-opinion setting. This is interesting to my argument and methodology—using the Internet as a place to compile assumptions regarding poverty and to gauge stereotypes of the poor. For more information on this topic, see Angela Thomas-Jones, *The Host in the Machine: Examining the Digital in the Social* (Oxford: Chandos, 2010); and Mia Consalvo et al., eds., *Internet Research Annual: Selected Papers from the Association of Internet Researchers Conferences 2000–2002*, vol. 1 (New York: Peter Lang, 2004).

people who are too stupid to work for very much money, and people who are criminally inclined to steal from stupid or helpless people, etc. And there will always be people who want to take money away from the higher paid, smart, energetic and enterprising people who are the backbone of this country, and give it to those who are not. **Those are the people who refuse to believe what God has said. Poverty CANNOT be cured or eradicated, but there will always be people who try.**[9]

Though judgmental, this statement contains a number of core assumptions about poverty and interpretations of this biblical text to which most people subscribe. The author posits that poverty will never be ended and insists that to try to eradicate poverty is to refuse to follow God's intentions. Blaming poverty and economic hardship on poor people, the post does not follow assumptions of liberation theologians and social-gospel believers that poverty is a social, economic, and political problem, or that the poverty of many is the result of the wealth of a few. Instead, the author connects the inevitability of poverty and the stupidity and laziness of the poor with inattention to what the author sees as God's message. The author asserts that common responses to the poor, through either governmental services taken from taxes or individual charity and acts of benevolence, are not only ineffectual but counter to God's will.

The following quotation from another post further connects theology to pathologizing the poor:

From time to time I think that I should mount a defense of what could (incorrectly) be described as my anti-charitable political policies, in light of all the "love they neighbor" stuff in Christianity. . . . I've spent weekends and one spring break helping to build houses for the poor . . . when they labored alongside. **Given that we each also labored every year to pay taxes to support the poor, to educate the poor and—when both of those fail—to incarcerate some lower-tier fractionate of the poor, I think my job is pretty well done** . . . and, really, the fact that all of us—by going to work each day—support the capitalist underpinnings of our society, we could skip the taxes and still consider it a job well done.[10]

9. "How Can Poverty Be Eradicated?" http://wiki.answers.com/Q/How_can
_poverty_can_be_eradicated.

10. This appeared on the right-wing political blog "Dispatches from TJICistan," http://tjic.com/?p=1839. Accessed May 16, 2009; the site has since been discontinued.

Here, the author critiques generosity, admits that he contradicts the Golden Rule, and blames poor people for their poverty, asserting that capitalism is the final act of civilizing ourselves. Such a defense of capitalism—as the best Christian response to poverty—indeed is touted by many in our society.[11]

Some blame the economic crisis that began in 2007 on poor people rather than on systemic problems with our economic system. In the case of the following quotation, the author actually asserts that this is what Jesus was trying to tell us when he said, "The poor you will always have with you":

> We have hashed over and over the causes of the banking crisis. Basically, the democrats forced banks to make loans to people with BAD credit (because they were "underprivileged"—due to racial, gender, sexual, and other types of discrimination). We couldn't bring in illegal Mexicans to build all the new houses fast enough. There was a "feeding frenzy" in the lending world and even though the democrats created those opportunities, we had to hear "predatory lending, predatory lenders, predatory this, predatory that," *ad nauseam*, attempting to make us feel sorry for the financially irresponsible, discriminated-against, underprivileged "groups" that "fell prey" to those "bad old" predatory lenders. **Naturally, the mortgage payments stopped coming in. That's what financially irresponsible people do. They don't honor their contracts.** As Jesus said, "the poor will be with you al-

---

11. Aryeh Spero writes a defense of capitalism as the best antipoverty response in an editorial in the *Wall Street Journal*: "More than any other nation, the United States was founded on broad themes of morality rooted in a specific religious perspective. We call this the Judeo-Christian ethos, and within it resides a ringing endorsement of capitalism as a moral endeavor. Regarding mankind, no theme is more salient in the Bible than the morality of personal responsibility, for it is through this that man cultivates the inner development leading to his own growth, good citizenship and happiness. The entitlement/welfare state is a paradigm that undermines that noble goal. . . . The motive of capitalism's detractors is a quest for their own power and an envy of those who have more money. But envy is a cardinal sin and something that ought not to be. God begins the Ten Commandments with 'I am the Lord your God' and concludes with 'Thou shalt not envy your neighbor, not for his wife, nor his house, nor for any of his holdings.' Envy is corrosive to the individual and to those societies that embrace it. Nations that throw over capitalism for socialism have made an immoral choice" (Aryeh Spero, "What the Bible Teaches about Capitalism," *Wall Street Journal*, January 30, 2012, http://online.wsj.com/news/articles/SB10001424052970203806 50457717930333047134).

ways." You can't even get rid of them with a letter bomb, especially if it looks like a bill. **The rich keep getting richer and the poor keep getting poorer because the rich continue to do the things that got them rich, the poor keep doing the things that keep them poor** and the democrats—who wouldn't have it any other way—keep being re-elected by the poor.[12]

Prosperity-gospel preachers and self-help gurus also believe in the inevitability of poverty and personal responsibility, proposing higher standards of personal responsibility for the poor than for the wealthy. This author claims that he has a solution to the economic insecurity that some face but does not claim that poverty can end:

> Poor is a condition I find very sad. Sad, yet inevitable. Jesus said, "The poor will be with you always." And they will. . . . **I didn't write this book for the poor people of the world. I know it is going to take a lot more than a book to help truly poor people.** . . . Broke is NOT a condition like being poor. Broke is a situation you find yourself in because you are either under earning or overspending. **I can't fix poor, though I would love to. I'm good, but I'm not that good. I can fix broke. . . . I will show you how, step by step. I wrote this book for the average person who has a job, makes a living, and still can't seem to get ahead.**[13]

While the quotations I have highlighted so far embody a more conservative and partisan portrayal of attitudes toward poverty and in some cases demonize the poor, even people who think of themselves as more sensitive to the plight of the poor often follow a similar logic.[14] Many "politically conscious" and self-identified "liberal" Christians come up to me after I speak on poverty and complain about seeing poor people use their food stamps to buy shrimp and steak rather than the hot dogs they can afford and should therefore buy. They claim that poor people lack the guid-

---

12. Russ J. Alan, "Your Home Value Is Falling . . . Refinance?" February 8, 2009, http://www.renewamerica.us/columns/alan/090208.

13. Larry Winget, *You're Broke Because You Want to Be: How to Stop Getting By and Start Getting Ahead* (New York: Gotham, 2009), 1-2.

14. Russ J. Alan, author of one of the quotations above, identifies himself as politically conservative. His articles have appeared on several web sites such as *USA Today, The Wall Street Journal, USNews*, and *NPR*. He is also a journalist for DigitalJournal.com.

ance to make informed, responsible financial decisions and argue that this is the reason they continue to be poor. In effect, they still blame the poor for their own poverty and hardship. This is shown in the following quotation from a post entitled "Why the Poor Will Always Be with Us":

> Why does poverty exist? In the case of my family it was a number of factors. My father—dad was born in 1876. He was also a coal miner. My dad was a child from a second marriage. And so far as I am able to learn, none of the family members were ever college educated. More importantly, we were never pushed or guided to want to go to college and thereby and hopefully, better our lives. This happened because of a lack of education to begin with. One cannot appreciate to the full extent what one has never experienced. **So . . . my answer to the question of why does poverty exist will be . . . a lack of guidance and understanding of what is required to escape from poverty. An education, opportunity, and the willingness to work and the discipline to keep working to get those keys to escape. Poverty will always be with us. As will the sick. As will be any unfortunate circumstance. It IS the human condition.**[15]

In this quotation, the existence of poverty is naturalized and ultimately attributed to the faults of individual poor people. Rather than accusing the poor of living off the largesse of others or acting irresponsibly with the limited resources they have, the author asserts that it is for lack of guidance that so many people in our country and in the world are poor. Referring to the Bible, this statement and others like it assert that poverty is an eternal part of the human condition. That some people have inadequate access to basic necessities is accepted, and individual human behavior, sometimes referred to as "sin," is identified as the cause of poverty and dispossession.

Another take on "sin" comes from an evangelical who refers to the example of the unnamed woman in the story in Matthew 26. She pours valuable oil onto Jesus, which scandalizes the disciples, who say that the oil could have been sold and the proceeds distributed to the poor. This author separates Jesus from the poor and comments that a deep commitment to

---

15. A. Dean, "Why the Poor Will Always Be with Us," *LifePaths 360*, http://www.helium.com/items/549625-why-the-poor-will-always-be-with-us. Accessed August 24, 2007; the site has since been discontinued.

the poor rather than to Jesus in many cases is misdirected and can lead to burnout and confusion:

> There is an important lesson here for Christians who do relief and development work among the poor. Too many Christian activists are ruining their health and destroying their families while justifying the zeal because of their commitment to the poor. In the name of the poor, activist workaholics suffer from poor health and burnout, and they damage their spouses and children. This is not a gospel stance. This is not what Jesus asks us to do. **Our devotion must be directed at Jesus, not the poor themselves.** While we certainly are supposed to love our neighbor, especially our poor neighbor, we are to worship only Jesus. The woman understood this and the disciples did not. **Getting your spirituality and worship right is key to sustaining one's service to God and the poor.**[16]

Unlike statements in which poor people are directly blamed for their poverty or God is thought to be justifying poverty, the author below, a mayoral candidate in a small city in Illinois, subscribes to the idea that individual charity is the best response to poverty:

> **Jesus said the poor will be with you always. It has been over two thousand years and this statement still holds true. We cannot eradicate poverty but if a neighbor comes to us and asks for a loaf of bread, we should care enough to share if we can meet that need.** With that in mind I propose establishing a directory with a Website containing all organizations offering various types of assistance. It would include churches, nonprofit organizations and government agencies to better connect the providers with recipients. . . . I would also like hard copies of the directory to be distributed to all participating organizations connecting the groups with one another for a unified approach to poverty in Galesburg.[17]

---

16. Bryant Myers, "Will the Poor Always Be with Us?" http://www.evangelicalsfor socialaction.org/holistic-ministry/will-the-poor-always-be-with-us/.

17. "Mayoral Candidate Eric Delawder: Galesburg Mayoral Candidate Eric Delawder Answers Questions from the Register-Mail Editorial Board and Speaks on Video about Why Voters Should Elect Him," *Register Mail*, March 20, 2009, http://www.galesburg.com/ x1331535567/Mayoral-candidate-Eric-Delawder.

As can be seen here, invoking charity and social service is still done with the assumption that the poor have no agency in addressing poverty.[18] The role that charity plays in sustaining a structure that creates poverty is left unexamined;[19] charity, and never larger social transformation, is thus put forward as the only Christian response possible to growing suffering and misery.[20]

But such assumptions and statements don't only come from people with little day-to-day experience among the poor, those seeking to justify their inaction in the face of growing poverty, or those trying to promote a self-help book or political platform. These assumptions are internalized

18. About charity, William Sloane Coffin, sometimes called a father of the peace and justice movement in the church, former chaplain at Yale and senior pastor at Riverside Church, writes, "Many of us are eager to respond to injustice, as long as we can do so without having to confront the causes of it. There's the great pitfall of charity. Handouts to needy individuals are genuine, necessary responses to injustice, but they do not necessarily face the reason for injustice. And that is why so many business and governmental leaders today are promoting charity; it is desperately needed in an economy whose prosperity is based on growing inequality. First these leaders proclaim themselves experts on matters economic, and prove it by taking the most out of the economy! Then they promote charity as if it were the work of the church, finally telling us troubled clergy to shut up and bless the economy as once we blessed the battleships" (*The Collected Sermons of William Sloane Coffin: The Riverside Years*, vol. 2 [Louisville: Westminster John Knox, 2008], 188).

19. Joan Roelofs focuses on the role that foundations, especially liberal foundations such as Ford and Carnegie, play in upholding the current economic system: "Tax evasion and public relations have motivated most foundations (along with indeterminable amounts of guilt and benevolence). However, [foundations'] greatest threat to democracy lies in their translation of wealth into power. They can create and disseminate an ideology justifying vast inequalities of life chances and political power; they can deflect criticism and mask (and sometimes mitigate) damaging aspects of the system; and they can hire the best brains, popular heroines, and even left-wing politicians to do their work" (Joan Roelofs, *Foundations and Public Policy: The Mask of Pluralism* [Binghamton: State University of New York Press, 2003], 8).

20. Teresa Funicello exposes the role of the "poverty industry" in making money off the poor. Her book has been influential in the Poverty Initiative network: "Charities come and go, some lasting only long enough to promote the promoters, others enduring a century or more. Sooner or later they involve money, often vast sums of it, and multiple agendas. Some may have been started with truly beneficent intentions, but even these finally give way to pragmatism that shifts focus away from 'helping the poor' and toward sustaining the institution. These dual objectives come increasingly to be at odds; the motivations behind them begin to diversify and encompass a host of additional interests" (Teresa Funicello, *Tyranny of Kindness: Dismantling the Welfare System to End Poverty in America* [New York: Atlantic Monthly Press, 1994], 212).

by some of the very leaders, including poor people themselves, involved in efforts to respond to the conditions and social causes of poverty.

Although homeless for much of his life, Ron Casanova became a significant leader in the movement to end poverty and an organizer for over twenty years. Yet even he, in his book *Each One Teach One: Up and Out of Poverty, Memoirs of a Street Activist*, comes to the conclusion that we may not be able to end poverty.[21] Although Glenda Adams believed that God had called her to work with other poor and formerly homeless people, she pulled back from her engagement with Poor Voices United (PVU) in Atlantic City, New Jersey, because her pastor told her that Jesus said you cannot end poverty. She focused her energy on building the church instead. Social worker Isaac Macon is skeptical that poverty can really be eliminated or even alleviated, even though he has seen hundreds of families acquire housing and gainful employment and come together to win better policies and build a larger movement.

Although her conscience and business ethics remind her to care for the poor, a supporter and donor to the Poverty Initiative/Kairos Center questioned whether she should donate to organizations dedicated to ending poverty, because poverty can only be managed, not ended. She believed it was not practical to support a group with such a lofty and unachievable goal. And one paid organizer from the United Workers of Baltimore City, after working with a group of over four hundred day laborers who won unprecedented living-wage victories, quit his job, saying he could not work for a group that believes in ending poverty, because Jesus says there will always be poverty.[22] Indeed, this biblical passage is a roadblock for many committed to abolishing poverty.

Academic Treatments

Interpretations of Matt 26:1–13 similar to those mentioned in the previous section characterize the writings of biblical scholars today. Referring to "the poor you will always have with you, but you will not always have me," New Testament scholar Craig Evans insists that the poor are a concern for Jesus

21. Ron Casanova and Stephen Blackburn, *Each One Teach One: Up and Out of Poverty, Memoirs of a Street Activist* (New York: Curbstone Press, 1996), 249.
22. These anecdotes come from my personal experiences in organizing among the poor for the past twenty years.

and his followers but that, in the Matthew 26 text itself, Jesus is more important: "Jesus is not indifferent to the needs of the poor—the disciples will have many opportunities to care for them—but they will not always have the opportunity to minister to Jesus."[23] Grant Osborne writes, in reference to the actions of the unnamed woman in the story: "The disciples were thinking of the external ministry of their apostolic band rather than the internal reality of Jesus as he faced destiny . . . for her thoughts were on Jesus while the disciples' minds were on others. Hers was an act of love or piety rather than an act of almsgiving."[24] Similar to the post quoted above from the evangelical leader about not becoming so focused on the poor that we lose sight of Jesus, each of these interpreters separates Jesus and the poor. Osborne even goes so far as to separate love and piety from care for the poor.

In a similar vein though coming from a Jewish perspective, Amy-Jill Levine writes that the poor and poverty are not central to the meaning of the story. She emphasizes the role that people with wealth play in the Gospel, and she positions Jesus's heavenly mission opposite more earthly matters such as helping the poor, as though they are mutually exclusive:

> The disciples' complaint that she has wasted the funds that might have been given to the poor contrasts the woman's true understanding of Jesus' fate with their focus on earthly—albeit important—matters.[25]

Levine sets up a dichotomy between heaven and earth, between Jesus and the poor. She also interprets this passage as saying that those who have a responsibility and ability to ameliorate poverty are the wealthy:

> Like the other evangelists, Matthew emphasizes the costliness of the ointment. The economic notice is consistent with the identification of Joseph of Arimathea as a "rich man" ([Matt] 27:57) and the beatitude about the "poor in spirit" ([Matt] 5:3) rather than simply the poor (cf. Luke 6:20b). The rich are welcome in the church, as long as their money is appropriately used (i.e., in service to others).[26]

23. Craig Evans, *Matthew*, New Cambridge Bible Commentary (Cambridge: Cambridge University Press, 2012), 426.

24. Grant R. Osbourne, *Matthew*, Zondervan Exegetical Commentary on the New Testament (Grand Rapids: Zondervan, 2010), 951.

25. Amy-Jill Levine, "Matthew," in *Women's Bible Commentary*, ed. Carol A. Newsom and Sharon H. Ringe (Louisville: Westminster John Knox, 1998), 349.

26. Levine, "Matthew," 348.

Levine asserts that money is the solution to poverty at the same time as she deemphasizes the agency of, and Jesus's association with, the poor. She minimizes any structural critique of wealth.

And Levine is not alone in her interpretation that this passage foregrounds the responsible use of wealth and the instruction of believers to give to the poor. Many scholars argue that the message from Matthew 26 and its parallels—drawing especially on the connection between Deut 15:11 (part of the Jubilee instructions) and Matt 26:11—is meant to inspire Jesus's followers to give amply to those in need. Among the writers who focus on giving to the poor, Donald Hagner insists that Deuteronomy 15 signals the inevitability of poverty and thus the necessity for charity: "The poor are a reality in every society of every age (cf. Deut 15:11a). Jesus, on the other hand, will not always be physically with the disciples. . . . One cannot miss what is implied: there will be opportunity in the future to minister to the needs of the poor."[27] And New Testament scholar and Jesuit priest Daniel Harrington insists that the overall concern with money in Matt 26:11 is particular to the Gospel of Matthew: "The story had a particular message for the Matthean community, whose wealth made it unduly concerned with money."[28]

However, as will be explored in the rest of this book, Matthew 26 is not only about the actions of the middle class and wealthy, nor is it simply about distributing money. Interpretations that focus on the responsibilities of individuals with resources, interpretations that assert that giving to the poor is the best response to poverty, fail to grapple fully with the passage's intertextuality. They miss the possibilities of a much more fulsome interpretation, an interpretation that asserts that economic justice—therefore structuring society around the needs of the poor—is God's will.

The final assumption that dominates the biblical commentaries on "the poor you will always have with you" is the separation of religion and politics. Many scholars hesitate to see Jesus as political or as advocating anything more than personal piety which, according to this view, has nothing to do with caring for your neighbor. As I will elaborate more fully later in this book, many scholars do not believe that Jesus is anointed as king and Christ in Matthew 26. For example, Ulrich Luz writes:

27. Donald Hagner, *Matthew 14–28*, Word Biblical Commentary 33B (Dallas: Word, 1995), 758.
28. Daniel Harrington, *The Gospel of Matthew*, Sacra Pagina 1 (Collegeville, MN: Liturgical), 362.

As attractive as the idea itself might be, at the very least the present narrative in no way suggests that the unknown woman anointed Jesus as the messianic king. It is a careless assumption that later narrators would have so completely obscured this original sense of the anointing.[29]

Therefore, it is assumed that Jesus's instruction about the poor is meant simply on a spiritual, not a material level. Many biblical scholars thus cordon off the concepts of love, piety, and discipleship from Jesus's mission to transform society politically and economically.

In general, the claims about the relationship of Jesus to the poor that we quoted from pop culture, politicians, and public forums online share similar themes with the interpretations of these biblical scholars: spiritualizing (heaven rather than earth), ritualizing (Jesus counts more than the poor), individualizing (individual charity or almsgiving is the only solution), and moralizing (we must help the poor because they cannot help themselves) about Jesus and the poor.

Theological Obstacles

Given the ways that Matt 26:11 conditions popular and scholarly ideas about poverty, I have identified five main biblical obstacles—from Matthew 26 specifically and from the New Testament in general—that have been cited as arguments for naturalizing poverty and marginalizing the poor. I encourage others to examine, elaborate, and add to these assumptions as I explain them in brief here: (1) poverty was not an issue in Jesus's time (sociohistorical); (2) Jesus believed in the inevitability of poverty (text-based); (3) poverty is an individual problem and not a social problem (sociological); (4) poverty is the result of individual sin, not structural sin (theological); and (5) Jesus is concerned solely with spiritual poverty and other spiritual matters rather than material poverty and problems (theological).

Allow me to expand on this. First, I have heard many people assert that poverty was not an issue in Jesus's time. Proponents of this belief argue that there was no significant poverty experienced by Jesus or his follow-

29. Ulrich Luz, *Matthew 21–28: A Commentary*, ed. Helmut Koester, trans. James E. Crouch, Hermeneia (Philadelphia: Fortress, 2005), 337.

ers, that Jesus was not primarily concerned with poverty nor did he make major prophetic statements about poverty and injustice in his own words. Among those who pay attention to the historical context of the New Testament and Jesus's ministry, many allege that the Roman Empire improved the lives of the majority of people during Jesus's time, including the poor. The *Pax Romana* spread peace, infrastructure, and order by building roads and sewage systems, sponsoring banquets, and handing out a dole to the poor. They argue that these programs did more to lift up the poor than ever before in history. Then, to connect these assertions with Matthew 26 specifically, some say that, because Jesus's statement was made during a plentiful meal and the unnamed woman appeared out of nowhere with ointment that cost a year's salary, clearly Jesus and his followers were not struggling economically.

Another prominent methodology used supports the inevitability of poverty by focusing specifically on biblical texts and stating that Jesus understood poverty to be inevitable, then reading the whole Bible through this lens. Proponents of this view assert that poverty will never end, and it is an affront to God to contradict the words of Jesus. They contend that, just as Jesus could not prevent his death, poverty cannot be prevented. They comment that if Jesus had wanted to end poverty, he would have done so. These proponents reveal their presumption that the only agent for ending poverty is the God of the Heavens. They assume that God blesses some people with prosperity; therefore, the rich should be generous with their wealth. This view never challenges the polarization of wealth and poverty itself. Many people argue that Jesus does not present an earthly alternative to poverty in his message or ministry. These same people say that while justice for the poor is a main theme throughout the Bible, Jesus's statement that "the poor you will always have with you" in Matt 26:11 makes it the key text for interpreting his other teachings on poverty. What he means by this statement is that poverty cannot be ended.

The third assumption about poverty and the Bible that is considered common sense in our society today is that poverty is an individual problem, not a social problem. Some argue that the stories about poverty and healings in the Bible are about individuals, not social groups. Poor or unwell people move up and out of poverty individually at the same time that others fall into poverty. These commenters indicate that the Bible is intended for individual reflection and practice: to treat it socially and sociologically is to misuse Scripture. In connecting this sense of personal responsibility and piety to particular biblical texts, they use the example of Jesus's anointing, where Judas (or one of the disciples) is the one who brings up poverty and says that the money spent on the ointment could have helped a number of poor individuals. People argue that the reference to Deut 15:11 in Matt 26:11 means that because people are disobedient to God's commandments, individuals are being implored to give to poor people even though it will have no impact on poverty generally. Giving money is the way to address poverty, and therefore those with money/wealth are the ones with a solution to poverty. This individual/charity response to poverty is connected to the way that many modern Christians assume Jesus addresses poverty: Jesus is about helping out individuals in need, not coming up with a larger social program. To some, this is backed up with a traditional view of Jesus as a figure who fit comfortably into Roman imperial structures. Many assume that Jesus was executed alongside petty criminals and robbers (27:38) and therefore is a misfit on the cross, because Jesus is lawful while the others are lawless. These interpreters do not realize that crucifixion was a punishment for revolutionaries. These sociological assumptions also tend to view Jesus's actions and message in our contemporary, individualized context rather than in the collective and melded political-religious culture of the Near East during the Roman Empire.

The other two primary assumptions about the Bible and poverty are deeply theological. First, many believe that poverty is the result of individual sin, not structural sin. Proponents of this position argue that poverty occurs because of individual failure; if someone is poor, he or she lacks sufficient faith. Many assert that the desire and aim of Jesus (and his ministry) is personal piety and faith, not systemic analysis or solutions. When Jesus announces in Matt 26:11–12 that he will die soon, a death brought about by the individual betrayal of Judas (Matt 26:14–16) and the complicity of the Temple elites (Matt 26:57–67). These are individual behaviors and actions, not something plotted to maintain the status quo. This connection between Jesus and the Roman imperial powers is possible because of the other main theological assumption, which is that Jesus's central concern is spiritual poverty rather than material poverty. Proponents of this view claim that the Kingdom of God is otherworldly, and teachings in the Bible, including the Lord's Prayer, are metaphysical and ephemeral rather than being concerned with survival and materiality. This is why there are statements about not worrying about what one will eat or wear (Matt 6:25) and admonitions that humans should not live by bread alone (Luke 4:4). Therefore, people posit, we can only end poverty in heaven and at the end of time; the role of Christians is to evangelize people. While meeting material needs might be necessary for followers of Jesus to assist people in finding God, it is secondary to the real mission of the church, which is to save souls. In Matthew 26, Jesus is impatient with the disciples' talk about material things such as ointment and helping the poor, so he reorients the conversation: he is going to leave and go to heaven. These interpreters assert that Jesus thinks the disciples should be focused on preparing spiritually for his death.

So what does all this mean? Why does it matter? Or in the words of Luke 3, "What then shall we do?" I maintain that the dominant interpretations of "the poor you will always have with you" and the assumptions drawn from these interpretations are central aspects of the paradigm that most people use to interpret the role of Jesus in relation to the poor and the whole of the Bible. The assumptions and interpretations listed above dominate beliefs and actions regarding religion, the Bible, and poverty. Popular invocations of Matthew 26 are widespread—from across the political spectrum—and pose significant obstacles to understanding the real causes of poverty, taking on the moral responsibility for combating poverty, and developing an action plan for poor people and other people of conscience to end poverty. If one explores these assumptions and statements in the context of growing, deepening poverty and inequality, the need to reinterpret this passage becomes all the more urgent.

CHAPTER 2

Reading the Bible with the Poor

One of the important things about the Bible is that it talks about poverty more than almost anything else. And one of the reasons that I identify with the story of Christ is not only that he came to preach good news to the poor, he was poor himself when he was on earth. He was a Jewish man living under Roman rule and living under a system of exploitation and oppression. So, he wasn't someone who was over me, he was someone who was in my reality.[1]

—Onleilove Alston (Kairos Center/
Poverty Initiative Poverty Scholar)

Alston's assertions above challenge the way many of us have been taught in our families, churches, and schools to think about poverty, the Bible, and Jesus Christ. Most of us did not grow up learning that poverty is a major focus of the Bible and came to believe that separation of church and state means that there is nothing political about the Bible. The biblical question of poverty is too often cloistered in the walls of the academy as New Testament scholars debate the socioeconomic position of Jesus and the early Christians, the validity of the assertion that Jesus was "poor and dispossessed," and the role of the Roman Empire in the life of Jesus of Nazareth. But when the subject of poverty does make it into the broader

---

1. Alston made this observation at a Poverty Scholars Strategic Dialogue at Union Theological Seminary on September 19, 2008. The Poverty Scholars Program is the cornerstone of the Poverty Initiative focused on leadership development and on networking low-income organizers. I will describe this more in this chapter and in the Conclusion.

discussion, it typically is through Jesus's words "the poor you will always have with you" in Matt 26:11.

Matthew 26:11 has been interpreted either to establish that God condones poverty or that, although God condemns poverty, it is an unfortunate but unalterable reality of the human condition. For many people, the fact that Jesus is the one communicating this statement about the "poor" and that he uses the word "always" makes the meaning clear and unequivocal: they may not know where this phrase falls in the biblical story or in the context of the Gospel of Matthew, but they posit that this biblical statement establishes poverty as perpetual and inevitable. For those more versed in the Gospel of Matthew, this passage is still used to come to similar conclusions. For some, Jesus and the poor are juxtaposed in Matthew 26, and attending to Jesus and the spiritual realm is rendered more important. For others the discussion of the ointment and the invoking of Deuteronomy 15 suggest money and charity are the biblical solution to poverty, giving agency to the wealthy in this story.

However, a more robust contextual exegesis of Matt 26:1–16 with an emphasis on vv. 6–13, in their intertextuality with Deut 15:1–11, reveals a critique of charity and the Roman imperial economy, the promotion of the agency of the poor, and the primacy of material security and prosperity for all humanity. Jesus reacts strongly to the disciples in v. 11. Echoing Deut 15:4 ("However, there need be no poor people among you"), Matt 26:11 is to be read as a warning (not a statement) about the perils of disobedience to God's commandments (resulting in poverty and inequality) and Jesus's call to the disciples (to take up the struggle for justice for the poor even after his death). That the woman who anoints Jesus in this passage is not named and does not follow charity-based patterns of benefaction and patronage, that Jesus's reaction to the practice of buying and selling suggested by the disciples is so strong, and that the potter's field donation of money for the poor (from Judas's blood money that the Temple elites make) in the passion narrative is treated negatively—all point to a strong criticism of money, charity, and Roman imperial economics.

Unpacking the context and implications of this passage in an exegetical and political project that centers on biblical interpretations by the poor today is where this chapter and book begin and end. Located at the intersection of poverty and the New Testament, this project examines the way the Bible has been used to justify and condemn poverty and the way poor people are simultaneously confronting and using the Bible in their quest to end poverty. By gathering and analyzing the perspectives of

Poverty Scholars—grassroots antipoverty organizers and leaders—such as Alston and the KWRU leaders mentioned earlier, who are working to build a social movement to end poverty, led by the poor, this work offers these interpretations as revealing, legitimate, and important for scholars, religious leaders, and others in our communities to hear. Finally, this interpretation establishes that the Messiah Jesus in the Gospel of Matthew is the leader of a social movement of the poor that proclaims and embodies God's Kingdom and the end of slavery, debts, and poverty on earth.

At the same gathering where Alston noted the centrality of poverty in the Bible, Poverty Scholar Charlene Sinclair underscored the power of the biblical texts and the impact of traditional interpretations:

> Whether we like it or not, a lot of people use the Bible and what their pastors have told them about the Bible to determine what their spirituality really is. And unfortunately what that means is that the pastors tell them to deal with their oppression, to suck it up, and to look forward to some land out there, some heavenly thing, that they don't know anything about. And so, we believe that fighting injustice is not the mandate of the Bible. [The biblical] text has been stripped of its power, its organizing power, its resistance power. We want to reclaim the text so that people can have another tool to use in their resistance towards social transformation.[2]

With the power of the texts in mind (to constrain and inspire social-justice work), let us turn to biblical interpretation work done by leaders of poor people's organizations, some of the most important twenty-first-century liberation theologians, interpreting from their perspective as the least of these who represent most of us.

Poverty Scholars Interpret

In August 2009, the Poverty Initiative at Union Theological Seminary held a weeklong Poverty Scholars Leadership School. The school brought over 160 low-income community and faith leaders, including 25 youth leaders, representing over 40 organizations, 15 states, and 4 countries, to Camp Virgil Tate in Charleston, West Virginia. In the optional Bible study track

---

2. Charlene Sinclair at Poverty Scholars Strategic Dialogue, September 2008.

(which ran alongside tracks on "Human Rights," "Multi-Media Production," "Arts and Culture," "New Labor Organizing"), grassroots, antipoverty leaders representing many organizations gathered for three hours a day, four days in a row, and studied the Bible together. The organizations gathered included:

> **The Philadelphia Student Union (PSU):** Because one-quarter of the kids in Philadelphia are poor, and Philadelphia public high school students are more likely to go to jail than graduate from high school, since 1995, the Philadelphia Student Union has organized campaigns on issues ranging from textbooks to school safety.
>
> **The Media Mobilizing Project (MMP),** which uses media to tell stories of taxi workers who drive "sweatshops on wheels," transporting people for full days but ending up poorer than when they started working in the morning; multiracial families whose homes have been destroyed and kids have been killed because of firehouse brownouts due to budget cuts; and public sector workers who find themselves too poor to afford health care, housing, and other basic necessities for their families.
>
> **The Direct Action Welfare Group (DAWG):** With 20 percent of West Virginians on food stamps, Walmart as the number one employer in the state, and mountaintop removal thrusting more families into economic devastation, a statewide grassroots organization comprising current and former public-assistance recipients, low-wage workers, and concerned individuals formed to share information and advocate for each other.
>
> **The Jesus People against Pollution (JPAP),** a grassroots environmental justice organization located in Columbia, Mississippi, which is a multiracial, poor community living in FHA- and HUD-subsidized housing built on a federal superfund toxic-waste site. Created in response to an explosion at a local chemical plant that resulted in severe exposure of the community to toxic substances, JPAP has set out to educate and inform impacted communities about the availability of toxicology and environmental health information so that the community can better understand the relationship between environmental exposure, racism, poverty, and disease.
>
> **The Michigan Welfare Rights Organization (MWRO)** based in Detroit, where the 1996 welfare reform eliminated the safety net for

hundreds of thousands in Michigan; 20,000 homes have had their water shut off for lack of payment each year since 2000, and unelected emergency managers control all public services including libraries, schools, sanitation, parks, etc. A statewide organization, MWRO has been in the forefront of efforts to expose and respond to the poisoning of the water in Flint, Michigan, and other cutting-edge struggles for justice for poor people across the state.

The United Workers (UW), an organization of low-wage workers advocating for dignity, living wages, and health care for all. In Baltimore's Inner Harbor, the United Workers have documented violations of the right to work with dignity and the right to health and have worked to overcome these violations, including: systematic failure to pay workers a living wage (or even a minimum wage in some cases); chronic wage theft; and working conditions offensive to human dignity, including verbal and sexual abuse and bribery by supervisors; widespread lack of health insurance; lack of sick days; and failure to respond adequately to workplace injuries, including pressure on employees to work while ill or severely injured, under threat of termination.

These realities informed the Leadership School in general and the Bible study track in particular.

On our last day, we looked at the passage "the poor you will always have with you" in Matt 26:6–13. The assembled group of Poverty Scholars reanalyzed this passage as being supportive of a growing social movement to end poverty rather than justifying poverty's existence and growth in modern times. The Bible study was dynamic, as energy and camaraderie built among the participants. We audio-recorded the session, and when I listen to the recording, I am brought back to the circle of thirty in their chairs, hunched over their Bibles, in a makeshift, crowded room. The youngest participant was fourteen years old, the oldest in her sixties. People came from a variety of religious backgrounds, socioeconomic backgrounds, and theological and political beliefs. There were pious and non-pious, churched and un-churched, organizers and pastors. They included an evangelical Christian who was moved by God to research the environmental pollution in her community only to discover evidence of toxic waste and off-the-chart rates of cancer and disease; a lawyer who grew up in poverty and has dedicated many years to working for the human right to housing; a seminarian who was raised in a conservative Christian community who found that empire-critical biblical studies and other forms of critical biblical scholarship actually deepened her faith and piety; a low-wage worker who did not attend church on a regular basis but prayed daily and found inspiration from Jesus Christ and those with whom she organized. What the group had in common was a desire and urgent need to end poverty for everyone. Three of us were charged with leading the Bible study: Onleilove Alston, Rev. Jessica Chadwick Williams, and me.

It is difficult to describe this Bible study, with laughter and a wide span of emotions running through it. I have modified some answers slightly and not included every single comment in order to try to communicate its meaning and energy better in the written word. This is always a problem where oral traditions meet written manuscripts. But what is contained in this text is testament to the fact that when we turn to Scripture, especially collectively, leaders of poor people's organizations with varied levels of familiarity and training in biblical studies are nonetheless interpreters of sacred texts.

In fact, beginning with the assertion that Jesus was poor and living under Roman imperial rule, these poor leaders and Poverty Scholars were able to make a series of connections and important interpretational moves. For those gathered, Jesus became recognizable as a poor person and a popular social-movement leader, given the New Testament depictions of early Christian communities as a budding social movement. Poverty Scholars suggested that what happens to Jesus throughout the Bible and in the anointing scene specifically shares similar characteristics with other poor people's experiences (including being surrounded by and finding shelter among other poor people, being concerned about debt and resources, valuing dignity over money at times, criticizing charity) as well as the experiences of social-movement leaders in particular (including holding other leaders to high standards, emphasizing political education among movement leaders and participants, evoking movement teachings and sacred traditions, suggesting nonparticipation in dominant economic systems, and assuming that controversy will arise). Similarities between early Christian communities and contemporary poor people are not surprising; social theorist James C. Scott notes, "To the degree structures of domination can be demonstrated to operate in comparable ways, they will, other things equal, elicit reactions and patterns of resistance that are also broadly comparable."[3] Such connections

---

3. James C. Scott, *Domination and the Arts of Resistance: Hidden Transcripts* (New Haven, CT: Yale University Press, 1990), xi.

suggest that a depiction of Jesus as a movement leader, popular messiah, and pedagogue of the oppressed is historically possible, and interpretations of biblical texts that presume this are valid.[4] I will explore these roles of Jesus more in later chapters in this book.

The background and experience of contemporary poor people who are engaged in the work of social transformation helps these Poverty Scholars participating in the Leadership School Bible study understand and draw meaning from the words and actions in the Gospel of Matthew. This Bible study also shows that diverse people can interpret together across their differences of experience, racial and gender composition, formal education levels, and theological persuasions.

We began our session together by reading the passage aloud in an effort to bring attention, reflection, and meditation to the text. With our heads bowed and minds turned to the Bible, we listened as one volunteer read Matt 26:1–13:

> When Jesus had finished saying all these things, he said to his disciples, "As you know, the Passover is two days away—and the Son of Man will be handed over to be crucified." Then the chief priests and the elders of the people assembled in the palace of the high priest, whose name was Caiaphas, and they schemed to arrest Jesus secretly and kill him. "But not during the festival," they said, "or there may be a riot among the people." While Jesus was in Bethany in the home of Simon the Leper, a woman came to him with an alabaster jar of very expensive perfume, which she poured on his head as he was reclining at the table. When the disciples saw this, they were indignant. "Why this waste?" they asked. "This perfume could have been sold at a high price and the money given to the poor." Aware of this, Jesus said to them, "Why are you bothering this woman? She has done a beautiful thing to me. The poor you will always have with you, but you will not always have me. When she poured this perfume on my body, she did it to prepare me for burial. Truly I tell you, wherever this gospel is preached throughout the world, what she has done will also be told, in memory of her."[5]

4. This follows the work of Stevan Davies, who relies on the presence of contemporary exorcisms in parts of West Africa similar to the exorcisms found in the New Testament to demonstrate that Jesus's exorcisms may be historically reliable. See Stevan L. Davies, *Jesus the Healer: Possession, Trance, and the Origins of Christianity* (New York: Continuum, 1995).

5. Biblical citations throughout this book come from the NIV translation unless otherwise noted.

We sat in silence for a few minutes following this reading. We then read the passage a second time, this time asking participants what words or characters really stood out to them. These were some of the responses:

Kym McNair (Antioch Baptist Church, Bedford Hills, NY): There's something I never heard before. Jesus is at Simon's house. Simon the Leper is an outcast; the woman is an outcast. The disciples are not necessarily the favorites in the community. You've got a couple of tax collectors mixed in there. Once they align themselves with Jesus they are outcasts. But they are also criticizing the woman. So it's like when you get to a certain position in life you forget where you came from. Once you're elevated, you find the liberty to criticize people who are where you were just yesterday. So there's a vicious cycle going on here.

Veronica Dorsey (United Workers, Baltimore, MD): The woman stuck out to me, because she could have made money off of the oil in this world. But instead of making money, she did not eat that worldly food. She made sure she was secure in her spiritual food. She knew once she anointed Jesus then he anointed her and blessed her back. The disciples questioned Jesus about her, but she didn't have any doubt about what she had done. And what also struck me was that women rule. And I am so grateful to see that women play such an important part in the Bible because when I was coming up in religion, there were some churches that wouldn't let women be pastors and I never understood why not. With all that women did in the Bible, you won't let them stand up behind the pulpit to give testimony to it? So, it is wonderful to see all these lovely ladies here doing this work in ministry to see how far we have come.

Koby Murphy (Philadelphia Student Union, Philadelphia, PA): The first word that stood out to me was "disciple." And the group of people that stood out to me that I could relate to were the disciples because they were not in their right mind to actually pay attention to what the woman was doing and the reasons behind her actions. And that's how I feel as an organizer and just as a regular person. I'll look at things and think why on earth would somebody do that? And by the time I want to retract my statement, it's too late. It made me think of the whole idea of discipleship period. You think you have people around you who ought to know what

37

needs to happen or what's really going on, but then it turns out that sometimes it is the last person you would think of who actually is exactly in accord with you. And that's what stood out to me, that the woman, she knew exactly what she was doing. While the disciples were following him in his every way, they still couldn't understand how simple and important an act by that woman that was.

We then read the text again and asked what we noticed about the unnamed woman in this passage. We also asked how this Bible passage related to the purpose of the Leadership School and its intention of building a social movement to end poverty. There were a few responses:

Aaron Scott (Chaplains by the Harbor, Aberdeen, WA): This story made me think about the Poor People's Campaign that we're studying and talking about at this Leadership School and how much that movement suffered after the loss of one leader. Here Jesus is trying to point to what the woman is doing, showing the qualities of leadership the whole community needs in order to get on board with what Jesus is about. Jesus knows what he is about to go through so he's working to develop other leaders in his disciples. But the group is resistant because they only want to have that one leader, him. They don't want to hear him saying, "Look, she's got it. She's on point."

Charlotte Keyes (Jesus People Against Pollution, Columbia, MS): Well, I will add something here. In the Bible, Jesus talks also about being poor in spirit: "Blessed are the poor in spirit" [Matt 5:3]. "I have come that you may have life, and have it more abundantly" [John 10:10]. "Thy will be done on earth as it is in heaven" [Matt 6:10]. So why do we feel we have to wait to leave earth to enter heaven? Life is not about stacking money from floor to ceiling or filling barns like the man in the story [Luke 12:13–21]. The poor that God was talking about are the poor in spirit in this passage.

Jesus became poor so that people can become rich [2 Cor 8:9] ..., and once a person receives Jesus, we have become a royal heir [Rom 8:17]. Like with the economy, we say if people are lacking money they are poor. But I was just in Atlanta and I met a man on the street. We ministered to him with food and items. Then we came back again and that young man was there and he flagged us down and told us that we had helped him several years ago: "I used to be homeless and you helped me and I want to bless you because you blessed me and now I am able to receive resources from someone."

From these introductory comments on the Bible and poverty, and participants' initial impressions and connections of Matthew 26 to their work, we turned to the text itself. We began with a discussion about the teachings of Jesus directly before this passage. Participants noticed that the transition, the first verse of Matthew 26, was "when Jesus had finished saying all these things." We looked at Matt 25:34–40, the passage about the "least of these" in the pericope about the "Final Judgment," and read aloud:

> Then the King will say to those on his right, "Come, you who are blessed by my Father; take your inheritance, the kingdom prepared for you since the creation of the world. For I was hungry and you gave me something to eat, I was thirsty and you gave me something to drink, I was a stranger and you invited me in, I needed clothes and you clothed me, I was sick and you looked after me, I was in prison and you came to visit me." Then the righteous will answer him, "Lord, when did we see you hungry and feed you, or thirsty and give you something to drink? When did we see you a stranger and invite you in, or needing clothes and clothe you? When did we see you sick or in prison and go to visit you?" The King will reply, "Truly I tell you, whatever you did for one of the least of these brothers and sisters of mine, you did for me."

Participants had much to say about this teaching that connects Jesus with the impoverished and oppressed: the poor, the prisoner, the stranger, and the hungry were the people with whom Jesus associated himself. We noticed that poor and despised people are those who in the first century CE did not benefit from the Roman Empire and Caesar's infrastructure developments. We examined Jesus's teachings on the poor: the poor will inherit the Kingdom of God;[6] it will be difficult for the rich to make it to heaven;[7]

6. "Now when Jesus saw the crowds, he went up on a mountainside and sat down. His disciples came to him, and he began to teach them. He said: 'Blessed are the poor in spirit, for theirs is the kingdom of heaven'" (Matt 5:1–3).

7. "Then Jesus said to his disciples, 'Truly I tell you, it is hard for someone who is rich to enter the kingdom of heaven'" (Matt 19:23).

God will provide for the poor.[8] Focusing on the "reign/empire of God" and how this empire actually contrasts with the Roman Empire of Caesar, we did a brief Greek word study: the Greek *basileia* means "empire," and that empire in Jesus's day belonged to Caesar (who was considered God). We discussed how Jesus's use of the phrase "empire of God" may have been polemic against Caesar's Roman Empire.

Then, we turned our attention to the actual anointing of Jesus, beginning with Jesus's entering the house of Simon the Leper in Bethany in Matt 26:6 and ending with Jesus's proclamation that we will remember the woman who anoints him in Matt 26:13. Here are select responses from the workshop:

> **Liz Theoharis (Poverty Initiative, New York, NY):** We have just discussed what it could mean when Matt 26:1 reads, "After saying these things," and have discussed the question with whom Jesus identifies his kingdom. We've heard from Jesus that you can't worship God and mammon; it's either God or wealth. Jesus has established that poverty and the poor are central to his ministry before this passage. Turning to our passage, we need to think about the setting. Before this scene with the woman coming and anointing Jesus, Jesus has been in the Temple for the Passover holiday. And what are the elite's reactions to Jesus when he's in the Temple turning over the tables?
>
> **Veronica Dorsey:** They want to hang him.
>
> **Tiffany Gardner (Housing Is a Human Right Campaign, National Economic and Social Rights Initiative):** They want to kill him, but who are they afraid of?
>
> **Group:** The people.
>
> **Liz Theoharis:** Why?
>
> **Veronica Dorsey:** Because there are too many of them.
>
> **Liz Theoharis:** It's divide and conquer; it's crowd control. They have to isolate him so that they can get to him. This is the culmination of this Gospel. He has come and turned over the tables, and they are afraid of him. Then he moves to somewhere else. Does anybody know what Bethany means?

---

8. "So do not worry, saying, 'What shall we eat?' or 'What shall we drink?' or 'What shall we wear?' For the pagans run after all these things, and your heavenly Father knows that you need them. But seek first his kingdom and his righteousness, and all these things will be given to you as well" (Matt 6:31–33).

Kym McNair: House of the Poor.

Liz Theoharis: Now in our story, Jesus isn't in the busy-ness of Jerusalem during a major festival or in the vast Temple anymore. Now he's in the house of Simon the Leper in the small town of Bethany. So what does it mean to us that he is in a place called "House of the Poor"?

Veronica Dorsey: He's in the hood!

Onleilove Alston (Federation of Protestant Welfare Agencies, New York, NY): And he's in the house of a leper, where he wasn't even supposed to be if you are Jewish. He wouldn't be allowed in the Temple after being with a leper; he would be considered ceremonially unclean. This is a lesson about giving what God needs and receiving a blessing. Because Simon offered his house, now he is mentioned every time the woman is mentioned. It shows that God can use anybody, and maybe a historic thing will happen in your midst.

Charlotte Keyes: Also God does things that don't make sense. When you have it all figured out, God will come and show you something totally different. What he did with this story is break down traditions. Many traditions of man are terrible, because they don't line up with God's idea. He wants to bless humanity, and sometimes humanity gets in the way.

Liz Theoharis: One of the things that doesn't line up is this woman. . . . How does she get in here? Where does she come from? Where did she get her alabaster jar? This is expensive ointment; does anyone know how much it is worth?

Veronica Dorsey: A whole year's salary.

Liz Theoharis: So if we know that it is very expensive and cost one year's salary, and this unnamed woman comes out of nowhere with this ointment, we should be thinking: what is going on? And if we know the word that Matthew uses for the ointment—this Greek-English Bible Interlinear translation says it's myrrh—where else have we heard about myrrh? What else does the mention of myrrh make us think about?

Tiffany Gardner: Jesus's birth.

Liz Theoharis: And what does it remind us of?

Tiffany Gardner: Burial and death. Herod killing babies at his birth.

Liz Theoharis: And what else?

Onlielove Alston: Kingship, the three kings. Anointing for kingship. We are reminded that Jesus is royalty bringing in a new reign.

Veronica Dorsey: Yes. Jesus is Kings of the Jews, the King of Kings.

Liz Theoharis: This is also the only place in the Gospel of Matthew where we hear of anointing. This woman uses the ointment to anoint Jesus. The Greek word for "an anointed one" is "Christ."

Jessica Chadwick Williams (First Baptist Church, Des Moines, IA): So this is where Jesus becomes anointed as Christ! He is made Jesus Christ in the house of the poor by this woman-out-of-nowhere with myrrh (usually associated with kings) that's worth a whole year's salary. And what is the reaction of the disciples?

Onleilove Alston: What are you doing!? What's wrong with you!

Koby Murphy: Wow!

Veronica Dorsey: I think the disciples were jealous. It's like they're thinking: "We've been working with him all this time. We're on a break, and here you come and touch him like that. Who does she think she is?" She beat them to the punch.

Aaron Scott: Or she has been there the whole time, but she was in the background doing the cooking and the work that keeps the community and movement going, and now she comes into this different role.

Jessica Chadwick Williams: Having just heard Jesus preach this judgment in Matthew 25, it could be that the disciples are trying really hard in this passage. They are trying to have the right answer to Jesus's questions. They're trying to take seriously how Jesus has said to care for the poor, and now this woman is doing this wasteful thing. So, the disciples are pointing to this to say: "We just heard you, Jesus. We're supposed to be caring for the poor, but she's wasting this money that could care for the poor."

Erika Almirón (JUNTOS, Philadelphia, PA): She was listening in the background, and she comes forward and anoints him before he's killed. She understands what's going to happen, and she better understands what he was saying. She gets it and they don't!

Liz Theoharis: And what specifically are the disciples complaining about?

Veronica Dorsey: She's wasting the oil. And imagine what could have happened if she hadn't!

Charlotte Keyes: If you pay attention to things like Judas being in charge of the moneybags [John 12:6], it makes even more sense. Like today, there are those in charge of God's resources, and they do foolish things and are intimidated by those who do the right

42

thing. And here's a lesson for us in this story. He didn't specify a name; the passage just reads about the woman with the alabaster box. And when you really look at that, it could be any one of us. So we have a lot to think about from this lesson. There is no one of us who can fully interpret the message of the word. Over and over I've had messages preached to me, and each time you hear preaching on a text something different comes out. That is why we need one another to study the Bible together.

Jessica Chadwick Williams: I noticed that in v. 10, right after the disciples say this, it says that Jesus was aware of this. He knew this was going to be the disciples' response. Jesus knew what their response would be and was ready to say this to them. He was prepared with his lesson.

Zakia Royster (Philadelphia Student Union, Philadelphia, PA): So what I want to know is, how can you think about wasting anything on Jesus? The disciples have been with him all this time and yet they don't see Jesus as something more important than the oil. (Laughter)

Veronica Dorsey: I hear it, but we still hear this story, and feel the same way. How can that year's salary be wasted? We have that reaction too.

Liz Theoharis: In John's Gospel, it has this extra line about Judas stealing from the treasury. John explains that Judas raises this question not because he cares about the poor but because he used to take the money donated to the poor. In our context today, we see this too. We might call Judas a "Poverty Pimp," someone who makes money off of people being poor.

Onleilove Alston: Yeah, Judas is concerned about his salary. The other disciples could be the same.

Liz Theoharis: So if we remember what Jessica was saying, the disciples in this story were trying to do the right thing. But when we look at the disciples' response here, it sounds like charity. They are looking at this year's worth of salary, which seems big, but really goes only so far to feed some people, clothe some people.

Veronica Dorsey: But Jesus is priceless.

Liz Theoharis: Yes, Jesus is priceless, and Jesus represents a program that is a complete disruption of the economic order. In the program of Jesus, the poor will inherit this kingdom. Perhaps we should consider the quotation we discussed earlier at this Leadership School by Rev. Dr. Martin Luther King Jr. that says that "true compassion is more than flinging a coin to a beggar but restructuring the system that produces beggars."

Vanessa Cardinale (CATA, Norris Square, PA): In this passage, we might see the disciples as those flinging a coin to a beggar. But Jesus stands for restructuring the system that produces beggars.

Liz Theoharis: Let us now turn to the passage in question itself: "The poor you will always have with you, but you will not always have me." Any thoughts?

Charlotte Keyes: I think it goes back to the poor in spirit. You have to look at things in reality. There is going to be good and evil. You have to examine—when you see the poor—what is the reason. Some people start out without, without the Lord or access to resources, even when help is right in your midst. If you can't access resources, you stay poor. Poverty exists.

Rachel Barnhart (Riverside Church Youth Program, New York, NY): I think Jesus, in his ministry, he wasn't asking for us to always have poverty. You've got this woman who is investing a year's worth of salary in him. She's basically making it so that people can see that it is the systematic structure that is the problem, not just having or not having money. She's not buying into the system of using the money to buy a few things for the poor. Instead she's pouring it all out!

Vanessa Cardinale: When I hear this phrase, I think of Deuteronomy 15. As I study the Bible and how different passages are connected to each other in the Bible, I notice that our passage in Matthew is not the first time that "the poor you will always have with you" appears. Jesus as a rabbi, as a teacher, is teaching from the Torah in this setting. Deuteronomy 15 starts out saying poverty is not acceptable, and we have to do something about it. Then it says, because we don't follow God's commandments, we will always have poverty.

Koby Murphy: Our world is not a perfect world; people have different circumstances. It has hurt all of us. So even the rich people in our world are hurt. They might be the poor in spirit that we already mentioned in our discussion. So Jesus isn't saying that it's okay that people are poor, just that it's the reality that this system is hurting us all and making many of us poor in spirit.

Phil Lindsay (Philadelphia Student Union, Philadelphia, PA): He is talking about what they have to do when he's gone. They will all have to pour themselves out when he is gone. It reminded me of the Pharisees asking about fasting. They aren't poor in faith while he's there, but they may be when he's gone.

Erika Almirón: I know that leadership development is crucial in the work that we do, and he's saying, "Dude, I'm going to be gone in a few days so get your act together."

Mary Ellen Kris (St. Paul and St. Andrew's United Methodist Church, New York, NY): My comment was very similar. I don't think the passage is about giving to the poor or curing poverty by giving away money. He's two days away from his death, and the people who are going to be taking over the fight in his absence don't even understand that he's going to be dying. They won't believe it, don't get it. She comes in and anoints him, the double meaning of anointing for burial and kingship, and there is a bigger point here that they are totally missing. And she gets it.

Aaron Scott: I think about this as Jesus saying there are always going to be ways that people will suffer. I hear people trying to naturalize things like poverty, disease, war, saying they are like nature's birth control. They try to naturalize things that are not natural. Poverty is not an accident; a tornado is an accident. Jesus is saying, "There is always going to be a chance to help the suffering and I am going to role model what you should do to those who suffer, and this woman who is anointing me is going to model for you that we are all entitled to these things . . . we're entitled to food, shelter, visits when we're in jail, AND a proper burial . . . all of it."

Onleilove Alston: I read a book called *The Last Week of Jesus*[9] that says this woman was the first minister or first evangelist through her actions. She is one of the first people to recognize and act.

Jessica Chadwick Williams: I was thinking about why Jesus would say this to the disciples. Maybe it is because that verse in Deuteronomy 15 about ending poverty will come into their heads. Then the reason you have the poor with you always is because the people haven't done what it says in Deuteronomy; they haven't followed God's commandments, including the Jubilee. The disciples would know that.

---

9. Marcus J. Borg and John D. Crossan, *The Last Week: What the Gospels Really Teach about Jesus's Final Days in Jerusalem* (San Francisco: HarperSanFrancisco, 2007).

Zakia Royster: He may have known that we would not get it—that we might not be poor but that we would suffer from being poor in faith. People with good faith know that God is going to be there. Jesus is saying that there will always be people who don't get it and don't do what God says we should do, and that leads to there being people who are poor (in spirit or faith).

Charlotte Keyes: Can you elaborate, Mary, about what you were saying?

Mary Ellen Kris: I think one way to look at this is that he is himself struggling with the idea that he is going to be dying and also frustrated that one of the things he's been saying is that the Son of Man is to be going up to Jerusalem and die and rise on the third day, and they don't get it. And this is his team; it's like the lights are on but nobody's home! This woman, maybe she's been lingering at the back of the pack: she believes that he is going to be killed, and she wants to anoint him as king before that happens. And she is right on the money (laughter), and they're out of the loop.

Veronica Dorsey: When you said that, a light came on and I am home—I get it! Jesus was probably nervous about dying, but God sent this woman to reassure this human part of Jesus—to say, "It's alright; your boys might not get it, but here is somebody who really gets it." So here is someone to give Jesus peace in this moment of fear in the flesh, as he was completely like us, even though his spirit saw beyond it.

Liz Theoharis: And that point goes back to caring for the least of these, from Matthew 25 that we discussed, and that's what this woman does. In this moment, Jesus is the least of these, who needs care and attention. And the passage from Deuteronomy 15 says that there will be *no* poverty if you follow God's commands, but because you are not following God's commands you will always have the poor. It continues with a little more about what those commandments are: redistribute things, don't hoard wealth, feed the poor, visit the prisoner, etc. So how this passage has been interpreted as Jesus giving up on the fight against poverty is actually the exact opposite. He is reiterating the lesson that God does not want poverty, and if we follow God's commandments we can end poverty.

When Jesus makes this strong statement about ending poverty, he says that what this woman has done will be remembered. But do we remember her? No! We don't have her name, and we don't know where she comes from. So first this story is an indictment on the disciples for not getting it, and then it's an indictment on us for still not getting it.

In the communion formula taught in Matthew, Jesus does not say: "Do this in remembrance of me" but instead: "Truly I tell you, wherever this gospel is preached throughout the world, what she has done will also be told, in memory of her." But we have all forgotten her because we have forgotten the poor. And so it points to our failure. Even when he's dying, even when he's being ministered to, Jesus remembers the poor. Jesus is reminding us that, first and foremost, our job is to end poverty as his living and dying wish.

This is just a short excerpt of this reinterpretation of Matthew 26. But even in this brief conversation, new ideas and exciting interpretations have been raised. Poverty Scholars asserted that Jesus himself was poor; that the unnamed woman was the only follower of Jesus who recognized his imminent death and what he stood for in his prophetic life; that the anointing was where Jesus was made Christ; that the anointing reminded us of Jesus's birth, his kingship, and the struggle over power; that this woman valued relationships and prophetic witness over money; that the money mentioned in the story was less important than Jesus's commitment and values; that Jesus may have been referring to Deuteronomy 15 when he asserted that we will always have the poor; and more. As one participant commented during the Bible study, with so many different interpretations of this passage even during this one short engagement with the text, using this passage to normalize and accept poverty in Jesus's time or today is problematic.

New Interpretations of Matthew 26

One of the most important lines of argument among the Poverty Scholars on this passage concerned the position and understanding of the disciples, with a number of different perspectives given. Indeed, the idea of discipleship is a complex one. In many ways the Poverty Scholars identified with the disciples and the challenges of discipleship. Many people saw the organizing and educating work they are doing in their communities to be similar in some ways to the work of the disciples alongside Jesus. This parallel is not often made; typically, disciples are compared to elders or deacons in a church, evangelists of the gospel, or leaders trying to build a congregation from the ground up. But these Poverty Scholars asserted that the disciples' spiritual work and commitment was focused on the social and economic needs of the people of Galilee and that Jesus's ministry of spiritual renewal included social and economic uplift as well.

McNair proposed that the disciples acted as "sellouts" because they were complicit in the ostracizing of the unnamed woman, although they too were social outcasts. Murphy was able to relate to their position and confusion, remembering that it is easy to be surprised by the individuals who do catch on to the new ideas of a leader and that it is often unlikely and unexpected leadership that arises in social justice movements. Alston asserted that the unnamed woman was the true disciple in this example. Williams humanized the position of the disciples, asserting that they were trying to demonstrate that they were taking Jesus seriously and following his call to care for the poor, but they were too mechanical in their application of those teachings. Almirón drew out the significance of the disciples as the leaders carrying on the teachings and actions of Jesus. Scott asserted that these leaders struggled to move away from the model of charismatic leadership to a new model, in which leaders must be teachers and a core of leaders is needed to push forward the work.

Overall, the Poverty Scholars emphasized the educational and practical aspects of the work of the disciples. As students of Jesus who studied his teachings, they worked to implement them, healing the sick, feeding the hungry, and ministering to the poor. The content of the teachings of Jesus is important in this comparison as well. Often we think that Jesus was focused on heaven and spiritual teachings, but the Poverty Scholars maintain that Jesus focused on the social and economic conditions of his followers and that Jesus's pedagogical method was about "waking people up" and teaching critical thinking in the present conditions of impoverishment and exclusion. In fact, the Poverty Scholars' analysis could pave the way for a new understanding of discipleship to be applied in religious congregations and community organizations.

Another observation on Jesus's response to the disciples was that Jesus was actually criticizing the way the disciples wanted to care for the poor, challenging the idea that the solution to poverty is charity that does not change the structures that make people poor. Some of the Poverty Scholars, although poor and homeless themselves, agreed that larger social change which grapples with the root causes of poverty is more important than servicing the needs of a smaller group of poor people for a limited time. The Poverty Scholars made a distinction between doing charity (simply meeting some of the material needs of a select group of people for a limited time) and practicing social justice (working to institute a larger program or platform that questions structures and works to end injustice). Royster and Almirón asserted that Jesus is priceless, rendering it impossible to put a monetary amount on his worth (or on any human being's, for that matter).

Barnhart commented that, by pouring the ointment out, the unnamed woman did not buy into a system where money was more important than people but anointed Jesus to uphold another system of values: people over money/profit. According to Scott, the fact that this woman prepared and provided for Jesus's burial demonstrates that all people should have the right to basic necessities, including burial, subverting a regular occurrence in Jesus's day as well as today where many are too poor to die (and be buried). The whole group also struggled with the idea that what Jesus stood for was larger social transformation and questioned the position of the disciples in the story, where they are depicted as wanting to raise money for the poor and perhaps protecting their personal livelihood in order not to end in poverty themselves.

Cardinale referenced Martin Luther King Jr.'s quotation on the nature of true compassion versus charity in her comments. King preached:

> A true revolution of values will soon cause us to question the fairness and justice of many of our past and present policies. On the one hand we are called to play the good Samaritan on life's roadside; but that will be only an initial act. One day we must come to see that the whole Jericho road must be transformed so that men and women will not be constantly beaten and robbed as they make their journey on life's highway. True compassion is more than flinging a coin to a beggar. . . . It comes to see that an edifice which produces beggars needs restructuring.[10]

Noting Jesus's critique of the disciples' interest in selling the ointment, Cardinale asserted that giving the money to the poor is like "flinging a coin to a beggar."

10. Martin Luther King Jr., "A Time to Break the Silence," in *A Testament of Hope: The Essential Writings and Speeches of Martin Luther King, Jr.*, ed. James M. Washington (San Francisco: HarperOne, 2003), 240–41.

49

Another major line of argument surrounding the Matthew 26 passage is that this is the moment when Jesus is anointed, not just for his burial, but as a "king." It was pointed out that Jesus is made Christ in this passage and that "Christ" is a political, economic, and social title as well as religious. The ointment/myrrh that the woman used was reminiscent of the three gifts at Jesus's birth, Gardner observed, and reminded us that Herod was threatened by a new "king" who would emerge to challenge him (which was why Herod ordered the killing of so many babies). Dorsey pointed out that if Jesus was anointed with the ointment for a king and anointed on his head (and not just his feet, as in Luke 7:38 and John 12:3), this act distinguished Jesus as an important political ruler. Williams was excited to show that this act of becoming "Christ" happened in the House of the Poor (not in the Temple or coliseum or Field of Mars, etc.), and this demonstrated that Jesus was about bringing in a new reign of peace and justice from the underside of history (as opposed to Caesar). Rather than simply hearing "Jesus Christ" as a religious title, the Poverty Scholars heard this title as signifying Jesus's being anointed as messiah/king and therefore as having—not only spiritual significance—but also social, economic, and political power. The group emphasized that this is the only place where Jesus becomes Christ in the New Testament; this conversation about Jesus as "king" and "Lord" had further significance. Poverty Scholars pointed out that Jesus is savior, king, and ruler, and this may be a polemic against Caesar's having these titles as emperor at the time. Anointing Jesus was viewed as a revolutionary act by the Poverty Scholars, just as the program and plan of Jesus was revolutionary to them as well.

Something special happened with the phrase "do this in remembrance" also. In Matthew's Gospel, the only place where the part of the communion formula "Do this in memory of . . ." is referenced is in relation to the woman in ch. 26. Jesus, in fact, declares that what the woman did will be told "in memory of her," rather than "me." Poverty Scholars pointed out the role of the unnamed woman in the remembering and honoring of Jesus as a new kind of ruler, who does not oppress but, instead, liberates hearts, minds, bodies, and souls. The unnamed woman is a model to be emulated today, but many have forgotten what she does for Jesus, and in doing so, have forgotten Jesus's teachings on how to remember and honor the poor (by ending poverty).

Another major interpretive move in the Bible study was to see Jesus's statement "the poor you will always have with you" as a social critique of poverty rather than a comment condoning the existence and prevalence of poverty. Keyes said that she understands this passage as explaining that some people are born poor or made poor, and so poverty exists in our society. Murphy suggested that this is what "poor in spirit" means when it is mentioned in Matthew's Sermon on the Mount (5:3); social problems in our world affect rich and poor, and the suffering associated with them is what makes someone "poor in spirit" and in need of faith, blessing, and healing, including doing these things by ending poverty for everyone.

The rich may be the ones who are spiritually poor in our society, Murphy asserted, because people's complicity with oppressive systems is spiritually impoverishing. The existing social problems are what Jesus is referring to when he says, "The poor you will always have with you," including lack of faith that ending poverty is possible. Instead of a blanket and future-oriented statement that Jesus condones poverty, these Poverty Scholars insisted that Jesus was making the point that poverty and oppression exist because of the way that society is organized. This line can be read as a social critique rather than an acceptance of the status quo.

Important intertextual points arose in our discussion. Cardinale told the group that Jesus's assertion "the poor you will always have with you" is a reference to the Jubilee codes in Deuteronomy 15, which state that there should be no poverty if everyone follows the commandments of God. God is explicit in the Jubilee codes about how to care for the widow and the foreigner, how to forgive debts, and how to allow the land to lie fallow. Poverty enters the picture in the disobedience of humanity to God's will. So any reference to this passage in Matthew 26 serves as a reminder that God has told people how to address poverty. Jesus is criticizing the disciples' suggestion to sell the ointment and give the money to the poor as a solution to the problem of poverty. Jesus responds by saying that God has already taught us how we are to address the problem of poverty through the Jubilee codes—a plan that is more than giving money to the poor. Williams concluded that Jesus anticipated the response of the disciples, and so his statement that "the poor you will always have with you" is a planned response or a teaching moment on the Jubilee. The fact that Poverty Scholars asserted that the New Testament was referring to and quoting the Old Testament shows a methodology of biblical interpretation whereby biblical stories speak and refer to each other, not just that the New Testament "corrects" the Old Testament.

The last major interpretive move made in this Bible study revolved around the social position of Jesus in the passage. Kris reminded the group that the comment of Jesus about the poor perhaps has more to do with the approach of the poor to Jesus's death than with other poor people or even the issue of solving poverty through money itself, in the moment. We discussed that Jesus of Nazareth is a poor person living under Roman rule, so Jesus is not dismissing the poor; he is a poor person experiencing hardship himself. Dorsey pointed out, as Jesus readies himself for his execution and burial, he is someone in need. The unnamed woman recognizes this need of Jesus and ministers to him. While it may not be easy for us to recognize Jesus Christ as ever being in need, if we are to take his humanity seriously and believe that in that humanity he was able to experience the poverty and oppression that many have faced throughout history, then it is important to see Jesus's vulnerability. This reminded the group of Jesus's teaching in Matthew 25 on the care for "the least of these" in the "Final Judgment." In Matthew 26 Jesus is "the least of these," in need of care as he prepares for continued hardship and death.

Poverty Scholars and Methodology

This Poverty Scholars Leadership School Bible study was community based and liberation oriented in both form and content. The preparation for the study drew lessons from academic and church-based sources that have made important contributions to the work of liberative interpretation and practice, including particularly the Christian Base Communities of Latin America and historical- and literary-critical Bible study (especially empire-critical biblical scholarship).[11] This poor-led process of biblical interpretation exemplified by the Poverty Scholars Leadership School Bible study exemplifies what I call "Reading the Bible with the Poor," a method that will be employed throughout the rest of this book.[12] I will return to

11. In 2005, the *Union Seminary Quarterly Review* published an entire issue (59.3-4) on the theme of "New Testament and Roman Empire." The articles there provide useful further reading on this subject, including Liz Theoharis, Noelle Damico, and Willie Baptist, "Responses of the Poor to Empire, Then and Now," pp. 162–71; and Liz Theoharis, review of *Paul and Empire: Religion and Power in Roman Imperial Society*, ed. Richard Horsley (Harrisburg: Trinity Press International, 1997), *Jesus: A Revolutionary Biography*, by John Dominic Crossan (San Francisco: HarperSanFrancisco, 1994), and *Jesus and the Politics of Interpretation*, by Elisabeth Schüssler Fiorenza (New York: Continuum, 2001), pp. 203–8.

12. Alexia Salvatierra and Peter Goodwin Heltzel argue that the call of the poor is the starting place for faith-rooted organizing for racial and economic justice. Alexia Salvatierra and Peter Goodwin Heltzel, "Our Starting Place, the Call of the Poor," *Faith-Rooted*

a more fulsome description of "Reading the Bible with the Poor" in the Conclusion to this book. This section describes its key influences, central practices, and insights gained by this hermeneutic for the interpretation of Matt 26:1-13. I will also demonstrate some of the important interpretational and methodological moves that practitioners of "Reading the Bible with the Poor" made in the Leadership School Bible study.

As evidenced throughout this chapter, "Reading the Bible with the Poor" has an emancipatory agenda and therefore posits that liberation and the agency of the poor and dispossessed are the focus of biblical texts. Putting liberation and the agency of the poor at the center of biblical interpretation produces a cohesive, directed way of doing biblical interpretation. It also connects with a theology of liberation that has emerged over decades from communities in struggle around the world. For instance, Ernesto Cardenal's *Gospel of Solentiname* unveils a liberationist model of interpreting Scripture developed while he was ministering on the Solentiname Islands on the southern end of Lake Nicaragua.[13] Holding open-air Bible studies with peasant farmers, Father Cardenal recorded the conversations to demonstrate an important model of liberative exegesis and community Bible study. After the Second Vatican Council (1962–65), bishops in Latin America met in Medellín, Colombia, in 1968 to discuss the implications of Vatican II for the Church in Latin America. One of the central concepts that emerged was "the preferential option for the poor."[14]

In the years since Vatican II and the flourishing of Christian Base Communities in Latin America, a paradigm shift in biblical studies has taken place at the same time as poor people in the United States and across the world have been compelled to mobilize, organize, and theorize in new ways. The development of empire-critical biblical studies has brought to the forefront a view of early Christianity as a transformative and counter-imperial movement. Scholars describe the early Christian movement—called the Jesus movement, the *basileia* movement, or Christ cults by different writers—as a social movement seeking to transform the violent and impoverishing empire into an egalitarian society. Although they differ in

---

Organizing: Mobilizing the Church in Service to the World (Downers Grove, IL: InterVarsity, 2014), 42–64.

13. Ernesto Cardenal, *The Gospel of Solentiname* (New York: Orbis, 2010).

14. Gustavo Gutierrez deepened and popularized the preferential option for the poor in *A Theology of Liberation*, trans. Caridad Inda and John Eagleson (Maryknoll, NY: Orbis, 1988); cf. idem, "Preferential Option for the Poor," *Gustavo Gutierrez: Essential Writings*, ed. James B. Nickoloff (Maryknoll, NY: Orbis, 1996), 143–46.

their approach and findings, together they illuminate early Christianity as a social movement developing from the subjected nations and people of the Roman Empire. This scholarship not only proposes new insights about the historical Jesus and Paul, but also offers a new paradigm in reading and interpreting the New Testament that intersects with ideas and activism developing out of poor communities responding to growing poverty and homelessness in the United States.[15]

Drawing from these influences, I want to walk through our process of contextual Bible study. A particularly useful outline for historical and literary biblical study comes from Gordon Fee, *New Testament Exegesis*.[16] In his book, Fee outlines the following process of biblical interpretation that I suggest as useful to my readers. Fee's outline includes:

1. Survey the historical context
2. Choose a limited passage or pericope
   a. Become acquainted with the pericope
   b. List exegetical difficulties (topics for special study)
   c. Explore the history of interpretation
   d. Read several translations
3. Analyze structure and syntax; that is, analyze grammar, significant words
4. Research historical background
5. Look at broader biblical and theological context
6. Explore secondary literature

Survey the Historical Context

Historical context was important in our Bible study. Before diving into the Bible study itself, we reviewed some key historical concepts and themes. We defined the Greek word *basileia*, or "empire," which during the first century CE would have stood for the Roman Empire, and saw that the

---

15. In 2004, Brigitte Kahl and Hal Taussig launched a series of New Testament and Roman Empire conferences and gatherings held at Union Theological Seminary, with the participation of Richard Horsley, Neil Elliot, Sze-kar Wan, John Dominic Crossan, Michael Hardt, and many others, including the founders of the Poverty Initiative/Kairos Center. Many of these scholars have long influenced this work and book.

16. Gordon Fee, *New Testament Exegesis: A Handbook for Students and Pastors*, 3rd ed. (Louisville: Westminster John Knox, 2002).

use of *basileia* in the New Testament, as God's Kingdom or empire, may have subverted the way the term was used in its larger historical context. We explored the social standing of lepers, the value of the ointment, the religious and social practice of Passover, and the Jerusalem Temple, as well as the polarization of wealth and poverty in the Roman Empire, and the social position of Jesus and his followers.

Choose a Limited Passage or Pericope

Our Bible study focused on the story of the unnamed woman anointing Jesus. Although we were interested in general themes of poverty and the Bible, we selected a passage that has a long history of negative interpretation with regard to these themes. We looked at Matt 26:1–13 with an emphasis on vv. 6 through 13. By focusing on this particular story, we aimed to draw larger themes and lessons on ways that the Bible has been interpreted to justify poverty and complacency to poverty.

Become Acquainted with the Pericope

At the beginning of the Bible study, we established our goal to explore Matt 26:1–13; we read these thirteen verses three times and urged all participants to identify key words, characters, and themes in the passage. By reading the passage multiple times, participants had the opportunity to familiarize themselves with the whole pericope. After soliciting some general themes and questions from the participants on the pericope as a whole, we then proceeded to explore the passage line by line.

List Exegetical Difficulties (Topics for Special Study)

Even in the first reading of the passage, the Bible study facilitators asked the participants to reveal any particular words, themes, or questions that occurred to them. Some of the areas for special study included: the meaning of *disciple* and *discipleship* (as explored above), the role of the unnamed woman (as a prophetess, disciple, and subservient follower of Jesus), the word *poor* and the attitude of this pericope to poverty and the poor, and the phrase "in memory of her." We also emphasized the poten-

55

tial intertextuality of Matt 26:11 and Deut 15:4 and 11; the connection of the anointing of Jesus with his words and teachings that came before and after this anointing; the role that the anointing in this passage played in Jesus's crucifixion and burial; and the evangelizing nature of the Gospel of Matthew and its connection to the call of the disciples to take up the struggle where Jesus left it.

Explore the History of Interpretation

The hermeneutical lens and history of interpretation were a starting point in this Bible study. The dominant interpretation of Matthew 26 is in line with the status quo; therefore, Poverty Scholars reading from a different social location bring enormous critical potential. Facilitators and participants alike shared their experience with the pericope, including the negative consequences of biblical scholars, pastors and preachers, and lay leaders interpreting this passage to condone poverty, or at least charity or limited action, in the face of poverty. During and even following the Leadership School Bible study, Poverty Scholars commented on the pervasive interpretations of Matthew 26 and John 12: Jesus believes in the inevitability of poverty, the best Christian response to poverty is charity, and Jesus and the poor are set at odds in this pericope. Facilitators raised some of the central interpretations throughout the Bible study. And participants commented throughout the session about the importance of knowing the history of interpretation in an effort to reinterpret and challenge traditional interpretations and paradigms.

Read Several Translations

The facilitators of the Bible study brought with them multiple translations of the text as well as some elementary exegesis and word study from the Greek Bible. Additionally, because participants brought their own Bibles to the study, numerous translations were in play. In fact, in the first three readings of the pericope, two different translations were read: the New Revised Standard Version and the Jubilee Translation of the Bible. In a number of cases throughout the study, participants and facilitators referenced the Greek, the King James Version, and the NRSV translations of the text. Although there were no significant differences emphasized in our Bible study, participants did recognize the importance of studying the Greek, in particular.[17]

Analyze Structure and Syntax

The Bible study followed a systematic reading of the thirteen verses themselves. As previously described, after reading the text in its entirety three times, we turned to a line-by-line exegesis of it. As we explored a verse or part of a verse, participants paused to study the text and the literary context itself.

Analyze Grammar, Significant Words

Facilitators and participants alike selected particular words when proceeding through the text. Some of these words were: *Bēthania* (meaning "House of the Poor" in Hebrew), *myron* (meaning "ointment" or "myrrh" in Greek), *chriō* and *ho christos* (meaning "to pour/anoint" and "an anointed one" in Greek), *basileia* (meaning "empire" or "the Roman Empire"). We also compared Matt 26:11 ("the poor you will always have with you") intertextually with Deut 15:11 ("there will always be poor people in the land"). And we looked at the connection and potential contradiction between Jesus's words "the poor you will always have with you" and "but you will not always have me."

17. It is important to say a word about the translation of Matt 26 here. Although the Leadership School Bible study did not focus on major translation differences of the text, there is a significant one to point out. The NRSV translation of Matt 26 reads, "For you always have the poor with you, but you will not always have me," while the NIV translation reads, "The poor you will always have with you, but you will not always have me." The presence of the future verb "you will always have" in the NIV versus "you always have" in the NRSV historically has had an impact on interpretation. The NIV has been used to imply that Jesus's words suggest inevitability while the NRSV lends itself to a reading that is more focused on describing the present. Nevertheless the presence of the term "always" has led to both translations being understood as unconditional and over a long period of time. Therefore a reinterpretation of the passage is needed for both.

Research Historical Background

Facilitators and participants brought their knowledge and study of historical background to the discussion. Whether it was a critique of Roman imperial patronage and philanthropy, the value of the jar of perfume, the poverty and social position of Jesus, the practice of the rituals and festivals including the economic and religious role of the Jerusalem Temple, it was important to situate the pericope in an accurate first-century historical context of poverty and dispossession for the majority and largesse for the few. Much of this historical knowledge came from participants who had attended seminary and thus had formal biblical training. However, some of the most relevant assertions about the Bible and history—including the fact that the ointment was worth a year's wages, the dire poverty of Jesus and his disciples, and the role of Herod in the killing of the babies—came from participants who had not attended seminary but had either learned about history through their religious congregation, community Bible studies, or self-study and personal interest.

Look at Broader Biblical and Theological Context

Concerned with the Bible's main teachings on poverty, we explored whether the traditional interpretation of "the poor you will always have with you" as meaning that Jesus condones poverty and believes in its inevitability was consistent with other teachings on poverty in the New and Old Testaments. Participants questioned a biblical theology that justified poverty or seemed to side with the wealthy; they supported their questioning with varied and multiple teachings on justice for the poor that they knew from their reading of the Bible: the Beatitudes and the rest of the Sermon on the Mount, the healings and miracles of Jesus, the theological instruction of Paul on the collection and practices of the poor, and a general biblical "arc" of justice for the poor. Numerous specific references to poverty in the Bible were made, including the Lord's Prayer, the woes against the Pharisees, the rich man and heaven, and more. Many of the Poverty Scholars pressed on to key issues in biblical criticism considering the poor. Although many scholars do not know what to do with passages like "poor in spirit" and the overall spiritualization of poverty, the Poverty Scholars made successful interventions and interpretations of these texts that neither ignored the common traps of not acknowledging the spiritual and pietistic elements of the Bible nor succumbed to the spiritualization of poverty.

Explore Secondary Literature

Participants and facilitators referred to secondary literature throughout the Bible study, including Crossan and Borg's *Last Week*, Martin Luther King's *Trumpet of Conscience*,[18] and various commentaries and articles about the anointing of Jesus from more-traditional biblical studies sources. In fact, the more that new questions and interpretations emerged from the Bible study, the more the participants wanted to know what others from secondary literature had to say about the issue. Indeed, an appreciation for study and scholarly engagement was present throughout the Bible study.

Poverty Scholars' Contributions

Following the outline from Fee, but suggesting that poor people can interpret the Bible in new and liberating ways as in the *Gospel of Solentiname* and the Leadership School Bible study, the Poverty Scholars employed a number of very important methods in this study, thereby making contributions on both interpretational and methodological levels. Indeed, I will illustrate this by exploring in depth six issues I highlighted above in the reflection about the Poverty Scholars Bible study, including (a) study of the text and context; (b) interest in the historical context; (c) study of the poor and poverty in the Bible as well as other intertextual work; (d) a look at the parallels of historical and contemporary context; (e) interest in the Christ of faith and the Jesus of history; and (f) communal Bible study. As is the case in more traditional exegesis, the Poverty Scholars were interested in connecting the "anointing at Bethany" to the stories that came before and after it in the text. This resistance to proof-texting or other forms of taking a text out of its literary context was motivated by a desire to see if the message about poverty, anointing, and burial was a major shift from the way those issues were discussed throughout the whole Gospel or if it was consistent with an overall biblical framework of justice for the poor. One of the first questions in the Bible study concerned the content of Jesus's

18. Martin Luther King Jr., *The Trumpet of Conscience* (Boston: Beacon Press, 2011).

teachings in Matthew 1–25 that lead to the transition, "When Jesus had finished saying all these things . . ." (Matt 26:1). Instead of reading Matthew 26 separately from the rest of the stories leading up to it, Poverty Scholars insisted that what came before (and after) informed our understanding of the passage.

Consistent with critical biblical scholars' approaches, Poverty Scholars connected Old Testament and New Testament passages, finding "intertextuality" between Matthew 26 and Deuteronomy 15. Similarly, during our discussion of the meaning of *poor* and *poverty* in our passage, the Poverty Scholars noted multiple additional references to the poor in the New Testament, including the Beatitudes in Matthew, the whole Sermon on the Mount, and some of Jesus's teachings on the rich and poor. Familiar with the famous texts about poverty, they had their own liberative interpretations of many of these texts that they brought to this Bible study. So, while no one pulled out an actual concordance in the session, the concordance in people's minds (and lives) was referenced throughout.

Another important aspect of the methodology used in this Bible study concerns historical and contemporary context, informed by mainstream historical-critical and literary-critical scholarship, especially reader-response methods. Poverty Scholars were quick to make connections to their contemporary context—the poverty, homelessness, and discrimination/ostracization that people have experienced in our society—and to parse out whether there were any similarities between history and the current day. These biblical readers insisted that they had special meanings and interpretations to bring to a text concerning poverty and the poor because of their own experiences of poverty and their role as the poor. What was particularly important was the urgency with which the Poverty Scholars approached both historical scholarship and contemporary application. The importance of poverty and poor people was not an abstract question to the Poverty Scholars. Finding lessons and parallels between the biblical text and the text of people's lives today was vital and held significant consequences.

Also important and potentially unique in a US context was the mixing and melding of personal spirituality and piety with social consciousness. A number of the Poverty Scholars are evangelical Christians who have a deep personal relationship with Jesus and believe that poverty and social change are central themes of the Bible. Rather than creating a divide between people who think that Jesus is a personal savior and others who see Jesus as a community organizer and revolutionary working to bring another political and economic reign to the world, the Poverty Scholars at this Bible study melded these two perspectives. People appreciated both the Jesus of history and the Christ of faith and did not see a conflict between the two. In a society where people are assumed to be either politically conservative and personally pious or politically progressive and socially minded, it is significant and instructional that the Poverty Scholars did not evidence this dichotomy.

Central to biblical exegesis in "Reading the Bible with the Poor" was storytelling. Participants connected the stories of their lives with biblical stories and drew parallels. This principle of storytelling is fundamental to the social-change world view of the Poverty Scholars and the Poverty Initiative Leadership School. The tagline of the Media Mobilizing Project, an organization whose leaders participated in the Bible study, is: "Movements begin with the telling of untold stories." This principle was a starting point and common thread in our Bible study method, both in how we read the Bible stories and how we approached the stories of the plight, fight, and insight of the poor organizing today.

Perhaps the most important and unique aspect of the methodology applied to this Bible study was the relationship of the Poverty Scholars to each other and to larger social issues. While many settings of Bible studies are churches or religious groups, where the participants are interested in learning about the text itself, the Leadership School Bible study had another layer of meaning. Participants were committed to the work of ending poverty as a united group and interested in biblical interpretations that were about ending poverty as well. This is a shift from many Bible studies, in which people have no shared dedication to the collective exploring of the Bible together as a community of interpretation. In these cases, often the differences in each interpretation are emphasized, and the urgency and relevancy of the Bible and biblical interpretations are deemphasized. In the case of the Poverty Scholars, because of the common endeavor to reclaim and reinterpret "the poor you will always have with you," people built on each other's interpretations rather than presenting competitive interpretations or allowing the dominant and traditional interpretations to take precedence. Even when people's ideas and interpretations differed, all participants emphasized their commitment to each other and their common approaches and campaigns to explore the Bible; the goal of building social-movement organizations remained prominent, and individuals did not divert from this socially responsible agenda to prove their personal interpretation was "right." This model of working across differing theological perspectives is potentially significant for our society today. Employing biblical study in an effort to empower the poor and transform society provides important learning and embodies core ideas of base community/liberationist Bible study—specifically, the preferential option for the poor and the melding of theory and practice.

Conclusion

The passage "the poor you will always have with you" is ripe for (re)interpretation in both methodology and meaning. During the Leadership School Bible study the Poverty Scholars revealed the limits of the existing interpretation, finding a source of inspiration and encouragement for their antipoverty organizing from a passage so often used to thwart and criticize their faith that God desires the end of poverty. The chapters that follow build on this experience in two ways. First, the Poverty Scholars' insights into the meaning of the anointing of Jesus at Bethany and the statement "the poor will be with you always" contribute to my exegetical exploration of Matt 26:1-13, which focuses on the interaction between contemporary context, Roman imperial context, biblical text, and biblical interpretation. Second, the method of biblical study engaged during the Poverty Scholars Leadership School is further elaborated as part of a new interpretative framework that I call "Reading the Bible with the Poor." This hermeneutic includes drawing parallels between New Testament stories and contemporary stories of poor people surviving and organizing, investigating important social issues both historical and contemporary (including taxation, debt, infrastructure and development, charity and patronage, poverty, wealth, and political power), and engaging in historical reinterpretation using primary sources about the Roman Empire. Through a reinterpretation of the passage "the poor you will always have with you" and the larger context of Matthew 26, this book is both a product and producer of this interpretative method. The insights and commitments of the Poverty Scholars are ever-present in the chapters that follow.

CHAPTER 3

No Needy among You

At the end of every seven years you must cancel debts. This is how it is to be done: Every creditor shall cancel any loan they have made to a fellow Israelite. They shall not require payment from anyone among their own people, because the LORD's time for canceling debts has been proclaimed. . . . However, there need be no poor people among you, for in the land the LORD your God is giving you to possess as your inheritance, he will richly bless you, if only you fully obey the LORD your God and are careful to follow all these commands I am giving you today. . . . If anyone is poor among your fellow Israelites . . . do not be hardhearted or tightfisted toward them. Rather, be openhanded and freely lend them whatever they need . . . do not show ill will toward the needy among your fellow Israelites and give them nothing. They may then appeal to the LORD against you, and you will be found guilty of sin. . . . There will always be poor people in the land. Therefore I command you to be openhanded toward your fellow Israelites who are poor and needy in your land.

—Deuteronomy 15:1–11

Undeniably, the most difficult line in the Bible for those committed to ending poverty is Matt 26:11, where Jesus actually says, "The poor you will always have with you, but you will not always have me." This line echoes Deut 15:4–11, one of the most liberating "Jubilee" passages in the Old Testament from the second giving of God's law to the people. Deuteronomy 15 has long been understood as an intertextual reference for Matthew 26: the editors of the *Jewish Annotated New Testament* connect Deut 15:4 with

Matt 26:11;[1] the editors of the *HarperCollins Study Bible* suggest that Matt 26:11 refers to Deut 15:11.[2]

Deuteronomy 15:11 reads that since there will never cease to be poor on the earth, it is the duty of the people of God to open their hands to the poor and needy neighbor. This latter echo has helped justify the traditional interpretation of Matthew 26: poverty will exist forever, and so people should give what they can/want to the poor. I claim, however, that the echo applies to the larger Deuteronomy 15 passage, in particular 15:4, which states that there will be *no* needy people if the people of God follow the commandments that God has given them. As a matter of fact, in this chapter and Chapters 4–6 below, I show that, by stating, "The poor you will always have with you," Jesus meant that ending poverty is possible and is God's will; indeed, this is one of the strongest passages advocating for religious responsibility to abolish inequality, with the poor in the lead.

Through his reference to Deuteronomy 15 in Matt 26:11, Jesus is demonstrating that poverty need not exist (and therefore the poor will not need loans or charity) if people follow God's law/commandments (especially through living out the "sabbatical year" and "Jubilee"). Jesus is criticizing the disciples with this echo of Deut 15:11, which establishes that poverty is the result of disobedience or following the "works" of the Roman Empire. Jesus may be warning that if the disciples continue their charity-like dealing and do not follow God's plan of bigger economic and social transformation, they will indeed never abolish poverty. I will return to a critique of charity in more depth in Chapter 6. Here, I explore the biblical theology of justice and abundance established in Deuteronomy, particularly Deuteronomy 15.

Deuteronomic Code and Sabbath/Jubilee

The Hebrew Scriptures, Deuteronomic Code, and the stories and instructions contained within them were important to the Jesus movement, especially to the Gospel of Matthew.[3] The most cited Old Testament book in the

1. Levine and Brettler, *The Jewish Annotated New Testament* (New York: Oxford University Press, 2011), 48.

2. Wayne Meeks, ed., *The HarperCollins Study Bible: New Standard Revised Version* (London: HarperCollins, 1989), 1906.

3. The Deuteronomic Code (Deuteronomy 12–26) is the second collection of legal material in the book of Deuteronomy. The change in king/leader in the ancient Near East

New Testament is the book of Deuteronomy;[4] it is the bridge connecting covenantal law, shalom justice, alternative power systems, and economic rights from the Torah through the New Testament. Theologian and social theorist Ulrich Duchrow writes:

> We may say that Deuteronomy, with the help of the ancient Israelite traditions about a free(d) people, updated by the prophets, Hosea and Jeremiah in particular, succeeded in reforming the kingship system fundamentally. The monarchy was fully bound into the social system of solidarity and participation and lost its instruments of economic exploitation and political oppression.[5]

Continuing in this vein of promoting justice and regulating economic exploitation, Walter Brueggemann writes, "Deuteronomy has a peculiar and persistent propensity for the poor and marginal and continually urges generosity and attentiveness towards widows, orphans, and sojourners, those who are legally and economically disinherited."[6]

Indeed, ending exploitation and caring for the poor is a major theme in the Deuteronomic Code.[7] The law codes exhibit "strong social concern"[8] for the poor and marginalized, including: mandating sabbatical and Jubilee years, prohibitions on charging interest to Israelites, protection of pledges given as collateral for loans, just weights and measures, prompt payment of wages, equity in legal proceedings, as well as direct provisions for the poor via tithing and gleaning.

Some of the individual regulations include the elimination of state tribute, setting a year for the remission of debts (15:1–11), freeing slaves (15:12–18), allowing the poor and weak to go on pilgrimage (16:11), forbid-

---

was accompanied by an oath of loyalty by the people. Therefore, Deuteronomy is not a covenant between two parties but a loyalty oath imposed by the sovereign on the people. See David Noel Freedman, "Deuteronomy," *Anchor Bible Dictionary* 2:168–83.

4. Ronald Clements, "The Book of Deuteronomy: Introduction, Commentary and Reflections," *The New Interpreter's Bible* 2:271–88.

5. Ulrich Duchrow, *Alternatives to Global Capitalism: Drawn from Biblical History, Designed for Political Action* (Heidelberg: Kairos Europa with International Books, 1995), 159.

6. Walter Brueggemann, *A Social Reading of the Old Testament* (Minneapolis: Fortress, 1994), 60.

7. Michael Coogan, *A Brief Introduction to the Old Testament: The Hebrew Bible in Its Context* (Oxford: Oxford University Press, 2009), 149.

8. Robert Wafawanaka, *Am I Still My Brother's Keeper? Biblical Perspectives on Poverty* (Lanham, MD: University Press of America, 2012), 11.

ding interest and pledges taken from the weak (23:20, 24:17), and mandating that harvest leftovers remain in the fields for the hungry (24:19). These instructions are given with reminders to the people that God led them out of slavery in Egypt and with the highest commandment, the *Shema' Israel*, in 6:4. The people bound themselves and all this in a covenant (26:16–19); keeping that covenant was viewed as a matter of life and death (30:15–20).[9]

The citation of Deuteronomy 15 in Matt 26:11 recalls the Hebrew *shabbat*, meaning rest or day of rest, and especially *shemittah*, meaning year of remission, remission of commercial debts, remission of private slaves, freeing security deposits, suppressing exactions, or a (temporary) remitting. Also called "the Sabbath or sabbatical year," *shemittah* is mentioned several times in the Bible, including: Exod 23:10–11, Lev 25:1–7, Deut 15:1–3, Jer 34:13–14, Neh 10:32, 2 Chr 36:20–21, and 2 Kgs 19:29–31.[10] Notably, the Sabbath—the

---

9. Duchrow, *Alternatives to Global Capitalism*, 156–59.

10. "For six years you are to sow your fields and harvest the crops, but during the seventh year let the land lie unplowed and unused. Then the poor among your people may get food from it, and the wild animals may eat what is left. Do the same with your vineyard and your olive grove" (Exod 23:10–11); "The LORD said to Moses at Mount Sinai: 'Speak to the Israelites and say to them: "When you enter the land I am going to give you, the land itself must observe a sabbath to the LORD. For six years sow your fields, and for six years prune your vineyards and gather their crops. But in the seventh year the land is to have a year of sabbath rest, a sabbath to the LORD. Do not sow your fields or prune your vineyards. Do not reap what grows of itself or harvest the grapes of your untended vines. The land is to have a year of rest. Whatever the land yields during the sabbath year will be food for you—for yourself, your male and female servants, and the hired worker and temporary resident who live among you, as well as for your livestock and the wild animals in your land. Whatever the land produces may be eaten"'" (Lev 25:1–7); "At the end of every seventh year you must cancel debts. This is how it is to be done: Every creditor shall cancel any loan they have made to a fellow Israelite. They shall not require payment from anyone among their own people, because the LORD's time for canceling debts has been proclaimed. You may require payment from a foreigner, but you must cancel any debt your fellow Israelite owes you" (Deut 15:1–3); "This is what the LORD, the God of Israel, says: I made a covenant with your ancestors when I brought them out of Egypt, out of the land of slavery. I said, 'Every seventh year each of you must free any fellow Hebrews who have sold themselves to you. After they have served you six years, you must let them go free.' Your ancestors, however, did not listen to me or pay attention to me" (Jer 34:13–14); "We assume the responsibility for carrying out the commands to give a third of a shekel each year for the service of the house of our God: for the bread set out on the table; for the regular grain offerings and burnt offerings; for the offerings on the Sabbaths, at the New Moon feasts and at the appointed festivals; for the holy offerings; for sin offerings to make atonement for Israel; and for all the duties of the house of our God" (Neh 10:32–33); "He carried into exile to Babylon the remnant, who escaped from the sword, and they became servants to him and his successors

rest required by God in order to worship God, and protect life, and ensure material well-being—is one of the earliest legislations in the Bible.

The Deuteronomic Code in Deuteronomy and the Covenant Code in Exodus[11] emphasize the humanitarian side of sabbath: slaves, animals, and everyone have a rest. But the priests also insist that observing sabbath is about copying/emulating God.[12] This combination of piety and economic practice are merged: rather than choosing between helping the poor and worshiping God, the Deuteronomic Code demonstrates that the way to worship God is to structure society around everyone's needs. God's intention with God's laws and commandments is to eliminate poverty and inequality on earth.

The Deuteronomist also connects debt forgiveness, land fallowing, and slave manumission. These verses broaden the law to apply to the entire society (rather than just the practices of particular families or clans). The message is that freeing slaves and forgiving debts is a moral obligation to God.[13] Rather than simply a suggestion to care for the poor in a more transitory and temporary situation, which is often the interpretation of Deuteronomy, the Deuteronomic Code offered a way of living with shalom justice at the center. It is a model for humanity's relationship with God that neither decenters the poor nor spiritualizes poverty. Rather than the Sabbath being about a holiday or taking a break on the backs of others who are unable to take a break, it is about economic equality and right relationship with humanity and God.

Indeed, the topic of Sabbath is taken up specifically in the Gospel of Matthew, where Jesus is considered the "Lord of the Sabbath" (Matt 12:8).[14]

---

until the kingdom of Persia came to power. The land enjoyed its sabbath rests; all the time of its desolation it rested, until the seventy years were completed in fulfillment of the word of the LORD spoken by Jeremiah" (2 Chr 36:20–21); "This will be the sign for you, Hezekiah: 'This year you will eat what grows by itself, and the second year what springs from that. But in the third year sow and reap, plant vineyards and eat their fruit. Once more a remnant of the kingdom of Judah will take root below and bear fruit above. For out of Jerusalem will come a remnant, and out of Mount Zion a band of survivors'" (2 Kgs 19:29–31).

11. The Covenant Code consists of Exodus 20–23 and includes the Ten Commandments as well as other economic and civil laws to govern the ancient Near East. See Coogan, *A Brief Introduction to the Old Testament*, 109–10.

12. Xavier Léon-Dufour, "Sabbath," in *Dictionary of Biblical Theology*, ed. X. Léon-Dufour (Boston: Word Among Us Press, 1988).

13. Mark Hamilton, "Sabbatical Year," *The New Interpreter's Dictionary of the Bible* 5:11–13.

14. Douglas R. A. Hare, "How Jewish Is the Gospel of Matthew?" *Catholic Biblical Quarterly* 62 (2000): 272.

The emphasis of this title on economic rights comes shining through with a fuller understanding of the Sabbath from the Deuteronomic Code. Roman lords were not interested in the well-being, prosperity, and rest of their subjects except to compel more work from them. This title for Jesus therefore emphasizes that he is from the underside of the empire—Jesus is truly on the side of the poor; he is a leader who represents the popular struggles of the poor. He values the lives and livelihoods of the other poor subjects of the Roman Empire and believes they deserve rest and justice. Matthew's Jesus is also focused on renewing Israel's covenant with God. Again, based on this broader understanding of Deuteronomy and the codes and covenants with God in the Hebrew Scriptures, we are reminded that the way to honor God is to structure society around the needs of everyone. Rest and remission from debts and slavery were terms used throughout Matthew. It is surely fitting, therefore, that there is in Matthew a strong echo of Deuteronomy, which promotes releasing slaves, forgiving debts, and treating neighbors with generosity. Jesus, his followers, and their contemporaries were looking for systemic solutions to poverty and dispossession and found them in popular prophetic tradition, especially the covenant as documented in stories, instructions, and the Scriptures.

Textual Analysis of Deuteronomy 15

Indeed, exploring Deut 15:1–12 and its three sabbatical-year provisions to alleviate the suffering of the poor, including remission when the poor cannot pay back their debts (15:1–6), generosity when they cannot obtain loans (15:7–11), and manumission when they face slavery or indentured servitude (15:12–18), is important to understanding the mission and vision of Jesus, according to Matthew 26.[15] Walter Brueggemann asserts that this debt remission (particularly as described in 15:1–2) is the most radical and astonishing call in the whole Bible. In the same passage, the people of God are promised blessing and prosperity and then asked to give it up to make sure that everyone has some level of economic security.[16] This passage should remind Christians of the Gospel passages where Jesus teaches, "For

---

15. Duane Christensen, *Deuteronomy*, 2 vols., Word Biblical Commentary 6a–b (Nashville: Thomas Nelson, 2001–2), 1:300–314.

16. Walter Brueggemann, "Conversations among Exiles," *Christian Century* 114, no. 20 (1997): 630–32.

whoever wants to save their life will lose it, but whoever loses their life for me will find it. What good will it be for someone to gain the whole world, yet forfeit their soul?" (Matt 16:25–26).

Deuteronomy 15:1 begins by stating that the people of God must make a release or remittance (Hebrew) or forgiveness (Greek) on the seventh year. It proceeds to detail how to make this release (to God), by canceling every private debt of one's neighbor. It explains that one is permitted to collect loans from foreigners, but anyone within the community (and therefore considered a brother) must have loans forgiven. Deuteronomy 15:4 states there should be no one lacking or in need, because people receive a blessing through the land that God has given as an inheritance. People are to listen to God and follow the commandments God has given. If followed, the people of God will lend to nations but will not need to borrow; they will control other nations but not be subjugated. In general, Deut 15:1–6 describes how the people of God should live and prosper. And importantly, these six verses suggest radical economic redistribution as being central to worship and obedience to God.

Deuteronomy 15:7 continues by indicating what to do if anyone is in need. The people are instructed to open their hands and lend to anyone who lacks. Verse 8 states that those who are able should lend whatever amount the person wants and needs. Verse 9 exhorts the people not to be tightfisted and not to hold anything back (in heart or in deed) by thinking that, as the seventh year approaches, anything they lend might not be repaid. In fact, in the Greek Septuagint it is called a sin (*hamartia*) against God if the brother seeking a loan or some form of economic resources must cry against the creditor to God because his need is unmet. Verse 10 instructs the people to lend whatever the person wants; the promise is that the Lord will bless them for following these commandments, and so they should not fear giving/lending. Deuteronomy 15:11 then states that the needy shall not fail from the land and therefore instructs the people to give/lend freely.

The core message of this passage is the elimination of poverty and inequality and God's will that all have enough. This is the goal. The structure of Deut 15:1–11 emphasizes v. 4 as the focus of the law. Verse 11 demonstrates what happens in a society that makes this sort of legislation and compassion necessary and central to its functioning and logic. In general, Deuteronomy 15 emphasizes that there will be no one in need if the people follow the commandments of God; it explains how God commands the people to live (and to share); and it reminds the people that creation is

God's and that humanity is supposed to take care of that creation including, especially, other human beings.

Not surprisingly based on what we have explored about the Deuteronomic Code, many of the words in Deuteronomy 15 are both pietistic and economic; they include commandment, blessing, God, brother, sin, inheritance, creditor, loan, needy, poor, possess, release/remission. The instructions include making a release of debts as a way to honor and worship God. They assert that people having to cry out against their creditors is considered a sin against God (not just the mistreatment of another person). They explain that God commands people to give to their neighbors and to ensure that all needs are met. Verses 4, 6, 10, 14, and 18 state that God will bless those who give.[17] Piety and economics are melded in this passage. In fact, they are melded throughout the Bible, including Matt 26:6–13.

History of Interpretation of Deuteronomy 15:11

In order to understand the application of Deuteronomy 15 to Matthew, I am specifically interested in the relationship between Deut 15:4 and 15:11 and their history of interpretation. Some scholars claim that in Deut 15:11, those with wealth are asked to show compassion and follow the laws that are given. In this interpretation the absence of poverty is the ideal, but with Sabbath and Jubilee regulations being too difficult for fallible humans, the instructions in 15:11 mitigate against the worst effects of poverty through the generosity of those with the ability to give. A related interpretation holds greater hope for the eventual ending of poverty and argues that the instructions for the care of the poor are included as the community moves towards that ideal. Other scholars argue that there should be no poverty within the community of Jewish worshipers but that poverty may exist in other lands. In this understanding Deuteronomy 15 and many additional laws are meant to set up a contrast between Israel and other nations.[18] Another interpretation is that poverty results from disobedience to God, and so 15:11 is speaking to this continued disobedience. One can also interpret

17. Christensen, *Deuteronomy*, 1:300–314.
18. Jeffries Hamilton, "*Hā'āreṣ* in the Shemitta Law," *Vetus Testamentum* 42 (1992): 214–22; M. Hamilton, "Sabbatical Year," 11–13; Christensen, "Protection of the Poor (15:1–11)," *Deuteronomy*, 1:300-314.

the passage not as proclaiming poverty's inevitability, but that the tension between vv. 4 and 11 demonstrates that when exceptional needs arise (because of disaster, crisis, widowhood, famine), the people of God know how to address it. In this understanding Deuteronomy 15 sets up a structure that addresses immediate need at the same time as it eliminates persistent, structural, and generational poverty.

Was Forgiveness of Debts Practiced?

The concept of Sabbath and Jubilee have been questioned, and their power and influence have been challenged based on various interpretations of the remission of debts, including: an assertion that only interest was forgiven, not the loan itself (although this seems unlikely, given the prohibition of usury in Exod 22:25 and Lev 25:36–37); the idea that people were required to pay back the loan if it happened before the seventh year (but an admission that remission did occur every seven years); and the question of whether creditors would have made loans if they were never going to be paid back. But as we read above, Deuteronomy 15 simply states that one should forgive debts on the seventh year, that people should continue to give loans (even if they will not be paid back), and that the goal of this release is to solve the problem of poverty—a very clear economic statement.

Nonetheless, a major question in regard to *shemittah*—especially its application in Jesus's day, but also the validity of our co-optation of the concept in our lives today—is whether this type of sabbath or remission was actually practiced historically or whether it existed only as an ideal. First Maccabees 6:49–53, Tacitus (*Histories* 5.4), and Josephus (*Antiquities* 12.378, 23.234, 14.202–6, 475)[19] all speak about Jews observing the sabbatical year.[20] In fact, Josephus's writings contain eight references to *shemittah* and Jubilee.[21] In the first century BCE, Hillel the Elder interpreted *shemittah* as being practiced only among Jews. After the destruction of the Temple in 70 CE, people are exhorted to observe *shemittah* so that no more misfortune befalls the people.[22]

---

19. Josephus writes that both Alexander the Great and Julius Caesar remitted Judea's taxes in the sabbatical year.
20. M. Hamilton, "Sabbatical Year," 13.
21. Brad Pruitt, "The Sabbatical Year of Release: The Social Location and Practice of Shemittah in Deuteronomy 15:1–18," *Restoration Quarterly* 52 (2010): 81–92.
22. Pruitt, "The Sabbatical Year of Release," 81–92.

Scholars including Edward McLeod assert that debt cancellation by those in power was applied more generally in the ancient Near East as well. This practice was usually at the whim of the people in power, however, rather than being the way that one showed obedience and loyalty to God. Debt cancellation follows a rhythm in this Deuteronomic passage. Economic restructuring is not left to bursts of good will or acts of selflessness but is structured into the society, with the authority being removed from any one earthly ruler. Commentators assert that this law is to avoid the establishment of a class of poor and indentured individuals. It is structured so that a people who have been slaves do not create slavery in their own society.[23] This should serve as inspiration to those who have been told all their lives that organizing the economy should be left to traditional economists and forgiving debts is not possible. It should be an example that, although we have known poverty and inequality for our whole lives, another way is possible and is in fact God's will.

In addition to the extrabiblical sources, evidence of debt remission also exists in the Hebrew Scriptures. Jeremiah 34:13–14 speaks about the manumission of slaves; Jeremiah is disappointed at the lack of adherence to *shemittah* law. Nehemiah 5:7–12 also speaks about debt remission and not charging interest.[24] First Maccabees 6:49 (referred to above) suggests that the king made peace with the people of Beth-zur because they had no provisions to withstand a siege due to the fact that it was a sabbatical year.

Whether or not the elimination of poverty happened in the ancient Near East, it does seem that during the Second Temple period (and around the time of Jesus) there were attempts to redistribute land and wealth among Jews, following the commandments. Indeed, the introduction of the *prozbul* should be evidence that there was a debate about the institution of debt release and *shemittah*. As Herzog writes,

> When the rabbis discovered that the rich refused to make loans to peasants in the year leading up to the sabbatical year, they introduced the *prozbul*, an oath taken by the debtor vowing that he would repay the loan whenever the lender stipulated (sabbatical or no sabbatical). . . . Just as Sabbath provided a physical respite from the endless toil of life, so the sabbatical provided debt relief from the endless cycle

23. Edward McLeod, "Between Text and Sermon: Deuteronomy 15:1–11," *Interpretation* 65 (2011): 180–82.
24. Pruitt, "The Sabbatical Year of Release," 81–92.

of poverty and misery. But it appears that both were undermined and eventually abrogated by the ruling class.[25]

The introduction of the *prozbul* would have meant both that debt would be perpetual (the elite could use debt to alienate peasants from their land) and that the pressure for loans must have been extreme (since the people were willing to modify such important Jewish principles). But, despite some evidence that *shemittah* was practiced, poverty was widespread in Roman imperial society (a subject to be discussed in more detail in Chapter 5). Therefore, Jesus's and his contemporaries' new attempts to forgive debts and release slaves in a more significant way were all the more necessary. This fact should inform any understanding of Deuteronomy 15 and Jesus's reference to it in Matthew 26.

Conclusion

Intertextuality between Deuteronomy 15 and Matthew 26 brings a liberative interpretation of Matt 26:11 into view. Having looked more closely at Deut 15:1-11 and explored the radical economic practice of *shemittah* in the ancient world, I return to Matt 26:11 itself, where an unnamed prophetess anoints Jesus to be ruler of God's Kingdom. His charge is to care for all, especially the poor. Indeed, when Jesus responds to the disciples, he quotes one of the most radical Sabbath and Jubilee prescriptions in the Bible. Deuteronomy 15 says that there will be no poor person among you if you follow the commandments God is giving today—those commandments are to forgive debts, release slaves, and lend money even when you know you won't get paid back. Deuteronomy 15 continues and says that because people will not follow those commandments, there will always be poor among you. So when Jesus quotes this phrase, he isn't condoning poverty, he is reminding us that God hates poverty and has commanded us to end poverty by forgiving debts, by outlawing slavery, and by restructuring society around the needs of the poor.

Therefore, the passage is a critique of empire, charity, and inequality, rather than stating that poverty is unavoidable and predetermined by God. Poverty is created by human beings—by their disobedience to God

---

25. William Herzog, *Prophet and Teacher: An Introduction to the Historical Jesus* (Louisville: Westminster John Knox, 2005), 140.

and neglect of their neighbor. Jesus shows another way: ending poverty is possible, through the practice of covenant economics, as seen in Deuteronomy 15. Matthew 26:11 both refers to people's failure to follow God's law and commandments (that is, the forgiveness of debts, the release of slaves, provisions for those in need without further benefiting only the wealthy) and instructs us on how to establish a reign of prosperity and dignity for all (that is, institute the Jubilee and Sabbath throughout the land). In God's Kingdom, there will be no poor because poverty (and perhaps wealth?) will not exist. This is what Jesus is saying when he proclaims, "The poor you will always have with you, but you will not always have me." Let us now turn to the economic conditions of Jesus's world to understand why this release was so necessary and urgent.

CHAPTER 4

"Don't Laugh, Folks—Jesus Was a Poor Man"[1]

In the gospels, canonical and noncanonical, and in Paul—in the broad memory and praxis of the early church—Jesus is recalled as living outside the system of brokered power and economy of Rome's Empire. . . . Jesus knew expendability, he knew expendables, and he invited those who had not fallen out of the Roman system of brokerage and patronage to step out voluntarily and to become part of a new thing, the Empire of God.[2]

—Stephen Patterson

To ignore the context of the Gospel of Matthew and Jesus's movement would be to miss the major motivating factors for the development and institutionalization of Jesus's mission and movement. It would be to miss why following the *shemittah* and larger Deuteronomic Code in the period of Roman Imperial rule was so necessary. As Richard Horsley writes in his book *Jesus and Empire: The Kingdom of God and the New World Disorder*, "Trying to understand Jesus' speech and action without knowing how Roman imperialism determined the conditions of life in Galilee and Jerusalem would be like trying to understand Martin Luther King without knowing

1. This quotation comes from a photo from the 1968 Poor People's Campaign called for by Rev. Dr. Martin Luther King Jr. only months before his death. It was a slogan written on the canopy of various "mule trains" that made their way from Marks, Mississippi, to Resurrection City in Washington, DC, where thousands of poor people from across the United States gathered to demand that the nation "lift the load of poverty."

2. Stephen J. Patterson, "Dirt, Shame, and Sin in the Expendable Company of Jesus," in *Profiles of Jesus*, ed. Roy Hoover (Santa Rosa, CA: Polebridge, 2002), 202–5.

how slavery, reconstruction, and segregation determined the lives of African Americans in the United States."[3] By taking up the Roman context as central to our understanding of Jesus's ministry, we can explore ways that the poor make history.

Jesus comes to his ministry from his own earthly poverty: from his experience of the severe dispossession and subjugation of the Roman Empire. John Dominic Crossan asserts that Jesus was a poor, illiterate worker, which is an understanding of his social and economic position that helps us emphasize the radical stance that Jesus takes in his teachings on and practice of economics and politics under the Roman Empire. In the Introduction to *Jesus: A Revolutionary Biography*, Crossan writes, "If, for example, we are tempted to describe Jesus as a literate middle-class carpenter, cross-cultural anthropology reminds us that there was no middle class in ancient societies and that peasants are usually illiterate, so how could Jesus become what never existed at his time?"[4] Instead, as Crossan asserts:

> If Jesus was a carpenter, therefore, he belonged to the Artisan class, that group pushed into the dangerous space between Peasants and Degradeds or Expendables. . . . Furthermore, since between 95 and 97 percent of the Jewish state was illiterate at the time of Jesus, it must be presumed that Jesus also was illiterate . . . like the vast majority of his contemporaries.[5]

Stephen Patterson has proposed that Jesus fits into the category of those most exploited and oppressed by the empire: "In the gospels, canonical and noncanonical, and in Paul—in the broad memory and praxis of the early church—Jesus is recalled as living outside the system of brokered power and economy of Rome's Empire."[6] Patterson asserts that the company that Jesus kept was poor and expendable and, by association, he may have fit into this category himself. He continues, "Jesus knew expendability, he knew expendables, and he invited those who had not fallen out of the Roman system of brokerage and patronage to step out

3. Richard Horsley, *Jesus and Empire: The Kingdom of God and the New World Disorder* (Minneapolis: Fortress, 2003), 15.

4. John Dominic Crossan, *Jesus: A Revolutionary Biography* (San Francisco: HarperCollins, 2009), xii.

5. Crossan, *Jesus*, 25.

6. Patterson, "Dirt, Shame, and Sin," 202.

voluntarily and to become part of a new thing, the Empire of God."[7] In Matt 8:20, Jesus says that he has nowhere to lay his head. This most likely is a statement that Jesus himself is homeless.[8] At his burial, Jesus is too poor to have his own tomb; instead, Joseph of Arimathea, a rich disciple of his, claims Jesus's body for placement in his own tomb (Matt 27:57–60). And William Herzog asserts that Jesus's poverty is established at his birth:

> The genealogies in Matthew and Luke may reflect the efforts of the early church to raise the honor level of Jesus by associating him with King David, or they may show that Jesus was profoundly related to the people of God known as Israel, but even these birth narratives depict Jesus as born into a peasant family.[9]

Jesus's poverty has political, economic, and spiritual implications. Jesus is a leader and ruler, a king and Christ/Messiah, as we will explore more fully in Chapter 6. But Jesus is poor: he is not a patron, benefactor, or wealthy leader/king like Caesar, Pharaoh, or other ruling authorities. As Patterson states in the quotation above, rather than insisting on adherence to the existing order, Jesus suggested that those with power and means step out of the patronage system that dispossessed and separated the poor. The poor Jesus is not in an economic or political position to benefit from the poverty of those around him. His ruling authority does not rest on an accumulation of wealth and the political power that assists appropriation and dispossession. Instead, Jesus is a new kind of savior, lord, and ruler: a savior of the poor who is poor himself.

Jesus's humility and poverty distinguish the type of Messiah he will become, from the beginning of the Gospel. In the genealogy (Matt 1:1–17), where Jesus is first titled "Messiah," he is compared and connected with King David. The Gospel notes that there were fourteen generations from Abraham to David, fourteen more generations from David to the deportation/exile, and now, fourteen generations later, Jesus—"the one being called Christ/Messiah" (1:16)—is born to Mary. This implies that he is the next "king of the Jews," who will usher the people out of exile, poverty,

---

7. Patterson, "Dirt, Shame, and Sin," 205.

8. Crossan, *Jesus*, 94.

9. William Herzog, *Prophet and Teacher: An Introduction to the Historical Jesus* (Louisville: Westminster John Knox, 2005), 81.

and empire. The suggestion of a "New Exodus" is based on the structuring presence in the genealogy of the Greek word *metoikesis*, meaning "exile." This Greek word *metoikesis* occurs in vv. 11 and 12, when the Israelites were exiled to Babylon; it is used again in v. 17 to connect David, the Babylonian exile, and Jesus Christ. It reminds readers that another exile and subjugation under Rome is occurring, and Jesus is here to lead the people to freedom.

But what particularly distinguishes Jesus in this genealogy is the presence of other leaders from the underside of Israelite history, especially women such as Rahab and Tamar, who remind readers of the horrors of exploitation, violence, and hegemonic power. Their inclusion in Jesus's genealogy raises a long-standing critique of king and kingship from the Hebrew Scriptures, where God sends a king to rule Israel with great reluctance, warning God's people of the problems with dominant and hegemonic power and authority. Jesus may be a new King David but not the sort of king one would expect; he is without a rule that values or privileges wealth, power, and authority. Jesus comes from a world of poverty, exclusion, and illegitimacy, and Jesus's rule will not simply mirror the rule of those with power and wealth.

At Jesus's birth, in Matt 2:1–12, a star rises—a sign that was said to be present for the birth of Caesar Augustus—signaling to the wise men of the east that Jesus has been born.[10] Jesus is born in a humble manger and, although visited by three magi sent to determine whether he is a threat to Herod's kingship, Jesus is of low birth himself. Herod the Great is so intimidated by the birth of this new king (2:3), born to an unwed teenager with no place to call home, that he instructs the wise men to inform him of Jesus's whereabouts so that he can dispose of him. When that fails, Jesus and his family run away into exile in Egypt because a messenger of God instructs them to flee (2:13–15)—perhaps a reference to the exile (*metoikēsis*) of the genealogy and to the poverty and slavery of the exodus.[11] Richard Horsley writes about this passage to Egypt and its connection to the rest of Jesus's earthly life as a new Moses, a leader of an antislavery and antipoverty movement:

10. Discussion of Augustus as divine son and of the birth narrative in general runs throughout these two books: John Dominic Crossan and Jonathan Reed, *In Search of Paul: How Jesus's Apostle Opposed Rome's Empire with God's Kingdom* (San Francisco: HarperSanFrancisco, 2004), 160; and Paul Zanker, *The Power of Images in the Age of Augustus* (Ann Arbor: University of Michigan Press, 1990), 35.

11. Reza Aslan, *Zealot: The Life and Times of Jesus of Nazareth* (New York: Random House, 2013).

As an infant [Jesus] descends to and then journeys out of Egypt, recapitulating Israel's exodus from Egypt (Matt. 2:13–23). He is then tested in the wilderness, like Moses (4:1–17). Jesus is still in the role of the new Moses at the climax of Matthew's Gospel when, at the Passover Festival celebrating Israel's exodus, he presides over the Last Supper as a meal of covenant renewal (26:27–28).[12]

At Jesus's baptism in Matthew 3, God claims Jesus as God's son, yet another parallel with Augustus, who actually deified his adopted father, Julius Caesar, in an effort to become God's son.[13] The fact that God identifies Jesus as his son and sets him apart in this story is important to his becoming Christ/Messiah. In the Hebrew Bible, prophets and kings were selected and raised up by God (see Conclusion). But this singling out of Jesus by God happens in the wilderness, not the arena or any location of political power. While there are witnesses present, this adoption of Jesus by God is not a public performance for the wealthy and powerful. The God of justice from the Hebrew Scriptures does not have a wealthy son but one who is poor like the majority of the people living around him.

In the temptation scene in Matt 4:1–11, Jesus demonstrates that he does not aspire to or desire the trappings of other rulers; rather than seeking riches and power or promoting himself, Jesus is obedient to God. The temptation scene indicates that the devil is the real power figure behind earthly empire, especially the concentration of wealth and power in 4:8–10. This is analogous to Rev 13:1–4, where the dragon/devil gives his throne and power to the imperial "beast."[14] Furthermore, the contentious yet poor and humble nature of Jesus as king, prophet, and messiah is raised in his trial and crucifixion scene. Jesus's poverty and political exclusion are signaled by the very fact that he is crucified—a punishment reserved for

12. Richard Horsley, *Covenant Economics: A Biblical Vision of Justice for All* (Louisville: Westminster John Knox, 2009), 149.

13. Michael Peppard, *The Son of God in the Roman World: Divine Sonship in Its Social and Political Context* (London: Oxford University Press, 2012), 31–85.

14. "The dragon stood on the shore of the sea. And I saw a beast coming out of the sea. It had ten horns and seven heads, with ten crowns on its horns, and on each head a blasphemous name. The beast I saw resembled a leopard, but had feet like those of a bear and a mouth like that of a lion. The dragon gave the beast his power and his throne and great authority. One of the heads of the beast seemed to have had a fatal wound, but the fatal wound had been healed. The whole world was filled with wonder and followed the beast. People worshiped the dragon because he had given authority to the beast, and they also worshiped the beast and asked, 'Who is like the beast? Who can wage war against it?'" (Rev 13:1–4).

those who are considered enemies of the state, leaders who do not serve the interests of or go along with the status quo.

Perhaps most relevant to any reading of Jesus as a poor man is the Last Judgment in Matt 25:31–46, where Jesus says feeding the hungry, clothing the ill-clothed, and welcoming the poor and outcast are caring for him (Matt 25:35–40), and failure to care for the needy is a rejection of him (Matt 25:41–43). These passages read:

> "For I was hungry and you gave me something to eat, I was thirsty and you gave me something to drink, I was a stranger and you invited me in, I needed clothes and you clothed me, I was sick and you looked after me, I was in prison and you came to visit me." Then the righteous will answer him, "Lord, when did we see you hungry and feed you, or thirsty and give you something to drink? When did we see you a stranger and invite you in, or needing clothes and clothe you? When did we see you sick or in prison and go to visit you?" The King will reply, "I tell you the truth, whatever you did for one of the least of these brothers of mine, you did for me." Then he will say to those on his left, "Depart from me, you who are cursed, into the eternal fire prepared for the devil and his angels. For I was hungry and you gave me nothing to eat, I was thirsty and you gave me nothing to drink, I was a stranger and you did not invite me in, I needed clothes and you did not clothe me, I was sick and in prison and you did not look after me." (Matt 25:35–43)

Jesus is the embodiment of the poor in this passage, and he proclaims judgment for those who neglect people in need.

Empire-Critical Context

Above, we looked at how Jesus's poverty is established in the gospels themselves. Here, we will deepen our understanding of the economic and social conditions of Jesus and his followers by looking at what historians and others have learned about the world Jesus was born into and fought to transform. Exploring this context in some detail brings the poverty of Jesus and the Jesus movement, as well as the main concerns of Jesus and those around him, into clear view.

During the lifetimes of Jesus, his followers, and the authors and audience of the Gospel of Matthew, the growth and consolidation of the Roman Empire was an engine for both accumulation of wealth and increasing impoverishment. As social historian and biblical scholar Richard Horsley explains:

> The fundamental conflict evident in ancient Jewish literature, such as Josephus's histories, was not between Judaism and Hellenism, the Jews and the Romans, or Judaism and Christianity. Rather, the fundamental conflict was between the Roman, Herodian, and high priestly rulers, on the one hand, and the Judean and Galilean villagers, whose produce supplied tribute for Caesar, taxes for Herod, and tithes and offerings for the priests and temple apparatus, on the other.[15]

A major part of the expansion and development of the Roman Empire (and thereby the position and security of the Herodian Dynasty and Jerusalem Temple elites) was bringing new lands and nations under its control through military conquest, forcibly taking natural resources including timber and minerals as well as gold, jewelry, and other luxury items of the conquered people.[16]

Horsley and Silberman describe this process:

> Just as smaller family farms were consolidated into large agribusiness with tenant farmers working the land of mainly absentee landowners, the fishing industry was shifting in a similar direction. Fishing, farming and other modes of the economy were starting to be produced on an "industrial" level rather than simply for subsistence. This led to a growth of low-wage work for the population of the rural areas of the empire and a migration into urban areas as the poor got pushed off their land and needed to find paid work elsewhere to survive. With this subsistence economy, the economic changes from small farms to agribusiness that developed as the Roman Empire expanded and consolidated brought about greater inequality and misery. While most people were poor in a subsistence economy, the shift to production on an "industrial" level for distribution across the whole Roman Empire

---

15. Richard Horsley and John Hanson, *Bandits, Prophets, and Messiahs: Popular Movements in the Time of Jesus* (Harrisburg: Trinity Press International, 1999), xi–xii.

16. K. C. Hanson and Douglas Oakman, *Palestine in the Time of Jesus: Social Structures and Social Conflicts* (Minneapolis: Augsburg Fortress, 2002), 5.

resulted in more families losing their ancestral lands and being forced into low wage work and expendability.[17]

Military conquest also resulted in the appropriation of slaves and other forms of human resources. The new people and nations brought into the empire were taxed. Relatedly, a central feature of the Roman Empire was the *Pax Romana*, where the "known world" was unified through a developed transportation and communication infrastructure that required human and material resources for its construction. These resources were gathered through heightened taxes, accumulated surplus, and ready labor.[18] In general, both extensive and intensive appropriation of resources played their role in this process.[19] Appian, a Roman historian from Alexandria who lived between 95 and 165 CE, discusses this reality of inequality:

> The rich had got possession of the greater part of the undivided land. They trusted in the conditions of the time, that these possessions would not be again taken from them, and bought, therefore, some of the pieces of land lying near theirs, and belonging to the poor, with the acquiescence of their owners, and took some by force, so that they now were cultivating widely extended domains, instead of isolated fields. Then they employed slaves in agriculture and cattle-breeding, because freemen would have been taken from labor for military ser-

17. Richard A. Horsley and Neil A. Silberman, *The Message and the Kingdom: How Jesus and Paul Ignited a Revolution and Transformed the Ancient World* (Minneapolis: Augsburg Fortress, 2002), 5.

18. Horsley and Silberman, *The Message and the Kingdom*, 27.

19. For some single-volume resources that further describe the economic and political system of the Roman Empire, see Douglas Oakman, *Jesus and the Peasants*, Matrix: The Bible in Mediterranean Context (Eugene, OR: Wipf & Stock, 2008); David Fiensy and Ralph K. Hawkins, eds., *The Galilean Economy in the Time of Jesus* (Atlanta: Society of Biblical Literature, 2013); Ekkehard W. Stegemann and Wolfgang Stegemann, *The Jesus Movement*, trans. O. C. Dean Jr. (Minneapolis: Fortress, 1999). See also, Catherine Hezser, ed., *The Oxford Handbook of Jewish Daily Life in Roman Palestine* (New York: Oxford University Press, 2010); Anthony Blasi et al., eds., *Handbook of Early Christianity: Social Science Approaches* (Walnut Creek, CA: AltaMira, 2002); Justin Meggitt, *Paul, Poverty, and Survival* (Edinburgh: T&T Clark, 1998); Hanson and Oakman, *Palestine in the Time of Jesus: Social Structures and Social Conflicts*; Warren Carter, *Matthew and the Margins: A Sociopolitical and Religious Reading* (Maryknoll, NY: Orbis, 2000); Jennifer Glancy, *Slavery in Early Christianity* (New York: Oxford University Press, 2002); Gerd Theissen, "The Social Structure of Pauline Communities: Some Critical Remarks on J. J. Meggitt, *Paul, Poverty, and Survival*," *Journal for the Study of the New Testament* 24 (2001): 65–84.

vice. The possession of slaves brought them great gain, inasmuch as these, on account of their immunity from military service, could freely multiply and have a multitude of children. Thus the powerful men drew all wealth to themselves, and all the land swarmed with slaves. The Italians, on the other hand, were always decreasing in number, destroyed as they were by poverty, taxes, and military service. Even when times of peace came, they were doomed to complete inactivity, because the rich were in possession of the soil, and used slaves instead of freemen in the tilling of it.[20]

Then as now, the state played an important role in maintaining the inequality that defined empire: "The distribution of what little income was available in the Mediterranean world was entirely dependent upon political power: those devoid of political power, the non-elite, over 99 percent of the Empire's population, could expect little more from life than abject poverty."[21] As Hanson and Oakman explain: "The Palestinians did not elect their rulers. . . . Taxes, tolls, and tribute were not open to referendum, but imposed from above; and they were not collected to benefit the populace, but only the elites."[22]

The nature of the economy, with 80–90 percent of the populace of Galilee (the base of Jesus's ministry) and the larger Roman Empire participating in agricultural work, further indicates the great economic divide.[23] An elite class of slaveholders and landowners controlled most of the land, people, and wealth in Galilee, Judea, Syria, and the greater Roman Empire.[24] Biblical scholar Justin Meggitt controversially, but in my opinion convincingly, demonstrates that 99 percent of the population was living

20. Appian, *Bell. civ.* 1.7 (White, LCL).

21. Meggitt, *Paul, Poverty, and Survival*, 50.

22. Hanson and Oakman, *Palestine in the Time of Jesus*, 66.

23. For more information on agricultural societies, especially ancient Palestine in the Second Temple period, see Jack Pastor, *Land and Economy in Ancient Palestine* (London: Routledge, 1997). For a deeper exploration of the Herodian period from the perspective of the bottom, the poorest agricultural workers, see David Fiensy, *The Social History of Palestine in the Herodian Period* (Lewiston, NY: Edwin Mellen, 1991). For a report and analysis of the economic conditions of the first century, based on new archaeological findings, see David A. Fiensy and Ralph K. Hawkins, *The Galilean Economy in the Time of Jesus* (Atlanta: Society of Biblical Literature, 2013). Many of these authors paint a fuller picture of peasant dispossession as well. For an important treatment, see Victor Tcherikover, *Hellenistic Civilization and the Jews* (Peabody, MA: Hendrickson, 1999).

24. Herzog, *Prophet and Teacher*, 50.

in dire poverty, and even conservative scholarly estimates agree that at least 70, 80, or 90 percent of the population were peasants living at a subsistence level, just barely surviving.[25] Around the Sea of Galilee and the harbor region of Antioch, fishing, in addition to farming, was central to the economy.[26] Similar to the way that the elites controlled agricultural production, there were also a select few who controlled the organization of and profits from fishing.

In order to maximize profits from both the ownership of land (which was [re]distributed through inheritance, conquest, or debt) and labor in fishing, building, and other areas of the economy, the ruling elites extracted taxes, tribute, and raw agricultural materials from the cities and countryside, further impoverishing the peasants and profiting from the dispossession of the poor.[27] Coercion was an important factor in the appropriation of resources and the polarization of wealth and poverty across the Roman Empire. Indeed, in the Roman agricultural economy, peasants did not voluntarily supply labor or work for wages. Instead, they were dispossessed of their land and other means of subsistence and forced to work under the control of elites. As many small farmers defaulted on loans, elite landowners acquired their land and wealth. Horsley and Silberman explain some of the ways that coercion through taxation functioned to polarize wealth and poverty within the empire:

---

25. There is a debate about the economic conditions of ancient Israel and in particular the early Christian communities, in large part responding to the work of Justin Meggitt. This debate was presented in the *Journal for the Study of the New Testament* and included reviews of Meggitt's book *Paul, Poverty, and Survival* by Gerd Theissen, Dale Martin, and others. For more information on this debate and the poverty of the early Christian communities, see: Justin Meggitt, *Paul, Poverty, and Survival*; Dale Martin, "Review Essay: Justin J. Meggitt, *Paul, Poverty, and Survival*," *Journal for the Study of the New Testament* 24 (2001): 51–64; Theissen, "The Social Structure of Pauline Communities." Both Steve Friesen and Bruce Longenecker also pay special attention to the issue of status and poverty (and wealth) levels in the Roman Empire, contributing to the debate on the social conditions of the followers of Jesus. For more information on this and poverty levels in general, see Bruce Longenecker and Kelly Liebengood, *Engaging Economics: New Testament Scenarios and Early Christian Reception* (Grand Rapids: Eerdmans, 2009); Bruce Longenecker, *Remember the Poor: Paul, Poverty, and the Greco-Roman World* (Grand Rapids: Eerdmans, 2010); and Steven Friesen, "Poverty in Pauline Studies: Beyond the So-Called New Consensus," *JSNT* 26 (2004): 323–61.

26. Horsley and Silberman, *Message and the Kingdom*, 25.

27. Hanson and Oakman, *Palestine in the Time of Jesus*, 113.

Antipas was granted the right to collect taxes from his subjects in Galilee and Perea, a privilege that, according to Josephus, yielded an annual equivalent of two hundred talents (or about nine tons) of gold. Of course there was no real gold to be found in the hills and valleys of the tetrarchy—just wheat, barley, grapes, olives, vegetables, and livestock. Antipas therefore had to dispatch a veritable army of auditors, tax collectors, and soldiers to the groves, vineyards, and threshing floors of every village at harvest time to ensure that his share of the harvest (estimated by modern scholars to have amounted to as much as a third of the total crops and other agricultural products) was duly handed over to the Herodian authorities.[28]

Trade and commerce were other avenues for the accumulation of wealth by elites.[29] Although those who made their wealth through these means were not as respected or as likely to be called for political office as the landed gentry were, it is clear from the archaeological evidence in Syria and from the numerous references to trade, money, and wealth in Matthew that both commerce and the money economy were prominent and expanding in the empire.[30] Elites traded luxury items (such as those listed in Rev 18:12–13) and other goods that had the potential to bring high profits.[31]

Poverty, Debt, and Dispossession

The imposition of taxes and the transition to an economic and monetary system characterized by mass-scale development and urbanization produced hardship and suffering among the empire's inhabitants.[32] This

28. Horsley and Silberman, *Message and the Kingdom*, 26.

29. Ze'ev Safrai asserts that the economy of Palestine was based on trade and commerce. For more information on this ancient economy as an "open market economy," see Ze'ev Safrai, *The Economy of Roman Palestine* (New York: Routledge, 1994).

30. Carter, *Matthew and the Margins*, 31.

31. The resources traded in Rev 18:12–13 include gold, silver, pearls, fine linen, silk, ivory, costly wood, bronze, iron, marble, spices, myrrh, frankincense, wine, cattle, sheep, horses, carriages, and slaves.

32. Taxation was central to the impoverishment of the population of the Roman Empire. There were two forms of taxation imposed on the Jewish people living in the Roman Empire: Jewish Temple taxes/tithing (which were paid as the *fiscus judaicus* to the Temple of Julius Capitolinas after the destruction of the Jerusalem Temple) and the numerous taxes

system led to displacement from ancestral land, and tax burdens caused suffering, slavery, debt, and in many cases debt bondage.[33] Debt grew as people needed to borrow money, especially after poor harvests.[34] Residents took loans from local elites, including those who sat in the very same courts that enforced their payment of taxes.[35] Oftentimes, debtors would become tenants to the elites as well as submit themselves as clients to these patrons in an effort to avoid the court (which favored and were controlled by the wealthy), the special police that enforced payments, and debt prison.[36] At the time of Jesus and the writing of the Gospel of Matthew, all of these debt records were accounted in *denarii* (Roman silver coins), rather than bushels of grain or fish. The circulation of imperial coins was not simply about a standard measure of exchange:

> When tribute was collected in Roman coinage, it was part and parcel of Roman political propaganda. The denarius was the most stable and extensively circulated coin of Tiberius's reign, a coin that doubled as currency and propaganda. The obverse of the coin contained a profile of Tiberius's head "adorned with the laurel wreath, the sign of divinity," and was inscribed with an epigram that claimed divinity for both Augustus and Tiberius.[37]

Therefore, money played both an economic and an ideological role in perpetuating Roman rule.

The move from debt to dispossession—losing one's land and livelihood—did not happen silently or without protest.[38] Resistance was displayed in the attitude toward tax and toll collectors throughout the

---

of the Roman Empire (Sean Freyne, *Galilee from Alexander the Great to Hadrian: A Study of Second Temple Judaism* [Wilmington, DE: Michael Glazier, 1980], 183).

33. Freyne, *Galilee from Alexander the Great to Hadrian*, 181; and Horsley and Silberman, *Message and the Kingdom*, 28.

34. Freyne, *Galilee from Alexander the Great to Hadrian*, 182.

35. Freyne, *Galilee from Alexander the Great to Hadrian*, 181.

36. Carter, *Matthew and the Margins*, 19; and William Herzog, *Parables as Subversive Speech: Jesus as Pedagogue of the Oppressed* (Louisville: Westminster John Knox, 1994), 61–66; and Herzog, *Prophet and Teacher*, 43–171.

37. Herzog, *Prophet and Teacher*, 185.

38. "In Judea, under the direct rule of Rome since the ouster of Archelaus more than two decades earlier, the issue of imperial taxation had led to widespread agitation and public resistance" (Horsley and Silberman, *Message and the Kingdom*, 83). This type of resistance occurred throughout the empire.

Roman Empire. It was also seen in the crowd control issues at festivals and other public events in provinces all over Rome. Indeed, a bureaucracy of courts and judges was set up to address peasant resistance to tax collection.[39] Richard Horsley and John Hanson explain the rise of banditry and other revolutionary groups around the time of Jesus: "Banditry, prophetic movements, and messianic movements (and oracular prophecy) occurred primarily among the peasantry—that is, were primarily popular social forms, different from the tax resistance and terrorist resistance that occurred among scribal circles."[40] Because slavery, taxation, and debt were major institutions within the Roman Empire, they remained central concerns of Jesus and his followers, who developed and propagated critiques of indebtedness and slavery. As "peasant concerns for debt-forgiveness and redistribution of labor are well-represented in the legal traditions of the Old Testament,"[41] Jewish prophets (and other messiahs) preached about debt release and slave manumission. Jesus himself proclaimed that he had come to forgive debts, set the slaves free, and preach good news to the poor in his inaugural speech in Luke 4:16–30.[42]

Alongside this agitation and resistance, the Roman economic system nevertheless had significant influence on the values of the population: "Under the pressure of debt and taxation, Roman legal standards, not the Torah, began to take precedence."[43] People moved away from the community-oriented ethics of the Torah, especially the Sabbath and Jubilee prescriptions discussed in the previous chapter.

39. Horsley and Silberman, *Message and the Kingdom*, 83.

40. Horsley and Hanson, *Bandits, Prophets, and Messiahs*, xv.

41. Hanson and Oakman, *Palestine in the Time of Jesus*, 119.

42. Throughout the ancient Near East and especially around the time of Jesus and before the destruction of the Temple in Jerusalem, there were many other prophets and messiahs. Martin Hengel, citing Josephus, writes, "There was apparently a Samaritan prophet or pseudo-Messiah who caused unrest under Pilate. A second pseudo-Messiah appeared at the time of Cuspius Fadus (who ruled from 44 AD onwards)—one Theudas, 'who claimed that he was a prophet', but who was, in Josephus' opinion, no more than an ordinary deceiver" (Martin Hengel, *The Zealots: Investigations into the Jewish Freedom Movement in the Period from Herod I until A.D. 70*, trans. John Bowden [Edinburgh: T&T Clark, 1989], 229; trans. of *Die Zeloten* [Tübingen: Mohr Siebeck, 1976]).

43. Horsley and Silberman, *Message and the Kingdom*, 55. Also discussed in Hanson and Oakman, *Palestine in the Time of Jesus*, 152.

Poverty, Wealth, and Power in Galilee and Antioch

As was true elsewhere and is often still the case around the world today, poverty in Galilee existed right next to great wealth. Sean Freyne asserts that under the control of the Roman Empire, the region went through rapid economic development. This created the conditions for the growth of a new social consciousness, in turn opening up new possibilities for major social changes.[44] This pattern played out in both urban and more rural areas across Galilee.

As we saw above, the state power of the Roman Empire was the leading agent in much of the economic development of the time. One of the clearest ways to see the tight control this power had over Galilee and surrounding areas is in the close patron-client relationship between Emperor Augustus and the Herodian Dynasty. One of the predecessors of Herod Antipas, who ruled Palestine during the time of Jesus, was known as Herod the Great. He served as a functionary beholden to the Roman Empire, instituting taxes and pursuing building projects and other economic policies that were consistent with the larger plan of Augustus for the further development of the empire but that severely hurt the poor residents of Galilee. He supported the imperial cult practices of Augustus and the Roman Empire, a religious and ideological program that went hand-in-hand with the economic one: "Herod the Great not only expanded the Jerusalem Temple mount with tax monies, but built Temples in honor of Roman emperors and gods,"[45] most notably Caesarea Maritima. He benefited greatly from his allegiance to and involvement in the growth, consolidation, and wealth-creation strategies of the Roman Empire, claiming 25–33 percent of grain and half of the fruit tree production from the areas of Palestine in his jurisdiction.[46] He even left Augustus and his wife a significant inheritance in his will.[47]

Although the imperial economic program imposed heavy tax burdens on the residents of Galilee, many also became dependent on the jobs produced through the building and infrastructure projects at its center. As Justin Meggitt points out: "Josephus' account of the completion of Herod's rebuilding of the Temple also indicates something of the signif-

---

44. Freyne, *Galilee from Alexander the Great to Hadrian*, 197.
45. Hanson and Oakman, *Palestine in the Time of Jesus*, 5.
46. Hanson and Oakman, *Palestine in the Time of Jesus*, 114.
47. Hanson and Oakman, *Palestine in the Time of Jesus*, 48.

icance of large scale construction projects for urban employment: it led to 18,000 men being made unemployed in Jerusalem and forced Herod to concoct another project almost immediately (they were put to work paving the city)."[48] Herod the Great's successors followed the same line of building, urban development, taxation, and further impoverishment of the citizenry.[49] He was succeeded by Archelaus in Judea (who was deposed in 6 CE), Herod Antipas (who ruled Galilee and Perea until 39 CE), and eventually Agrippa (who was king from 41 to 44 CE). The fact that Herod could not pass on his rule to the individual he chose (a choice that was documented in his will but not followed by the imperial elite) is further evidence that supreme power over Palestine, both political and economic, was in Roman hands.[50] Indeed, as imperial powers often do, Augustus took the wealth inheritance of Herod but ignored the land-inheritance suggestion laid out in his will.

The Jerusalem Temple, which was rebuilt by Herod the Great, was one of the places where imperial-cult practice was present among the Jewish people. The Temple was the community bank and the center of economic activity and religious ritual for Jerusalem, Judea, Galilee, and the diaspora.[51] Although Jews were generally given an exemption from imperial-cult worship per se, a daily sacrifice for the health and well-being of the Roman emperor was made at the Temple. Jews across the empire were required to send in a Temple tax to pay for these sacrifices, along with other taxes to the Roman Empire until the Temple's destruction in 70 CE. Therefore, Herod and other elites, while responsible for rebuilding the Temple with money gathered from the population, were able to raid the Temple treasury and use the money collected there for projects in service to the economic and political aspirations of the empire.[52]

The complicity between the Jerusalem Temple and the Roman imperial system raised concerns for many during Jesus's day. As Hoppe writes: "The major portion of Palestine's wealth was channeled through the Temple, whose priests collected taxes for themselves and for the Romans. The Jews of Palestine hated the Romans because they saw their wealth going to the empire, though the intensity of the opposition to Rome varied. The priests were coopted by the Romans and were the least likely to support

48. Meggitt, *Paul, Poverty, and Survival*, 57.
49. Horsley and Silberman, *The Message and the Kingdom*, 24.
50. Herzog, *Prophet and Teacher*, 44.
51. Hanson and Oakman, *Palestine in the Time of Jesus*, 16.
52. Hanson and Oakman, *Palestine in the Time of Jesus*, 150.

a revolution."[53] The impetus and demands of the Jewish revolutionaries leading up to and during the Jewish Wars demonstrate just how central debt and economics were in the uprising/Jewish Wars in 66–70 CE. In fact, reports document that the factors that led up to war were, for the Jewish people in 66 CE, firmly rooted in the economic pressures facing them. Indeed, the first act that eventually led to Rome's burning the Temple was Jewish leaders entering the Temple to burn the debt records.[54]

About 250 miles north of Galilee sat Antioch, which during the time of Jesus was part of the Syrian territory of the Roman Empire. This is where the Gospel of Matthew, and so also Matthew's version of the anointing at Bethany, was most likely written, rather than in Galilee or elsewhere in Judea, where the story of Jesus takes place.[55] Antioch, located on the Orontes River, fourteen miles from the Mediterranean Sea, was a point of convergence for north–south and east–west trade routes.[56] By the first century, it may have been the third-largest city (after Rome and Alexandria) in the empire.[57] It had a population of about 150,000–200,000, and was so small geographically—half the land was taken up by public buildings, gymnasiums, baths, and so on—that the population density was most likely higher than Mumbai or Kolkata, or six times that of New York City today. People were packed in tightly, leading to a lack of privacy and great potential for conflict, especially among the lower strata.[58] Its location also contributed to its primary position in the imperial economic order: the grains produced and the fish caught all throughout the empire had to be sold along trade routes that extended for hundreds of miles, and some of the most important ran through Antioch.

Warren Carter writes that there were two social groups who lived in Antioch: the elites (making up 5–10%) and the rest, who were poor and dispossessed or made their living serving the elite (the remaining

---

53. Leslie Hoppe, *There Shall Be No Poor among You: Poverty in the Bible* (Nashville: Abingdon, 2004), 13.

54. Freyne, *Galilee from Alexander the Great to Hadrian*, 193.

55. Andrew Overman demonstrates in his book that scholars historically have placed Matthew's community in Sepphoris or Tiberias in Galilee, Jerusalem or Palestine, or Caesarea Maritima in addition to Antioch (Andrew Overman, *Matthew's Gospel and Formative Judaism: The Social World of the Matthean Community* [Minneapolis: Fortress, 1990], 159).

56. Carter, *Matthew and the Margins*, 17.

57. L. M. McDonald, "Antioch (Syria)," *Dictionary of New Testament Background*, ed. Craig A. Evans and Stanley E. Porter (Downers Grove, IL: InterVarsity , 2000), 34–36.

58. Carter, *Matthew and the Margins*, 18.

90–95%).[59] The elites acquired resources from taxes, interest on loans, inheritances, and rents (often paid in kind), as well as from land ownership, trade, military conquest, and the exploitation of slave work. The elites had access to two types of retainers: (1) priests who were appointed and elected to various temples, often based on their beneficence to the city, and who were supported and in some cases even salaried; and (2) tax collectors, bureaucrats, soldiers, judges, and others who derived their power and authority from the political and economic elites. These groups, while not a part of the elite themselves, still had a vested interest in helping the elites maintain their wealth and power and in keeping the existing system intact.

The nonelites included workers of all types: artisans, construction workers, sailors, longshoremen, dyers, weavers, tailors, tanners, metalsmiths, dancers, food vendors, and many other specialists. At the bottom of this group were day laborers, slaves, and other expendables.[60]

Slavery was a central institution within the Roman Empire; people became slaves through debt, being sold or selling themselves into slavery, being born into it or being conquered in war by the Roman Empire's mighty military. Because of the variety of paths toward enslavement, slaves spanned a number of professions, educational levels, and social and religious backgrounds. In fact, many slaves were doctors and other professionals who were essential for the running of society. The majority of slaves, however, were unskilled and did much of the most difficult and degrading work available.

A major distinction between the labor conditions of slaves and those of free people was that slaves could be punished. Slaves were sometimes used in situations where they handled money,[61] such as household financial management, because there could be greater repercussions if they squandered money. Slave owners were sometimes allowed to substitute their slaves for their own prison sentences. Largely, it was people with means who were able to afford slaves, but there was a constituent of nonelite people who acquired slaves to keep their households running. Small-scale domestic slave ownership did not necessarily mean wealth; for example, it did not cost a family much to raise an abandoned child as a slave.[62]

59. Carter, *Matthew and the Margins*, 18–20. Carter goes on to explain that these percentages regarding the elites may be too high.

60. Meggitt, *Paul, Poverty, and Survival*, 50.

61. This idea comes from the lecture notes of a class on parables taught by Luise Schottroff at Union Theological Seminary in the City of New York, February 17, 2005.

62. For more information on slavery in the Roman Empire, see Glancy, *Slavery in*

The most serious problem for the residents of Antioch and other urban centers, both slave and free, was securing enough food. Starvation was prevalent.[63] The poor of these urban centers were also wanting in clothes, housing, health care, and any form of an adequate standard of living. They also suffered from injuries at work and regular violence.[64] Indeed, old age was not common because of these harsh conditions of life.[65]

Despite the Roman Empire's prevalent peace propaganda, *Pax Romana*, the social order's agricultural production, trade and commerce, infrastructure development and enrichment of elites was firmly dependent on military power. Antioch, for instance, was a staging ground for Roman legions of 15,000–20,000 soldiers for the Jewish War (66–70 CE). The economic support for the entire military apparatus came from taxes and levies.[66] While many poor Syrian residents were starving, the corn and other supplies they harvested and produced went to feed the army that maintained and protected the empire and its elites.

Popular History and the Jesus Movement

My understanding of Jesus's ministry is grounded in the idea that the poor make history—driving needed social, economic, and political transformations in their societies and eras—but that history is often documented on behalf of and from the perspective of the wealthy and powerful. Scholars have claimed that there were multiple messiahs and prophets in the first century CE who proclaimed that they had come to bring good news to the poor, but few are remembered and recorded. Nor is Jesus remembered as such a prophet in the histories of his day.[67] Some of these prophets evoked Israelite history and teachings. In his groundbreaking work on this topic, *Bandits, Prophets, and Messiahs*, Richard Horsley describes these revolutionary prophets and rabble-rousers:

Early Christianity; S. S. Bartchy, *First-Century Slavery and the Interpretation of 1 Corinthians 7:21* (Eugene, OR: Wipf & Stock, 2003); and J. Albert Harrill, *Slaves in the New Testament: Literary, Social, and Moral Dimensions* (Minneapolis: Fortress, 2005).

63. Meggitt, *Paul, Poverty, and Survival*, 59.
64. Meggitt, *Paul, Poverty, and Survival*, 71–72.
65. Meggitt, *Paul, Poverty, and Survival*, 67.
66. Josephus, *Ant* 2.186 (Feldman, LCL).
67. Richard A. Horsley and John S. Hanson, *Bandits, Prophets, and Messiahs: Popular Movements in the Time of Jesus* (Harrisburg, PA: Trinity Press International, 1985), xv.

Judging from several reports by Josephus, there were a number of prophetic figures that appeared among the people around the time of Jesus. Indeed, Jesus was understood as a prophet (see Mk 6:15–16). . . . The classical oracular prophets and others like them whose memory is preserved in prophetic traditions, can thus be discerned as spokespersons for the peasantry and the covenantal social-economic policy that served to protect their interests. Because of the blatant exploitation of the peasantry, these prophets felt compelled to oppose the ruling class, which was failing to observe the covenantal order. Rather than heed the prophetic warnings, the ruling groups appear to have responded with repression and persecution.[68]

To reconstruct profiles of these revolutionaries, Horsley and other social historians "read between the lines" of primary sources. One of the main sources of information about first-century prophets, bandits, and rabble-rousers is Flavius Josephus, who documented *The Jewish War* and *Jewish Antiquities* on behalf of the elites. In line with James C. Scott's arguments—"dominant elites attempt to portray social action in the public transcript as, metaphorically, a parade, thus denying, by omission, the possibility of autonomous social action by insubordinates. Inferiors who actually assemble at their own initiative are typically described as mobs or rabble"[69]—much of Josephus's attention to such popular leaders warns of their demagoguery and radicalism. This resonates with the Passion Narrative in Matthew and the other Gospels, where Jesus is portrayed as a popular leader who the elites fear will move the mob to riot and revolution, thereby making it necessary for them to control and eventually execute him.

As this social-history approach to the Jesus movement has gained ascendancy, some have questioned it on historical grounds, because other sources of the period do not seem to document anti-empire figures or movements. But this should not come as a surprise, given a more critical approach to historical preservation, because revolutionary stories do not tend to be recorded as such. They are usually either left out, co-opted, or rendered as disruptions. William Herzog in his book *Prophet and Teacher* lists key characteristics of popular-movement leaders (Herzog uses the term "reputational leaders") and demagogues of the poor and connects Jesus to this description:

68. Horsley and Hanson, *Bandits, Prophets, and Messiahs*, 135–45.
69. Douglas A. Knight, *Law, Power, and Justice in Ancient Israel*, Library of Ancient Israel (Louisville: Westminster John Knox, 2011), 45–46.

Reputational leaders emerge because they embody the values of the group they represent. Jesus, for instance, emerges out of the village life of Galilee, a peasant artisan steeped in the prophetic traditions of Israel and the little tradition of peasant villages like Nazareth. In his teaching and through his actions, he challenged the higher-order norms and institutions represented by the Torah as it came from Jerusalem and the Temple system, controlled as it was by the high priestly houses serving their Roman masters. Not surprisingly, scribal Pharisees and Pharisees challenged his role as reputational leader and broker of God's power, which was centered in Temple and Torah.[70]

Through scholars' search for such "hidden transcripts" in the Gospels and other early Christian writings as well as based on the reaction of the elites to Jesus and his ultimate crucifixion, a profile of Jesus as a revolutionary social-movement leader emerges.[71] His poverty is documented both through the biblical accounts of him and from a deeper study of the economic and political context of the Roman Empire, discussed earlier in this chapter.

Although the Bible may be the product of the powerful trying to acculturate lessons, traditions, and practices of the poor, the fact that societies erupt when they read it and those in power try to control oppressed people's access to it sheds light on the reality that it is also a revolutionary document. Within it, we can glean from the sources collected to form the Gospels and epistles that Jesus was a radical leader and teacher responding to fundamental social, economic, and political problems. The hermeneutic of the organized poor being used and elaborated in this book, "Reading the Bible with the Poor," seeks to gather these pieces of revolutionary history and fills in the historical gaps using contemporary experiences of poverty, oppression, and dispossession. The social, political, and economic context of the Bible is central to the message of Jesus and to any characterization of Jesus Christ himself.

---

70. Herzog, *Prophet and Teacher*, 23.

71. The anthropologist James C. Scott coined the term "hidden transcripts" to highlight disguised or covert acts of resistance that fall short of open insurrection. Biblical scholars have found this concept helpful in exploring the everyday acts of resistance to the Roman Empire performed by Jesus and the early Christians. See James C. Scott, *Domination and the Arts of Resistance: Hidden Transcripts* (New Haven, CT: Yale University Press, 1990).

Feasting in the House of the Poor

So how do we apply these lessons on historiography, the poor historical Jesus, and the humble Jesus of the Gospels to the story of the anointing at Bethany and the passage where Jesus states, "The poor you will always have with you"? In Matthew's story of the anointing of Jesus, an unnamed woman appears at Simon the Leper's house with a jar of very expensive ointment as Jesus and his disciples are gathered together.[72] This verse emphasizes the question of money and the context of impoverishment and marginalization with almost every word and detail: *Bethania* ("Bethany"), *lepros* ("with an infectious skin disease"), *gynē* ("woman"), *alabastros* ("alabaster"), *barytimos* ("expensive"), *myron* ("ointment"), just to name a few. Bethany means the "house of the poor" in Hebrew (from *bet*, meaning "house" and *'ani* meaning "poor"); it is not clear how much this literal sense was actually still "heard" in the name of this place, though the allusion could establish a metaphorical connection to the poor and poverty. Jesus is staying in Bethany, only a few miles from Jerusalem, where he has come to observe the Passover holidays.[73] While Jerusalem (and the Temple in particular) may represent a place of wealth and power, Jesus and his followers are staying in a place of poverty and marginalization. This could be out of convenience and due to the fact that they do not have the resources to stay somewhere else. It is also an indication of who Jesus is and with whom he associates.[74] Jesus is staying with Simon, the leper, in the "house of the poor,"[75] because Jesus

---

72. The anointing is at Bethany for Matthew, Mark, and John, but not Luke. In Matthew and Mark, the head is anointed; in Luke and John, it is Jesus's feet. In John, Mary anoints; in Matthew and Mark, the woman who anoints is unnamed; in Luke, the woman is called "sinful." In Matthew, the disciples are the ones who raise questions about the woman's actions; in Mark, it is some who were there; in John, it is Judas who raises the criticism. In Matthew, the story has fewer historical details than Mark, placing the emphasis on the actions and discipleship of the anointing woman. See Ronald Thiemann, "The Unnamed Woman at Bethany," *Theology Today* 44 (1987): 179–88.

73. Donald Hagner, *Matthew 14–28*, Word Biblical Commentary, 33B (Dallas: Word, 1995), 756.

74. John Dominic Crossan, *The Historical Jesus: The Life of a Mediterranean Jewish Peasant* (New York: HarperCollins, 1993), 94.

75. Brian Capper writes that, because semantically and etymologically Bethany can mean "House of the Poor" and based on some archaeological evidence of a poor house being built east of Jerusalem, Bethany may have come to be known as a "House of the Poor" (Brian Capper, "Essene Community Houses and Jesus' Early Community," in *Jesus and Archaeology*, ed. James H. Charlesworth [Grand Rapids: Eerdmans, 2006], 472–502).

himself is concerned with the problems of the poor. The fact that Simon has leprosy may also mean that he is poor, is considered ritually unclean, and is certainly not the type of person hosting and holding dinners for the Jewish high priests and Roman authorities in Jerusalem.[76]

In this scene in Matthew 26, Jesus is reclining over a meal with his disciples.[77] Jesus shares an open commensality; he socializes and eats with all kinds of people, including lepers and women with unknown backgrounds.[78] Jesus stood for a Kingdom/Empire/Realm of God that was challenging the very foundations of the Roman Empire. He practiced a "radical egalitarianism" that included people of all classes, statuses, abilities, and so on. For this, Jesus was called "a glutton and a drunkard" by his contemporaries. He asserts that God's Kingdom is made up of those who are considered to be expendable and are excluded from society: "In any situation of oppression, especially in those oblique, indirect, and systemic ones where injustice wears a mask of normalcy or even of necessity, the only ones who are innocent or blessed are those squeezed out deliberately as human junk from the system's own evil operations. A contemporary equivalent: only the homeless are innocent."[79]

The scene in Bethany follows Jesus's entrance into Jerusalem and his visit to the Temple in Matthew 21, and is a continuation of these actions and teachings. Some scholars argue that Bethany is a place of refuge or sanctuary for Jesus and his followers:[80] he has caused a stir at the Temple

76. The fact that Simon has a house, however, means that, although he is potentially poor or near poverty, he is not destitute.

77. Luzia Sutter Rehmann asserts that because of the poverty of Jesus and his followers, it is possible that they do not share food, although they gather to recline and have fellowship. See Luzia Sutter Rehmann, "Olivenöl als Zündstoff: Die vier Salbungsgeschichten der Evangelien im Kontext des Judentums des Zweiten Tempels," *Lectio Difficilior* 1 (2013): 1.

78. Lepers and women are brought together in three miracle stories of Jesus in Matt 8:1–15, where Jesus heals a man with leprosy, a slave of a centurion, and Peter's mother. These healings and other ministry among the poor and marginalized are connected to Jesus's anointing in this scene in part because of the role of Simon the Leper and the unnamed woman.

79. Crossan, *The Historical Jesus*, 62.

80. Elaine Wainwright says that Bethany is a place of refuge for Jesus, who has come into conflict with the Jewish and Roman authorities in Jerusalem. If we come to think of Bethany, the house of the poor, as a place where unknown women and lepers and people who pose a threat to the political and religious authorities have refuge, it shifts from being a place of rest and relaxation to a place where the *basileia* of God is being realized (in opposition to the *basileia* of Rome). See Elaine Wainwright, *Towards a Feminist Critical Reading of the Gospel according to Matthew* (Berlin: de Gruyter, 1991), 125.

during the Passover festivities and he has fled to Bethany for protection or cover among the poor and marginalized. Jesus may be staying in Bethany because the poor peasants of that town support him and his following and desire to welcome and protect Jesus, who is coming up against the Temple elite and Roman authorities. Horsley points out that "the Jewish peasants not only supported bandits and viewed them as heroic victims of injustice, but also protected them and were willing to suffer the consequences."[81] It is clear in the company that Jesus keeps that he is a popular-movement leader and budding revolutionary. By the anointing in this story, Jesus's teachings, feedings, and acts of protest are amplified and put in further contrast to his opponents and the ruling class of his day.[82]

Jesus Was a Poor Man

This context sheds particular light on "the poor you will always have with you," as well as the whole scene and setting. Through their interpretation of this verse, many scholars claim that poverty was not a main concern of Jesus, but that other things, such as religious observance, mattered more to him, separating these practices from the economic structure surrounding them. Scholars pit Jesus and the poor against each other and insist that Jesus desired luxury in this case because he was so close to his death, even though he valued simplicity in other situations. Still others deny that Matt 26:11 is focused on the topic of poverty at all.

The fact that it is a poor person who makes the statement "the poor you will always have with you" is significant. Rather than a person of wealth condemning those he has impoverished to everlasting poverty, Jesus is a poor person talking about the reality and brutality of being poor and marginalized. He is not romanticizing poverty; only those who are not poor can do that. He is not pitting himself against the poor, because that distinction cannot be made in his case: Jesus also is poor. Given a deeper understanding of the economic context of the Jesus movement, we realize it is inconceivable that Jesus would be spiritualizing the poverty and problems that people were facing around him. Given a longer biblical-theological arc of justice and the earthly poverty of Jesus, his stance on the issues of his day is clear: poverty is an abomination to

---

81. Horsley and Hanson, *Bandits, Prophets, and Messiahs*, 72.
82. Crossan, *The Historical Jesus*, 94–95.

God. This poor person challenges the status quo and promotes justice and peace for all.

When Jesus says, "The poor you will have with you always, but you will not always have me," he is not only reminding his followers of the Deuteronomic Code and God's admonition to forgive debts, release slaves, and be generous with one's possessions, as discussed in the previous chapter. He is also reminding his followers that he is soon to be executed for his vision of God's Kingdom on earth and his practice of these very commandments, as demonstrated through his feedings and healings; his teachings on what to do about wealth and taxes; his disruption of the Temple (all to be discussed in chapters below); and his audacity to do all of this while being poor himself.

Matthew 26:11 portrays Jesus as passing many of the responsibilities of building a popular movement on to his disciples—other movement leaders—right before he is killed. In this reading of the anointing scene, a turning point in the larger Passion narrative, Jesus is a threat to Rome because of what he stands for and also his role in developing leaders committed to his same vision. Jesus is himself poor; his disciples are also poor. His statement is not about pitting the poor against himself or even about pitting the poor Jesus against other poor people. Instead, Jesus is trying to suggest his significant role and the role of the disciples in the ending of everyone's poverty. He is reminding his disciples that with his impending death, they are charged with carrying on his legacy. This argument is backed up through the grammatical structure of his critique. There is no future prediction in his statement. The verbs used are not in the future tense. The disciples "have" the poor around them (the verb used here is *echete,* meaning "you have" in the present tense); they are the people on whom the Jesus movement is based. But time is running out for Jesus. His disciples need to understand what needs to be done to end poverty and to follow Jesus's vision for the realization of the Deuteronomic Code: the release of slaves, forgiveness of debts, and generosity in the face of economic hardship. They too must become popular-movement leaders, even though they too are poor and seemingly powerless.

The Gospel of Mark includes more details of the anointing and the entire scene than Matthew does. This includes Mark's making the point that, because the poor will be surrounding the disciples for some time, they have many opportunities to care for them. Matthew instead sets up the contrast: you always have the poor; you do not always have me. Therefore, the emphasis of Matthew's version is to juxtapose having the poor with not having Jesus.[83] Later in Matthew, in the Great Commission (28:16–20), Jesus tells the disciples that he will be with them to the end of the age. When we contrast this statement with Matt 26:11, it seems that Jesus is contradicting himself. But in Matt 26:11, Jesus could be saying that the disciples will not have him in the way they want him: as their leader and anointed ruler. He is passing on his responsibilities as teacher, leader, and anointed king/messiah of the poor. He is demanding that his disciples rise to the occasion.

At the same time, he is reminding the disciples that the poor are a stand-in for him (as he established in Matt 25:31–46, the Last Judgment); God's children are not the rich, not the usual philanthropists or change-makers, but the poor. They are the foundation of a movement to materialize God's reign on earth, corresponding to the new logic of God's Kingdom in their community practices. God is not only aligned with the poor but is, in fact, present in (and is of) the poor (see Psalm 14).[84] The movement-building disciples must understand this role of the poor and of themselves as the poor. They must accept both Jesus's untimely death and the fact that Jesus's memory and legacy will carry on as they are sent out to build this movement and recruit for this Kingdom of God. In the poor who are organizing to bring God's reign to earth, Jesus is forever present.

---

83. Hagner, *Matthew 14–28*, 756–57.

84. "The fool says in his heart, 'There is no God.' They are corrupt, their deeds are vile; there is no one who does good. The LORD looks down from heaven on all mankind to see if there are any who understand, any who seek God. All have turned away, all have become corrupt; there is no one who does good, not even one. Do all these evildoers know nothing? They devour my people as though eating bread; they never call on the LORD. But there they are, overwhelmed with dread, for God is present in the company of the righteous. You evildoers frustrate the plans of the poor, but the LORD is their refuge. Oh, that salvation for Israel would come out of Zion! When the Lord restores his people, let Jacob rejoice and Israel be glad!" (Ps 14:1–7).

CHAPTER 5

More Than Flinging a Coin to a Beggar

*A true revolution of values will soon cause us to question the fairness
and justice of many of our past and present policies. On the one hand
we are called to play the Good Samaritan on life's roadside, but that
will be only an initial act. One day we must come to see that the whole
Jericho Road must be transformed so that men and women will not
be constantly beaten and robbed as they make their journey on life's
highway. True compassion is more than flinging a coin to a beggar. It
comes to see that an edifice which produces beggars needs restructuring.*[1]

—Martin Luther King Jr.

If we are serious about understanding Jesus's economic and social critique,
we must read Matt 26:1–13 side by side with contemporary statements
by Martin Luther King Jr. and others. Willie Baptist, Poverty Initiative
Scholar-in-Residence and Coordinator of Poverty Scholarship and Leadership Development for the Kairos Center for Religions, Rights, and Social
Justice and a mentor of mine for over twenty years, asserts that in fact Rev.
Dr. King was thinking about the passage "the poor you will always have
with you" when he made the statement about "true compassion" cited in
the epigraph to this chapter. Baptist says that Jesus critiques the disciples'
concern over selling the ointment and argues that giving the money to
the poor is like "flinging a coin to a beggar." According to Baptist, this

1. Martin Luther King Jr., "A Time to Break the Silence," in *A Testament of Hope: The
Essential Writings and Speeches of Martin Luther King, Jr.*, ed. James M. Washington (San
Francisco: HarperOne, 2003), 231–44.

woman's act of anointing, recognizing, and honoring Jesus is a celebration of someone whose words and actions stand for restructuring the "edifice which produces beggars." Baptist connects flinging a coin to a beggar with the establishment of a potter's field for the poor with the money discarded by the Temple elites when Judas returns Jesus's blood money, which we will explore farther along in this chapter. Indeed, juxtaposing Matthew 26 and the Martin Luther King Jr. text helps us to bring forth a new liberationist reading of this passage. Rather than simply accepting that the only response to poverty is a "Band-Aid solution" with no critique of economic systems and structures that hurt communities and destroy lives, Dr. King reminds us, especially as Christians, that God requires justice and love for all and judges that which impoverishes and tramples on God's children. Dr. King suggests that to follow Jesus means to strive for economic dignity and justice for all. Although helping individuals is necessary, the only true help for individuals is bettering the whole society.

Baptist's reading of these two texts shatters the traditional and fatalistic interpretation of this passage; it insists that poverty should and could be ended, with the organized poor leading the way. Drawing this parallel between Dr. King's critique of poverty and charity and the passage in Matthew, which is regularly used to justify economic and social inequality and charity, pulls out new textual readings and connections. Using Dr. King's quotation on true compassion to (re)interpret Matthew 26 compels us to look more closely at the economic and social lessons in Matt 26:6–14 in particular. It emphasizes Jesus's economic focus and critique. And it insists that, rather than reading through the lens of the traditional interpretation of Matthew 26 (in which poverty is inevitable and individual), we should read the story of the Good Samaritan and other stories about compassion and shalom through the lens of Matthew 26, which shows that Jesus is about ending poverty.

Wasting Their Efforts: Jesus's Economic Critique

After the unnamed woman anoints Jesus, instead of acknowledging his imminent death or recognizing and celebrating the social critique implicit in her anointing of a poor person with a luxury item, the disciples chide her. They criticize her for wasting the ointment. They suggest that instead of breaking the alabaster jar and pouring out all the ointment, the woman should have kept it intact and sold the item.

Before we are too critical of the disciples for their shortsighted critique of the woman, we must recognize that access to large amounts of money was most likely infrequent or impossible for Jesus's followers. Some accounts (e.g., John 12:5) say that this ointment used by the woman was worth 300 denarii, a whole year's wages.[2] Although no price tag is attached in Matthew, the words used in this pericope—including *alabastros, barytimou,* and *myron*—show that the ointment was expensive. So, if the disciples had sold the ointment as they suggested, they could have had a large sum of money to give to the poor. At first, the disciples seem to be the practical (and compassionate/generous) ones in this passage, the people who are thinking about the needs of the poor. For people who are poor themselves or spend a good deal of time with poor people, the instinct to turn a luxury item into income that can be more reasonably spent on living expenses is a logical reaction. Their response also suggests a critique of luxury items in a world where so many lack basic necessities. Rather than pouring out all of the luxury ointment, could not the woman have poured a little and sold the rest for a profit to help fund Jesus's ministry?

But the disciples do not simply assert that she has wasted the ointment by using it to anoint Jesus; they claim that in doing so she has destroyed it. The Greek word *apōleia* is more accurately translated "destruction." The term is used by Matthew in only one other place, 7:13: "For wide is the gate and broad is the road that leads to destruction," which occurs immediately prior to a warning against false prophets. The use of this word in Matthew 26 could refer to the breaking of the vial containing the ointment, which is described in Mark and implied in Matthew by his

2. John's Gospel states that the *myron* was worth 300 denarii. In today's dollars, I suggest this could be equal to anywhere between $500 and $15,000. I base this broad estimate on what we know about the worth of the denarius and the wages of day laborers. We know that it was standard to pay day laborers one denarius per day, making 300 denarii worth about a year's wages. We also know that day laborers were at the lower end of the social class structure in ancient Israel. A modern-day comparison could be farmworkers or other labor-pool or temporary workers. The average pay for a day laborer today in the United States is somewhere between $5,000 and $15,000 a year. The median pay for all workers in the United States is $26,695. In the developing world, individuals living in extreme poverty survive on about $500 per year. Regardless of its precise value in today's dollars, something worth as much as a year of income would be a lot of money for the disciples, and in the story they respond to it accordingly. Drawing again from the experiences of today, we can imagine that a smaller value, something closer to $500, would seem like more money in an economy where the majority of people survived on only $500 per year. That this was a significant sum for the disciples gives us insight into their own meager economic positions.

specifying that the container was an alabaster jar, a type of container that must be broken to access its contents.[3] Once the jar is broken, it is no longer possible to trade the luxury ointment (*myron*) for cash for more-practical commodities.

The term *apōleia* could describe the unnamed woman's action as destroying the ointment because Jesus, the disciples, and even the woman herself could no longer benefit from the ointment; she destroyed the possibility of receiving the gratitude, status, social stability, and conformity that came with the exchange of such an expensive item in the Roman imperial system of patronage and philanthropy. In the same way, she destroyed the possibility of giving the ointment to the poor, who similarly could have received money or honor and status in exchange for it. In order to understand how the woman's actions could have been considered a form of destruction by the disciples, one needs to look in more detail at the concepts of buying and selling in their scriptural and social context.

Selling

In Matt 26:9 the disciples use the word *prathēnai*, meaning "to sell." There are two other references to selling in Matthew, 13:46 and 18:25.[4] Both references are in parables pertaining to buying and selling in the Kingdom of God in contrast to buying and selling as bankers and other ruling elites in the kingdom/empire of Caesar. Matthew 13:46 tells the story of a man who finds a pearl for sale and then sells everything that he has in order to buy the pearl.[5] In this story, the man is clearly not wealthy. If he needs to sell everything he has to buy the pearl, he is not a regular trader in luxury items. He does not invest the pearl in the Roman economy and use it to earn interest, as the wealthy commonly did in that economy. Instead, he invests it in the Kingdom of God, where there is no mention of using money to make more money. The parable in Matt 13:46 shows that the economics of the Kingdom of God are not the same as those of the Roman Empire:

3. Susan Miller, "The Woman Who Anoints Jesus (Mark 14:3–9)," *Feminist Theology* 14 (2006): 221–36.
4. Donald Hagner, *Matthew 14–28*, Word Biblical Commentary, 33B (Dallas: Word, 1995), 757. This verb also appears in Mark 14:5; John 12:5; Acts 2:45, 4:34, 5:4; and Rom 7:14.
5. "Again, the kingdom of heaven is like a merchant looking for fine pearls. When he found one of great value, he went away and sold everything he had and bought it" (Matt 13:45–46).

things of great value are enjoyed by the poor but not sold, and people living in the Kingdom of God do not worry about their basic necessities. The logic of this passage may be similar to the actions of the woman anointing Jesus. The woman takes the luxury ointment—perhaps she too had to sell everything she had to attain it—and uses it on Jesus to anoint him as king for the Kingdom of God.

It is important here to pay attention to the woman's social class and economic status as they are unknown to the reader. Many have asserted that she must be a woman of means, and often scholars argue that there seem to have been other wealthy woman followers of Jesus and supporters of the Jesus movement.[6] The fact that she has an alabaster jar of *myron* in her possession does raise the question of her economic status. I want to suggest that, although it is possible this woman did have means and did buy this ointment to anoint Jesus in the first place, it is also possible that she was not wealthy. She may have sold everything she had to acquire this *myron* (cf. Matt 6:19). She may have stolen the ointment in order to anoint Jesus. Perhaps this is why she is willing to use/waste it all. Perhaps trying to sell it would arouse suspicion or lead to arrest. The fact that we learn nothing about the origins of the woman, although Matthew does name tax collectors and other people of wealth, suggests that it was not the primary concern of Matthew. The ointment was necessary to anoint Jesus the Christ and is not inconsistent with the critique of luxury items and wealth throughout Matthew.

There is also some possibility that the unnamed woman is a prostitute, especially via traditional interpretations of the Luke version. Historically and contemporarily, prostitution pays better and more consistently than other jobs available to poor women, sometimes a lot of money (i.e., a year's wages) all at once. It also adds a layer of meaning to the disciples' sudden moral panic: she is not just wasteful/destructive because of how she gives her gift but also because of how she procures it. An anointing sex worker also fits with Jesus's Matthean genealogy, where he is descended from Rahab and Tamar. Sex workers are who Jesus comes from and to whom he belongs. Likewise, Matthew repeatedly highlights the legal, social, and religious "impurities" of the people with whom Jesus lives (lepers, tax collectors, etc.), with Jesus emphasizing that law is not about individual purity but about collective purity and a new kingdom,

---

6. See Ulrich Luz, *Matthew 21–28*, trans. James E. Crouch, Hermeneia (Minneapolis: Fortress, 2007), 340.

free of poverty and the humiliation and violence to which the poor are subjected.[7]

Whatever the unnamed woman's economic and social position, she invests everything she has in Jesus and his kingdom. These stories tell us that the use of a luxury item and its "investment" in the Kingdom of God are more important than any money or honor a person might receive for exchanging it in the Empire of Rome. These stories emphasize "not to store up treasures on earth" (Matt 6:19), where the hoarding or even exchanging of a luxury item is discouraged; and that in a world where it is possible to suggest that a luxury item is more valuable than the Son of God, "you cannot serve God and Mammon" (Matt 6:24). The overall message is that God is to be glorified, and all are to have enough in God's Kingdom. It suggests that the giving of everything to Jesus or the kingdom is an act of commitment, a giving wholly of oneself to others. It is an act of trust in the fact that God both desires and seeks for the needs of all to be provided.

Matthew 18:23–35 also speaks about selling in relation to both the Roman and God's empires. It tells the story of a man who has a debt with the king. The king demands that he pay back his debt by selling all that he has, including his wife and child, but then relents and shows compassion toward the man and forgives his entire debt. However, when the indebted man turns to collect from someone who owes him money and cannot pay, he shows no compassion and sends his debtor to prison, refusing to extend the forgiveness that has been shown to him by the king. The logic of this passage may be similar to Matthew 26. Instead of debt leading to the selling of one's family into slavery and being imprisoned, as was practiced in the Roman Empire, this parable tells a story of forgiving debts and being obliged to forgive the debts of others, just as Jesus prays in the Lord's Prayer in the Sermon on the Mount. Jesus as the anointed "king" in Matthew 26 defies the valorization of money, interest-making, and indebtedness that produces poverty and enslavement and reduces human beings to merchandise. Instead, Jesus professes the forgiveness of debts and the elimination of poverty in the Kingdom of God.

In ways similar to these passages in Matthew, Rev 18:11–19 critiques the buying and selling associated with the powerful in the Roman Empire. The inclusion of the "bodies and souls of human beings" in Rev 18:13's list of traded spices, dyes, and luxury items (including *myron*, the ointment used by the unnamed woman to anoint Jesus, which I will discuss in more

---

7. Avaren Ipsen, *Sex Working and the Bible* (Sheffield: Equinox, 2009).

depth below) challenges a system where human lives can be bought and sold publicly in the marketplace alongside other commodities.[8] In fact, the act of buying and selling proposed by the disciples in Matt 26:9 may have been a small building block in maintaining the very structure that was excluding and exploiting the poor from the farming and fishing industries and confining the majority of inhabitants in the empire to dispossession, misery, and slavery.

Indeed, Matthew uses the word for slave more than any other New Testament book and makes connections between slavery, poverty, and indebtedness. He reveals the inclusion of slaves and the poor in Jesus's reign, that those who desire to be great must be a slave, and that Jesus came not to be served but to serve (Matt 20:25–28); Jesus's followers are to come from the underside of history. Matthew's Gospel shows that conformity to the economic system of buying and selling impoverishes and enslaves (much like Revelation) and that Jesus himself has chosen sides: he has sided with the poor.

Giving: Justice or Charity?

On the other side of wealth accumulation in this passage—selling the ointment for a high price—comes the suggestion that someone give the proceeds to the poor. Biblical scholars and other interpreters usually consider the disciples' proposal to include almsgiving or meeting basic survival needs.[9] New

---

8. Part of the criticism being leveled here is that, if economic production is focused on luxury items, it isn't being devoted to growing and producing what people need to live. Even the food items in the list are not for common consumption, either in the place where the trade ship originates or in the destination. The economy, including shipping, is focused on the desires of the elite, not the needs of the people.

9. Many commentaries on and interpretations of Matt 26:9 recognize that Jewish almsgiving is what the disciples had in mind when they said the *myron* should have been sold and the proceeds given to the poor. Among these interpretations are Susan Miller, "The Woman Who Anoints Jesus (Mark 14:3–9)," 221–36; Luz, *Matthew 21–28*, 339–40; Daniel Harrington, *The Gospel of Matthew*, Sacra Pagina 1 (Collegeville, MN: Liturgical Press, 1991); Elaine Wainwright, *Towards a Feminist Critical Reading of the Gospel according to Matthew* (Berlin: de Gruyter, 1991). The Gospel of Mark includes the statement that Jesus's followers will have other opportunities to care for the poor, perhaps making a more direct connection to almsgiving and other ways of meeting the needs of the poor. Few interpretations make connections between the selling of the *myron* as a luxury item, the giving of the proceeds to the poor, and the overall role that euergetism played in the Roman economic structure.

Testament scholar Justin Meggitt describes almsgiving as having a minor impact on alleviating poverty; it was minor in terms of both participation and relation to the empire-sponsored benefaction system. I follow Meggitt's analysis and connect the selling of the luxury item and giving of the proceeds to the poor to the larger systems of patronage—the dominant way by which the poor were "cared for" in the Roman Empire, to the small extent that they were cared for at all.[10]

Despite the fact that poverty was widespread in the Roman Empire, there was little recourse for those who were destitute. Some were able to receive alms or other forms of charity from wealthy patrons and benefactors,[11] but the alms were insufficient compared to the actual needs of the poor. Patronage and charity were focused on raising up the wealth and status of the benefactor rather than the recipient. There is a relationship between the disciples' orientation to money, charity, and the poor and the Roman systems of charity and patronage. Jesus's response to the disciples gives us insight into his larger response to charity, patronage, and the economy as a whole.

The patronage system[12] permeated through and functioned on all

10. Justin Meggitt, *Paul, Poverty, and Survival* (Edinburgh: T&T Clark, 1998), 156.

11. K. C. Hanson and Douglas Oakman describe one form of patronage in which individual elites (male and female) cultivated a relationship of exchange with poorer and less powerful people. The patrons "provide benefits to others on a personal basis, due to a combination of superior power, influence, reputation, position, and wealth. In return for these benefits, patrons could expect to receive honor, information, and political support from clients" (*Palestine in the Time of Jesus: Social Structures and Social Conflicts* [Minneapolis: Augsburg Fortress, 2002], 71). Hanson and Oakman continue, "In Roman society patronage took on a very ritualized form. The clients of a Roman patron (especially his or her freedmen and freedwomen) were expected to appear every morning at the patron's home to salute the patron, pay deference, and find out if there was anything they could do for the patron" (Hanson and Oakman, *Palestine in the Time of Jesus*, 73). The patrons received more than they gave, with remuneration coming in the form of political power, prestige, and even financial gain. Roman historian Suetonius notes that, in the last twenty years of his reign, Emperor Augustus (the ultimate Roman patron) received 1.4 billion sesterces from his clients in wills (Hanson and Oakman, *Palestine in the Time of Jesus*, 74). There were other downsides to the patronage system, including that many of its forms were not designed for those who were truly poor. Meggitt points out that "a client had to have something to offer, and as is made clear again and again in Roman literature, the poor had nothing the rich wanted" (*Paul, Poverty, and Survival*, 168). For more information on patronage, see Hanson and Oakman, *Palestine in the Time of Jesus*; Meggitt, *Paul, Poverty, and Survival*; and Richard Horsley, *Paul and Empire: Religion and Power in Roman Imperial Society* (Harrisburg, PA: Trinity Press International, 1997).

12. These multilayered charity systems are sometimes called *euergetism*, from the Greek for "good" and "works." It is related to eucharist and is perhaps related to what Paul critiques as "good works" in his letters.

levels of society, from within families and villages to the organization of the empire as a whole. The Roman emperor himself was the most powerful patron and used his position to appoint political and religious offices, free slaves, raise individuals' status, grant citizenship, endow buildings, sponsor competitions, grant exemptions from taxes, and give preference in legal cases.[13] Augustus mastered the role of patron, inventing many of these forms of patronage.[14] He consolidated his popularity among the people by burning records of old debts to the treasury.[15] Although feigning care for

13. Hanson and Oakman, *Palestine in the Time of Jesus*, 72–80. The patronage of the emperor included public service. As the supreme patron, emperors attended to the material needs of their subjects with food, water, and housing. They entertained the public with shows and games and sponsored regular banquets for the masses and meals for elites. They even occasionally distributed sums of money, although only male citizens of Rome were included in the dole (Horsley, *Paul and Empire*, 98). The *Res gestae divi Augusti* publicly recorded Augustus's generosity, including: "To the Roman plebs I paid out three hundred sesterces per man in accordance with the will of my father, and in my own name in my fifth consulship I gave four hundred sesterces apiece from the spoils of war; a second time, moreover, in my tenth consulship I paid out of my own patrimony four hundred sesterces per man by way of bounty, and in my eleventh consulship I made twelve distributions of food from grain bought at my own expense, and in the twelfth year of my tribunician power I gave for the third time four hundred sesterces to each man. These largesses of mine reached a number of persons never less than two hundred and fifty thousand" (3.15).

14. Velleius Paterculus, *Res gestae divi Augusti* summary (Shipley, LCL).

15. Suetonius, *Aug.* 32 (Wolfe, LCL). Augustus understood how to rule politically and economically, including using patronage and euergetism to maintain his power. He mentions that he had to discern between using the carrot and the stick, relying on the military to subdue the mutinous in some cases and providing benefits to the masses in other cases. Augustus was also a master of divide-and-conquer tactics, even among those loyal to him, keeping social and political groups united through him but divided among themselves. This form of social control was important for the order of the empire, preventing the mingling of people from different backgrounds and status. He particularly maintained distinct social classes among the military. Suetonius describes the unusual decision to employ slaves and freedmen as soldiers when additional forces were needed to control a scarcity riot, but emphasizes that "even these he levied, when they were slaves, from men and women of means and at once gave them freedom; and he kept them under their original standard [i.e., he kept them apart from the rest in the companies in which they were first enrolled], not mingling them with the soldiers of free birth or arming them in the same fashion" (Suetonius, *Aug.* 25 [Wolfe, LCL]). Suetonius also describes Augustus's efforts to pay off his soldiers, readily giving prizes to even common soldiers, realizing that if he could keep those who coerced and controlled the masses satisfied, he could continue to withhold his wealth and power from the majority of the empire. "As military prizes he was somewhat more ready to give trappings [the *phalerae* were discs or plates of metal attached to a belt or to the harness of horses] or collars, valuable for their gold and silver, than crowns for scaling ramparts or walls, which

the masses of people, the caesars did most of their giving for the benefit of the elites. Augustus limited the number of Roman citizens by increasing the property and wealth requirements, and made it more difficult for slaves to become citizens. And of course, any generosity was made possible by extraction of wealth from the empire, giving the emperors the economic power to perform these public services.

Other elites similarly sponsored regional, local, and individual forms of patronage and benefaction. Meggitt explains that ultimately the patronage system had little effect on the lives it claimed to improve, arguing that "upper-class largesse seems to have been limited to providing the funds for an occasional meal and little else."[16] And while there were few real benefits, there were drawbacks. The system cemented the empire's hierarchal structure—with the emperor on top and the poor on the bottom—which was used as an instrument of social control. The benefits received by those who depended on the largesse of benefactors, even when substantial, were always precarious.[17] Those in power had the ability to deliver help and the ability to refuse this same help, undermining any attempts at mutuality or solidarity forged by the poor of the Roman Empire.[18] Patronage systems and charity divided the people of the empire in a way that helped to subdue and vanquish them.

Examining patronage through the teachings of the Scriptures and Jesus's teachings on poverty and wealth in Matthew 26 yields four levels of critique: ideological, political, spiritual/moral, and material. Ideologically, patronage and charity functioned as a way for the rich to demonstrate care for the poor. Inequality and verticality were both inherent to and reinforced by the patronage system. Caesars and other elites sponsored banquets, handed out the dole, and organized athletic and gladiatorial games for the financial health, enjoyment, and spiritual well-being of the people.[19]

conferred high honour; the latter he gave as sparingly as possible and without favouritism, often even to the common soldiers" (Suetonius, *Aug.* 25 [Wolfe, LCL]).

16. Meggitt, *Paul, Poverty, and Survival*, 169.

17. Richard Horsley and Neil A. Silberman, *The Message and the Kingdom: How Jesus and Paul Ignited a Revolution and Transformed the Ancient World* (Minneapolis: Augsburg Fortress, 2002), 83.

18. Horsley, *Paul and Empire*, 90.

19. The public shows and games were an important part of the ideological battle for the hearts and minds of the people of the Roman Empire. In this, Augustus was supreme, "He surpassed all his predecessors in the frequency, variety, and magnificence of his public shows. He says that he gave games four times in his own name and twenty-three times for other magistrates, who were either away from Rome or lacked means. He gave them

Therefore, rather than viewing the rich of the empire as responsible for the impoverishment of the poor, the rich were viewed as the saviors of the poor and common people.[20] This stands in marked contrast with Jesus's teachings and judgment of the rich.

Politically, patronage and charity helped the wealthy to gain a political base and following. The clients and subjects of benefactors pledged loyalty to them, supported their campaigns for political or social offices, and supported their tenure in those positions (even when positions were used against the interests of the poor), and backed them in the political office to which they aspired or social campaign they promulgated. The wealthy and powerful used the resulting social stratification and the monopolizing social, political, and economic positions to make their clients both more dependent and poorer. The wealth and political power of elite benefactors generated more wealth and political power through this exchange—all under the guise of great generosity on the part of the elites.[21]

Spiritually, patronage and charity were tied to the state religion and imperial cult of the Roman Empire. It was the Roman gods who justified and sanctioned the empire's social and economic inequality.[22] Richard Horsley argues, "Euergetism, established throughout the empire as the socially responsible use of wealth, proclaimed the necessity of social inequality, grounded in the divine world of the gods."[23] The gods deemed some people deserving and others undeserving, under the approving gaze

---

sometimes in all the wards and on many stages with actors in all languages, and combats of gladiators not only in the Forum or the amphitheatre, but in the Circus and in the Saepta; sometimes, however, he gave nothing except a fight with wild beasts. He gave athletic contests too in the Campus Martius, erecting wooden seats; also a seafight, constructing an artificial lake near the Tiber, where the grove of the Caesars now stands" (Suetonius, *Aug.* 43 [Rolfe, LCL]).

20. It is not simply poverty that causes social unrest but inequality and the public perception that some are living in extreme luxury while others are dying from extreme poverty. To keep the common people from erupting, "Augustus understood the need to put limits on the luxury and excess of the rich at the same time as enforcing legislation that helped protect the wealth and heredity of the wealthy. He maintained an image that he lived simply and did not flaunt his wealth. This legislation served to protect the overall wealth and power of the empire rather than undermining it" (Suetonius, *Aug.* 73 [Wolfe, LCL]).

21. Susan Sorek, *Remembered for Good: A Jewish Benefaction System in Ancient Palestine* (Sheffield: Sheffield Phoenix , 2010), 24–30.

22. Horsley, "Introduction: Patronage, Priesthoods, and Power," in *Paul and Empire*, 90–95.

23. Horsley, "Introduction," 95.

of the high priests of the temples, creating a theological justification for inequality and apologetics for its necessity in the cosmos.[24]

Materially, patronage and charity not only failed to meet the needs of the poor but also exacerbated poverty by making more money for the wealthy. Biblical and classical scholars argue that Roman imperial patronage only offered material assistance to individual poor people but failed to address the larger social problem of poverty. Instead, it undergirded systems of debt, taxation, and poverty-creation.[25] The wealthy were also rewarded for acts of patronage with appointments to paid positions of social, political, and religious functions. Therefore, those who were in a position to donate wealth and benefactions to the empire were better positioned to be honored with well-paying positions of status. In patronage systems, one had to have (and give) money in order to make money.[26]

The wealthy were able to enrich themselves off the poverty of the poor, particularly in times of disaster. Benefactors would come to the aid of a city during famine, economic crisis, or natural disaster, be recognized and honored for their generosity, and still make money from the crisis. One example shows that in a time of famine an elite from the Greek island of Amorgos lent other residents of the island money at a twenty percent interest rate so that they could buy grain from him at ten times the regular price. This elite was perceived to be a savior in a time of crisis, yet he not only profited from the exchange but caused the people to go into more debt and poverty.[27] The debts of the poor became a source of wealth and income for the rich.

---

24. Philosophical leaders also supported the rights of the wealthy to maintain this imbalance. Aristotle argued, "If one is a better man than the other, he thinks he has a right to more, for goodness deserves the larger share. And similarly when one is more useful than the other: if a man is of no use, they say, he ought not to have an equal share, for it becomes a charity and not a friendship at all, if what one gets out of it is not enough to repay one's trouble. For men think that it ought to be in a friendship as it is in a business partnership, where those who contribute more capital take more of the profits. On the other hand the needy or inferior person takes the opposite view: he maintains that it is the part of a good friend to assist those in need; what is the use (he argues) of being friends with the good and great if one is to get nothing out of it?" (Aristotle, *Eth. Nic.* 1163a [Rackham, LCL]).

25. Richard Horsley states, "Among the Roman urban poor, for whom we have at least minimal evidence of dependency on patronage, we should not imagine either that the poor were happy about their dependency or that patronage really alleviated poverty and hunger" (Horsley, "Introduction," 90).

26. Sorek, *Remembered for Good*, 24–30.

27. Meggitt, *Paul, Poverty, and Survival*, 167.

Taking into consideration what we now know about buying and selling, money exchange and luxury items, and Rome's patronage systems and charity for the poor, we can return to the disciples' critique of the unnamed woman's destruction of the *myron*. The woman's action not only disrupts one exchange of a luxury item for money for charity, but it subverts the whole system of buying and selling, especially the valuing and exchange of luxury items. She undermines patronage systems and charity rather than participating in them. She does metaphorically "destroy" something: she challenges the whole economic structure that creates wealth, including the system of patronage, which on its flip side impoverishes the poor.

Rather than being only about almsgiving, as the disciples' words have traditionally been interpreted (in the disciples' culture, a luxury item's value is its ability to access patronage or be offered as charity, especially in the Gospel of Matthew), their criticism reveals an uncritical willingness to participate in the larger patronage systems, which perpetuate the economic structure of Rome and impoverish both the disciples and those they seek to help.

Jesus's Economic Critique

In light of this understanding of the economics of the Roman Empire and its systems of patronage and charity, Jesus's response to the disciples and the unnamed woman reveals his multilayered social, theological, and economic assessment. He criticizes the system of patronage and charity and the role that it plays in masking the problems of poverty: this system allows further polarization of wealth and poverty. He judges the Roman economy for exploiting the poor and creating poverty in the first place. He perceives that the process of monetization further dispossesses the already dispossessed. And he critiques the religious and political authorities for their complicity in the impoverishment of the people.[28]

When Matt 26:10 reads, "Aware of this," Jesus realizes that the disciples propose selling a luxury item—and charity toward the poor in general—as the solution to poverty and dispossession. They have a vertical orientation modeled on the hierarchy of the Roman Empire and practiced in patronage systems. But the unnamed woman attends to Jesus and his kingship. She has a horizontal orientation modeled on mutual need and

28. Hanson and Oakman, *Palestine in the Time of Jesus*, 125–27.

solidarity.[29] Jesus is the woman's brother. She does not use her gift to him to lift herself up, as gifts are used by patrons; her luxury item does not help her produce more power, wealth, or status at the expense of others. On the contrary, her gift serves to comfort and acknowledge a humble but worthy poor person/messiah and her commitment to his way. Because of her understanding and actions, Jesus chides the disciples not to bother her or discredit her. Jesus's critique of the disciples in Matthew 26 may be strong because he is disappointed that they cannot see the possibility for a different world that the unnamed woman has demonstrated in their midst. Jesus wants the consciousness of his disciples to be where the woman's is, but instead, they fall short.

Good Works and Works of the Law

The other side of Jesus's appraisal of the disciples and the systems that they are upholding is his praise for what the unnamed woman has done for him. In the second part of Matt 26:10, Jesus says that this woman has done a *kalon ergon*, a "beautiful thing" or a "good work," by anointing him. Matthew mentions good works and good fruits several times, including in the Sermon on the Mount, where Jesus tells his followers to let their light shine and demonstrate their good works in an effort to glorify God in Heaven (5:16); John the Baptist reminds the Pharisees and Sadducees that every tree that does not produce good fruit will be cut down (3:10); Jesus warns about false prophets by stating that good trees produce good fruit (12:33) and all others will be chopped down (7:17–19); and Jesus tells the parable of the sower and reminds his listeners that good seed produces good fruit (13:8). Clearly, in Matthew, good works are those that benefit others in real ways and that glorify God. Works are associated with judgment when they produce bad deeds or seeds. These teachings on good works are connected to related biblical references. James 2:26 asserts that faith without works is dead. Philippians 1:6 states that "he who began a good work in you will

---

29. Those with property and wealth protect it by working together. Speaking to the elites of his day, Aristotle writes in *Nicomachean Ethics*, "Again, the proverb says 'Friends' goods are common property,' and this is correct, since community is the essence of friendship. Brothers have all things in common, and so do members of a comradeship; other friends hold special possessions in common, more or fewer in different cases, inasmuch as friendships vary in degree. The claims of justice also differ in different relationships" (Aristotle, *Eth. Nic.* 1159b [Rackham, LCL]).

carry it on to completion," rather than promising to do something good in the interest of receiving credit.

Jesus's praise of the unnamed woman's actions as *kalon ergon* defines the good works of the Kingdom of God as the opposite of the patronage and charity systems of Rome. Patrons were considered the *euergetai*, or "good workers/benefactors" of the empire of the Caesars.[30] This woman anoints a poor person. She prepares a poor, dying man for his burial. Her actions may even confer kingship and messiahship on the popular leader (a possibility discussed in Chapter 6 below). She affirms that beautiful things belong in the Kingdom of God for the betterment of everyone. As in the Sermon on the Mount, authentic "good works" are about glorifying God, not glorifying human patrons who lord their power over others. In the rabbinic tradition, good works include almsgiving, hosting strangers, and visiting the sick. Good works that are connected to doing justice are more highly valued by rabbinic standards, particularly works that will not be recognized or repaid. In fact, the Jewish benefaction system was different from Rome's. This system of euergetism, based on the Hebrew concept of loving-kindness (*ḥesed*), was about glorifying God, taking care of each other, and adhering to Jewish law which promoted justice and equality.[31]

Jesus's good news/works for the poor in Matthew raise an important question for believers about how to interpret and respond to God's will and law. Matthew offers two options: hypocrisy and righteousness.[32] Righteousness is following the will/law of God and emulating Jesus. It is another way of defining true "good works."[33] Hypocrisy is adhering to the laws, norms, and forms of charity that Rome considers "good," using

30. In contrast, Roman theological and philosophical ethics supported and endorsed the "good works" of patronage systems that were motivated by reward and repayment. Aristotle encouraged the wealthy to practice "doing good related either to personal security and all the causes of existence; or to wealth." He continued, "[gifts] are an acquisition for the latter and an honour for the former; so that they furnish both with what they want" (*Rhet.* 1361a 36–53 [Freese, LCL]).

31. Sorek, *Remembered for Good: A Jewish Benefaction System in Ancient Palestine*.

32. According to David Rhoads, there are four types of hypocrites in Matthew: (1) those who do things to be glorified by others rather than to glorify God; (2) those whose inward appearance is the opposite of their outward appearance; (3) those who act morally in some situations but not others; and (4) those who behave one way with God and another way with others. See David Rhoads, "The Gospel of Matthew. The Two Ways: Hypocrisy or Righteousness," *Currents in Theology and Mission* 19 (1992): 453–61.

33. Rhoads, "The Gospel of Matthew," 453–61.

the backs of others to prop oneself up in that political-economic system. I argue that Jesus's critique of the *euergetai* (benefactors and patrons of the Roman Empire), hypocrites (including teachers of the law who are conspiring with Rome), and "works of the law" is a polemic against Rome and empire; it is more than simply an internal message to Judaism. The Messiah Jesus insists that this interpretation of law and its relationship to justice/righteousness is important in relation to the Deuteronomic Code. Jesus's interpretation also reveals the ways in which those laws and scriptures are in contradiction to and irreconcilable with the laws and theologies of Rome.

Too Poor to Die

After Jesus criticizes the "good works" of Roman imperial charity, praises the good works of the unnamed woman, and reminds his disciples that creating a world without poverty is their responsibility, because "you will not always have me," he describes the woman's actions thus: "She has prepared my body for burial." This is Jesus's first announcement of his impending death at this dinner, and he calls attention to the fact that the unnamed woman is caring for his humble body while he is still alive.

Burial was sacred in all cultures and nations in the Roman Empire, but it had a particularly important place in Jewish practice and belief. Part of what was so devastating to Jews about crucifixion was that the body was not usually recovered or buried. Instead, crucified bodies hung for days or weeks, left on public display as an example to others, left to be consumed by wild animals.[34] Crucifixion was reserved for revolutionaries, insurrectionists, slaves, and provincials of the Roman Empire.[35] Martin Hengel writes:

> For the men of the ancient world, Greeks, Romans, barbarians and Jews, the cross was not just a matter of indifference, just any kind of

34. Philosophers and writers from antiquity as well as others discuss the horror of crucifixion, including Seneca, *Dial.* 6.20.3 (Basore, LCL); see Michael Licona, *The Resurrection of Jesus: A New Historiographical Approach* (Downers Grove, IL: InterVarsity, 2010), 304; and Colleen Conway, *Behold the Man: Jesus and Greco-Roman Masculinity* (New York: Oxford University Press, 2008), 67.

35. Martin Hengel, *Crucifixion*, trans. John Bowden, Facets (Minneapolis: Fortress, 1977), 22–52.

death. It was an utterly offensive affair, "obscene" in the original sense of the word.[36]

The unnamed woman's anointing of Jesus has multiple potential meanings. It both anoints him as king/Christ/Messiah (discussed in Chapter 6 below) and prepares his body for burial. In both these meanings, her individual act of care is also greater than her present context. His preparation for burial was significant given what we know about the denial of burial for the crucified. Does she know that he will receive the punishment of a revolutionary? Is her action one of civil disobedience, much like Jesus's tax evasion and actions in the Temple? Is this why her actions make the disciples uneasy? She associates herself with a revolutionary and prepares his body as though he were a king. She anoints him for burial before he is dead in an effort to take away from the imperial elite the power to deny him anointing at his burial.

Preparation for burial was a responsibility that Christians and other organizations assumed on behalf of the poor of the Roman Empire. In the early Christian tradition, it came to have anti-imperial and revolutionary significance. Throughout the empire there existed all kinds of institutions (*ekklēsia, koinon, synagōgē*) organized around various cultic figures (such as Isis or other Roman gods and goddesses), labor associations, and other aspects of life. One of the key functions of associations was ensuring the burial and memorializing of their members, almost taking on the role of mutual-aid societies or insurance policies for those too poor to provide for their own burial. When individuals died, members of their association would ensure that they were buried, honored, and remembered by a libational toast in a regular association meal—the early tradition from which communion derived. While many associations in the Roman Empire honored the Caesars and the gods of Rome, the early Christians honored a poor man executed as a criminal revolutionary. Hal Taussig notes:

> The . . . libational tradition concerning Jesus' death and its implication for resistance to Rome is the (possibly pre-Pauline and Pauline) injunction to do the libation as a remembering of Jesus . . . inasmuch as this libational injunction was a companion of the wine = Jesus' blood . . . the injunction to have a libation in Jesus' memory made the words much more charged. The meaning of this libational combination

---

36. Hengel, *Crucifixion*, 22.

would have been very strong in its anti-Roman character, both evoking the death of Jesus as a new sociopolitical bonding at the meal and promoting it as an ongoing practice.[37]

Both Jesus's and Paul's communion formulas follow the words these early Christian associations used to memorialize the dead: Luke 22:19 and 1 Cor 11:24–25 use the Greek word *anamnēsin* for "memory."[38] Interestingly, in Matt 26:13 when Jesus states that what the unnamed woman has done will be told in memory of her, he uses the Greek word *mnēmosynon*, meaning "memory" or "memorial offering."[39] This same word is used in Acts 10:4, when an angel of God tells Cornelius that his alms and generosity to the poor have ascended as a memorial offering to God. The use of *mnēmosynon* also echoes Exodus 12 and the manna scene of the exodus event. In the Jewish tradition, this language of memory, including its use in the Passover celebrations, predated the funeral associations of the Roman Empire. In the world view and religious knowledge of Jesus and disciples, the echoing of the language used for the exodus would be a reminder of God's dissatisfaction with the practices of Egypt/Rome and desire for liberation.

Nevertheless, in the communion formula in 1 Corinthians 11 and Luke 22, and the commemorating of the unnamed woman in Matt 26:13, the scriptures popularize and politicize the words said at the burial-association dinners/memorials by placing Jesus's death, burial, and resurrection alongside the death and burial of thousands of other poor subjects of the Roman Empire.[40] In Matthew, Jesus elevates the good work of the unnamed woman to the level of an instruction on how to honor and remember him and other followers. Indeed, this burial ritual is an important aspect of the economic practices of Jesus and God's Kingdom.

37. Hal Taussig, *In the Beginning Was the Meal: Social Experimentation and Early Christian Identity* (Minneapolis: Fortress, 2009), 133–34.

38. For more information on associations and the poor in the ancient world, see Taussig, *In the Beginning Was the Meal*, 87–144.

39. Also Mark 14:9.

40. "A variation of the funerary meal was the memorial meal, a form that is not widely attested but that this tradition certainly assumes. This seems to be the significance of the phrase 'Do this in remembrance of me.' . . . What is to be remembered is left somewhat vague. That is to say, presumably anyone's version of 'the Christ story' could be substituted here. This is important to note since we too easily assume that the canonical gospel story was the universal story of Jesus" (Dennis Smith, *From Symposium to Eucharist: The Banquet in the Early Christian World* [Minneapolis: Fortress, 2003], 189).

In Memory of Her

Jesus continues with more praise for what this woman has done for him, saying that, wherever the good news/the gospel is preached, what she has done will also be remembered. The unnamed woman appears in Matt 26:7, and then Jesus reminds the audience of her in v. 13; she is the opening and closing of this story.[41] She is praised unconditionally by Jesus—potentially contrasted with the disciples, the priests, and especially Judas—yet in the history of interpretation of this text, she is unnamed and forgotten. Elisabeth Schüssler Fiorenza observes that of the three most important followers of Jesus in the Passion Narrative, we are only given the names of Judas his betrayer and Peter who denies him, but not this woman who serves as a model disciple and even a prophetess.[42]

In light of the preceding reflections, I suggest that the lack of attention given to the unnamed woman may be in observance of Jesus's teaching on good works: she is not to be lifted up for caring for the poor Jesus; her actions are truly focused on the needs of the poor (individually and collectively) rather than on herself. This is how all of us are supposed to act. Perhaps the not-naming of the woman is a direct critique of patronage systems and charity relationships. If her name had been given in association with her gift, her actions would have been closer to the way patronage works, particularly in its elaborate public recording of gift-giving. This may have been especially true if she was wealthy. Perhaps the missing name was not misogyny but intentional anonymity, maybe even by her own choice. It is possible, in fact, that being unnamed is part of what makes her the model disciple and prophetess.

Jesus associates the unnamed woman with good news/gospel. The specific word *euangelion* is used only four times in Matthew: two usages specify "Gospel of the Kingdom" and another one aligns this "Gospel of the Kingdom" with Jesus's worldwide mission. When *euangelion* is used, it is in combination with keeping God's law, doing justice, and caring for the poor.[43] In fact, Matt 4:23 and 9:35 reveal that Jesus's proclaiming the good

41. Luz, *Matthew 21–28*, 334.

42. Elisabeth Schüssler Fiorenza, *In Memory of Her: A Feminist Theological Reconstruction of Christian Origins* (New York: Crossroad, 1983), xlii.

43. The other three uses of *euangelion* ("gospel") appear in Matt 4:23, 9:35, and 24:14: "Jesus went throughout Galilee, teaching in their synagogues, proclaiming the good news of the kingdom, and healing every disease and sickness among the people" (4:23); "Jesus went through all the towns and villages, teaching in their synagogues, proclaiming the good

news of the Kingdom is connected to "healing every disease and sickness." This coupling of proclamation and healing demonstrates the material nature of the good news. Matthew's use of *euangelion* in 26:13, therefore, is in line with Matthew's definition of "good works" and Deuteronomy's concept of "Jubilee/Sabbath." Significant to understanding the "good news" of the anointing scene is the preceding proclamation of the "good news" as God's worldwide mission. After Jesus leaves the Temple and travels to the Mount of Olives (24:1–13), his disciples approach him privately, seeking a sign about his return and the end of the age. It is in this setting that Jesus replies, "And this gospel of the kingdom will be preached in the whole world as a testimony to all nations, and then the end will come" (24:14).[44] Matthew 24:14 is a stepping-stone gospel proclamation of the materializing of God's Kingdom on earth, further developed and explained in Matt 26:13, where Jesus proclaims that what the unnamed woman has done is "good news": healing the sick and "release" for the poor.[45] Even if we are not to remember the anointing woman's name, it is clear from Jesus's statement that his followers are to emulate her actions: this is how she and others will be memorialized, and this is how God's mission to the world will be realized.

The combination of world mission and gospel in Matt 24:14 is further elaborated in 28:16–20, "Then Jesus came to them and said, 'All authority in heaven and on earth has been given to me. Therefore go and make disciples of all nations, baptizing them in the name of the Father and of the Son and of the Holy Spirit, and teaching them to obey everything I have commanded you. And surely I am with you always, to the very end of the age.'" Jesus shifts responsibility for his mission/movement "throughout the world" to his disciples. They are to take up Jesus's mission to proclaim the good news and heal every disease. The disciples are charged with

news of the kingdom and healing every disease and sickness" (9:35); "And this gospel of the kingdom will be preached in the whole world as a testimony to all nations, and then the end will come" (24:14).

44. Matthew 24:14 follows the incident in the Jerusalem Temple where Jesus drives out the money-changers (21:12–16), returns to Bethany to rest for the night (21:17), and then comes back to teach in the Temple (21:23–23:39). In response to his teachings there, the Temple elites want to move on him but do not because they realize the people recognize Jesus as a prophet (21:46). The people are amazed by his questions and answers (22:22) and eventually no longer dare pose questions to him (22:26).

45. These stories harken back to the temptation scene in Matt 4 where material wealth and power are demonstrated to be the purview of the empire elites and not God and the poor.

bringing God's Kingdom to earth. But they fall short. They try to emulate Jesus and obey God's law, but they have not internalized God's justice. Perhaps because the unnamed woman's actions fall outside the charity and patronage systems, the disciples do not follow Jesus's explicit instructions; instead, they try to reify poverty and oppression. They claim to follow Jesus, but right in the moment when Jesus is anointed Messiah—responsible for improving the lives of all and actually ending poverty—they are focused solely on the poor people in their midst, on ameliorating poverty rather than ending it. They fall back on the hegemonic stance of the empire and propose a "solution" to poverty that will only make it worse. They suggest participating in the dominant, oppressive economic system and assisting the poor through imperial charity. Unlike the unnamed woman, they fail to see the revolutionary potential in the kingship of Jesus and, as a result, they fail to commit themselves to ending poverty in the way that Jesus has done and calls his followers to do.

Judas and Money for the Poor

Directly following the anointing at Bethany, Judas goes to the chief priests and offers to betray Jesus for thirty pieces of silver. This is probably less money than the ointment cost but, nonetheless, is a significant exchange of resources. John's version of the story states that Judas raises the challenge to Jesus, not because he is concerned about the poor, but because he is the treasurer and takes from the donations to the poor in the common purse. Subsequently in John, Judas is accused of using the poor as an excuse to raise money (never passing these donations on to the poor, thereby stealing from the "least of these," as the poor are termed in Matt 25:40).[46] Even in our Matthean version, Judas's relationship to the poor and money is significant. Judas and the other disciples are unable to obtain the money they want by selling the woman's ointment, so immediately Judas turns to the chief priests and double-crosses Jesus.[47] Judas obtains his money (for

46. "But one of his disciples, Judas Iscariot, who was later to betray him, objected, 'Why wasn't this perfume sold and the money given to the poor? It was worth a year's wages.' He did not say this because he cared about the poor but because he was a thief; as keeper of the money bag, he used to help himself to what was put into it" (John 12:4–6).

47. It is significant that in Mark's version of Judas's betrayal (Mark 14:10–11), Judas does not ask for money, but the chief priests offer it. In Matthew, however, Judas asks what they will pay him for turning over Jesus. This has been interpreted by many as Judas's greed.

himself or the poor), and this results in the crucifixion of Jesus, another poor person. As was stated at the beginning of this chapter, perhaps Jesus's anointing as Christ/king/prophet is threatening or confusing to Judas (as well as the Jewish and Roman authorities). Perhaps the unnamed woman's disregard for the established practices of buying and selling, patronage and charity (which maintain the social and economic status quo of the empire), is unsettling to Judas and the other disciples (and the Jewish and Roman authorities again). Perhaps Judas thinks he is the one focused on poverty-amelioration through obtaining money by any means to give to the poor. Or perhaps Judas just does not believe that ending poverty, as discussed in Deuteronomy 15 and affirmed by Jesus, is really possible. He wants only his "due"; this is all that is possible.

If we follow Judas and the money issue further in Matthew, the situation becomes even more problematic. In Matt 27:3–8, Judas feels terrible about his betrayal of Jesus when he sees that Jesus has been condemned to death by the political and religious elite.[48] He returns the blood money to the chief priests and asks them to make it right, but the chief priests do not want to contaminate the Temple by putting the money into the treasury, so they give it away immediately. Their reaction shows the complicity between the religious authorities and the larger imperial powers in the economics of the day.

Although the Temple is supposed to be set up for absolving sins, the chief priests cannot help Judas find peace. And because they will not free Jesus, they refuse to save both Jesus's and Judas's lives. Judas kills himself, and the chief priests establish a "potter's field" (27:7) for poor people and

In any case, it emphasizes the money in Matthew; see Jesse Robertson, *The Death of Judas: The Characterization of Judas Iscariot in Three Early Christian Accounts of His Death* (Sheffield: Sheffield Phoenix, 2012), 56.

48. "Early in the morning, all the chief priests and the elders of the people made their plans how to have Jesus executed. So they bound him, led him away and handed him over to Pilate, the governor. When Judas, who had betrayed him, saw that Jesus was condemned, he was seized with remorse and returned the thirty pieces of silver to the chief priests and the elders. 'I have sinned,' he said, 'for I have betrayed innocent blood.' 'What is that to us?' they replied. 'That's your responsibility.' So Judas threw the money into the temple and left. Then he went away and hanged himself. The chief priests picked up the coins and said, 'It is against the law to put this into the treasury, since it is blood money.' So they decided to use the money to buy the potter's field as a burial place for foreigners. That is why it has been called the Field of Blood to this day. Then what was spoken by Jeremiah the prophet was fulfilled: 'They took the thirty pieces of silver, the price set on him by the people of Israel, and they used them to buy the potter's field, as the Lord commanded me'" (Matt 27:1–10).

foreigners with the money he leaves behind. One wonders whether their effort to prevent pollution of the Temple by the "blood money" is seen to be misguided by Matthew: the Temple is already contaminated, because money is part of a system that exploits, excludes, deprives, and kills. And in the establishment of the potter's field with the money from Judas, we have an example of money being given to the poor, as Judas and the disciples originally suggested to Jesus with regard to the woman's ointment. Yet the result is not liberative. It does not resolve poverty but instead establishes a horrible burial plot, where the poor are buried in mass graves.

The significance that the story about Jesus's anointment continues with Judas and the money he was trying to acquire on behalf of the poor should not be missed. It demonstrates what happens when charity and patronage are the only antipoverty solutions being offered. The vertical, hierarchical order of Rome—and the Jerusalem Temple—results in more impoverishment and misery, even when donations are made for the poor.[49] Matthew's juxtaposition shows that economic exchanges and debts are some of the very "sins" for which religion is supposed to atone, but in cases of complicity with power and wealth, religion serves to increase poverty rather than liberate.

That is what was at stake for Jesus. That is why he insisted that another way of addressing poverty was—and must be—possible. He stepped in as a messiah of the poor, a popular king and prophet in the tradition of the Hebrew Scriptures, who was anointed to bring good news to the poor and release to the captives. He was to usher in the vision and law of Sabbath and Jubilee. And yet, Judas and the disciples chose money and the ameliorating of some poverty when what was on offer was much greater: a world where everything is abundant, and all are loved and protected by God.

The "trail of money" in Matthew's Passion Narrative continues even after this episode with Judas and the potter's field. In Matt 27:64–66, the Roman authorities post guards directly following the crucifixion scene and Joseph of Arimathea's claiming of Jesus's body for burial in his own tomb. The charge of these guards is to watch the tomb, because the Roman authorities fear—much as they feared the mob following Jesus at the beginning of Matthew 26—the ramifications of Jesus's predicted resurrection.[50]

49. William Herzog, *Prophet and Teacher: An Introduction to the Historical Jesus* (Louisville, Westminster John Knox, 2005), 48.

50. "The chief priests and the Pharisees gathered before Pilate and said, '. . . So give the order for the tomb to be made secure until the third day. Otherwise, his disciples may come and steal the body and tell the people that he has been raised from the dead. This last

In alliance with the local elites, Rome has just crucified this revolutionary who was an anointed king and messiah, aiming to instill fear in his burgeoning following and to squash his vision of the Kingdom of God and a world without poverty. Now they worry that the story will not end with his execution if his followers assert that he is raised from the dead after three days. Pilate, the Roman governor, in fact, sends a guard to Jesus's tomb to secure it.

Then, in Matt 28:11–15, when the tomb breaks, the guards go to the chief priests and tell them what has happened. These guards are paid a large sum of money by the chief priests—recalling the money that the disciples could have acquired by selling the *myron* or the payment that Judas received for betraying Jesus—to spread a false story that Jesus was not immortalized and resurrected but that Jesus's followers stole his body.[51] In fact, at the death and then the resurrection of Jesus in Matt 27:51–53, the bodies of other saints who lived before Jesus are also raised,[52] thereby making it even more important to distract and divert the people from learning about and responding to this large-scale resurrection and rebirth of leaders.

The transaction of money in Matthew's Passion Narrative—Judas betraying Jesus to the Temple elites and the payment of the guards to spread false rumors—is used to try to quell the news of the resurrection of Jesus and the other saints, as well as the good news for the poor that his and the others' resurrection brings: although seemingly all-powerful, the Roman Empire does not have the last word over death or life. The Gospel of Matthew shares the true purpose and role of money: securing the political and economic power of the elites at the expense of the well-being of the poor.

---

deception will be worse than the first.' 'Take a guard,' Pilate answered. 'Go, make the tomb as secure as you know how.' So they went and made the tomb secure by putting a seal on the stone and posting the guard" (Matt 27:64–66).

51. "While the women were on their way, some of the guards went into the city and reported to the chief priests everything that had happened. When the chief priests had met with the elders and devised a plan, they gave the soldiers a large sum of money, telling them, 'You are to say, "His disciples came during the night and stole him away while we were asleep." If this report gets to the governor, we will satisfy him and keep you out of trouble.' So the soldiers took the money and did as they were instructed. And this story has been widely circulated among the Jews to this very day" (Matt 28:11–15).

52. "At that moment the curtain of the Temple was torn in two from top to bottom. The earth shook, the rocks split and the tombs broke open. The bodies of many holy people who had died were raised to life. They came out of the tombs after Jesus' resurrection and went into the holy city and appeared to many people" (Matt 27:51–53).

Thus the unnamed woman's "destruction" of the *myron* may be seen as an iconoclastic prophetic sign or action signaling the real use of money in upholding the status quo.

Conclusion

Rather than taking on the position of the empire that poverty is inevitable, and the poor are to be despised and buried in a potter's field, in Matt 26:1–16 Jesus stands for an era of justice and equality for everyone. It is no coincidence that Jesus is betrayed to the elites of the empire by a close follower for thirty pieces of silver. Matthew's Passion Narrative insists that participating in the Roman imperial economy—and specifically, the complicity of the Jerusalem Temple in the Roman imperial economy—is not the way to address poverty. The unnamed woman refuses to use the luxury *myron* to participate in patronage systems but instead anoints a poor man to lead the way in ending poverty and spreading good news to all. Therefore, "the poor you will always have with you" represents a disruption of imperial systems by reproaching the disciples, Judas, and society for their greed and lack of vision. The passage praises a woman for knowing about Jesus's death and appreciating the significance of his transformative vision of a world without poverty and oppression. To return to the opening quotation from Rev. Dr. King, the unnamed woman demonstrates true compassion toward Jesus, the poor, and the whole of society. Unlike the disciples' and larger society's suggestion of "flinging a coin to a beggar," she and Jesus demonstrate that the Kingdom of God on earth is a restructured edifice that produces no beggars.

CHAPTER 6

Christ, the Social-Movement Leader

I know a man. . . . He was born in an obscure village, the child of a poor peasant woman. And then he grew up in still another obscure village, where he worked as a carpenter until he was thirty years old. . . . He didn't have much. He never wrote a book. He never held an office. He never had a family. He never owned a house. He never went to college. He never visited a big city. He never went two hundred miles from where he was born. He did none of the usual things that the world would associate with greatness. He had no credentials but himself. He was only thirty-three when the tide of public opinion turned against him. They called him a rabble-rouser. They called him a troublemaker. They said he was an agitator. He practiced civil disobedience; he broke injunctions. And so he was turned over to his enemies and went through the mockery of a trial.[1]

—Martin Luther King Jr.

Weary of hearing the story that Rosa Parks just got tired one day and would not get up from her seat on a Montgomery public bus, proponents of the "Reading the Bible with the Poor" methodology, which informs this book's reinterpretation of Matthew 26, instead situate Mrs. Parks in her historical context. Parks had recently returned from a human-rights training session at the Highlander Folk School (where passive resistance and the problems

---

1. Martin Luther King Jr., *A Testament of Hope: The Essential Writings and Speeches of Martin Luther King, Jr.*, edited by James M. Washington (San Francisco: HarperOne, 2003), 259–68.

of segregation were discussed) when she refused to give up her seat. She was the secretary of the NAACP in Alabama, working with E. D. Nixon to turn it into a more activist branch. She was familiar with the driver who called the police when she refused to move, knowing that he was notorious for his staunch support of segregation. Her father was a social-activist follower of Marcus Garvey.[2] And the Montgomery Bus Boycott was not the last social-justice event or cause in which Mrs. Parks took leadership. As is the case with the lore around Rosa Parks and her "personal" stand against bus segregation, our society and educational institutions separate education from action, mobilization from organization, individual and spontaneous actions from deep-rooted social commitments and values. We have glorified historically unreliable accounts of Rosa Parks and other movement leaders in an effort to sanitize her beliefs and actions and protect us from having to make similar sacrifices, undergo significant risks, and commit to revolutionary movement building like she did.

Indeed, people often assume that resistance is only present and explicit when people are marching in the streets, protesting current policies and conditions, and covered by the mainstream media. Sometimes people say the only kind of education that is relevant to poor people is job-training programs, without recognizing that fewer and fewer jobs exist, and even the jobs that can be found do not necessarily pull a family out of poverty. Justice-minded people may suggest that the poor should be educated about how to organize to make those jobs pay better, but even this education is often limited to strike tactics and local-level power analysis. However, from the perspective of an organizer and educator in a social movement to end poverty, and a student of historical social movements including the Civil Rights Movement and the leadership of tireless fighters such as Mrs. Rosa Parks, each step in the development of this movement must be focused on education, critical thinking, applied action, values and commitment, and leadership development.

It is from this position that I (re)construct—gathering the fragments and excavating the hidden transcript of—a profile of Jesus Christ in the Gospel of Matthew, arguing that Jesus was a teacher, movement leader, and popularly acclaimed ruler with a revolutionary economic program. All of these roles of Jesus are connected and needed to struggle for dignity and justice and achieve social transformation.

---

2. For more information on the political life and commitments of Rosa Parks, see Jeanne Theoharis, *The Rebellious Life of Mrs. Rosa Parks* (New York: Beacon, 2013).

Against interpretations of Jesus's words "the poor you will always have with you" as resignation to or even approval of poverty, this book has traced an interpretation that finds exactly the opposite in Jesus's revolutionary economic and social program rooted in the Hebrew Scriptures. He and the movement he catalyzed were poor people moving to transform the oppressive and impoverishing Roman Empire into a justice and love-filled Empire of God. He critiqued charity and other Band-Aid solutions to injustice. This chapter returns to Matthew 26—the challenging and controversial character and actions of Jesus, the unnamed woman, and the movement in which they were leaders—in order to understand better how Matthew understood and communicated this revolutionary leadership theologically through the language of messiah and Christ.

A Riot among the People

The twenty-sixth chapter of Matthew opens dramatically. In the second verse, Jesus announces to his disciples that he is about to be crucified. Jesus does not say why he will be killed but only that it will happen at Passover. But Matthew gives us some more information. In v. 1, just before Jesus's reminder of his impending execution, Matthew writes, "when he had finished saying all these things," a reference to Jesus's teachings throughout Matthew, including ch. 25 and the line "whatever you did for one of the least of these brothers and sisters of mine, you did for me," where Jesus as king and judge identifies with the poor in the Last Judgment.

The Last Judgment separation of those who care for the hungry, the immigrant, and the imprisoned from those who do not (Matt 25:31–46) can be directly tied to the text about Jesus's crucifixion and his earthly poverty, especially the dividing up of his clothes, making him naked, and his captivity under Pontius Pilate and the Roman officials. Indirectly, this text echoes many of the critiques that Jesus makes of the Pharisees and scribes and even other rulers of the earth, especially in the "Warning against Hypocrisy" and "Woes to the Pharisees" in Matt 23:1–26.[3] He chides them for

---

3. "Then Jesus said to the crowds and to his disciples: 'The teachers of the law and the Pharisees sit in Moses' seat. So you must be careful to do everything they tell you. But do not do what they do, for they do not practice what they preach. They tie up heavy, cumbersome loads and put them on other people's shoulders, but they themselves are not willing to lift a finger to move them. Everything they do is done for people to see: They make their phylacteries wide and the tassels on their garments long; they love the place of honor at banquets

being hypocrites, for not following the commandments to care for others, and for being interested in furthering their own positions and ambitions.[4]

Matthew 26 moves immediately in v. 3 to tell us that, at the same time

and the most important seats in the synagogues; they love to be greeted with respect in the marketplaces and to be called "Rabbi" by others. But you are not to be called "Rabbi," for you have one Teacher, and you are all brothers. And do not call anyone on earth "father," for you have one Father, and he is in heaven. Nor are you to be called instructors, for you have one Instructor, the Messiah. The greatest among you will be your servant. For those who exalt themselves will be humbled, and those who humble themselves will be exalted. Woe to you, teachers of the law and Pharisees, you hypocrites! You shut the door of the kingdom of heaven in people's faces. You yourselves do not enter, nor will you let those enter who are trying to. Woe to you, teachers of the law and Pharisees, you hypocrites! You travel over land and sea to win a single convert, and when you have succeeded, you make them twice as much a child of hell as you are. . . . Woe to you, teachers of the law and Pharisees, you hypocrites! You give a tenth of your spices—mint, dill and cumin. But you have neglected the more important matters of the law—justice, mercy and faithfulness. You should have practiced the latter, without neglecting the former. You blind guides! You strain out a gnat but swallow a camel. Woe to you, teachers of the law and Pharisees, you hypocrites! You clean the outside of the cup and dish, but inside they are full of greed and self-indulgence. Blind Pharisee! First clean the inside of the cup and dish, and then the outside also will be clean'" (Matt 23:1–26).

4. Jesus begins Matt 23 with a warning about the authority and power of his contemporary political and religious leaders. He reminds his followers that they should follow the instructions of the authorities because they sit on Moses's seat. This reference to Moses's seat is on a few different levels. In ancient Near Eastern temples, the place where those with authority sat was called "Moses's seat." Jesus is telling his followers what to do in order to avoid unnecessary trouble with the law and authorities. As he will mention later, those in power have the authority to lock up and even kill. Since Jesus is a social and spiritual leader—a movement leader—he is instructing his followers on how to handle clashes with the authorities. But Jesus is not merely telling his followers to be strategic in their witness for justice. Jesus is judging the leaders who regularly sit in Moses's seat by saying that they administrate injustice and violence. He's also telling his followers not to do what they do. He's telling his followers that they should not administer laws that punish the poor, or follow orders to exclude, discriminate against, or divide the people. Jesus's mention of Moses is also a reminder of the exodus from slavery in Egypt: Moses was the liberator, the leader of the exodus, and a teacher who brought God's commandment of justice to the people. Jesus is reminding people to follow in the footsteps of the liberator Moses and not those in authority who sit in "Moses's seat." Tithing is also criticized in Matt 23. Matthew 23:23 says that giving a tenth of mint, dill, cumin is one of the lighter provisions of the law. Jesus insists that justice is heavier—justice is more important; it is more difficult to do. This reference to tithing also has to do with economics and power. On top of the taxes and other payments that went to landowners and the wealthy, economic pressures overwhelmed many farmers and fisherpeople in Jesus's day. Consequently, tithing on basic things such as dill and so on would have been something that only the rich could afford to do.

Jesus is gathered with his disciples trying to prepare them for his death, another meeting of leaders is taking place. Matthew explains that Caiaphas, the high priest, has assembled the chief priests and elders of the people in his house. The topic on their agenda is a conspiracy to arrest and kill Jesus. They are fearful of the crowd that is assembled in Jerusalem and following Jesus during the Passover festival. These holidays were events that sometimes turned into mass protests; at these huge assemblies, social, political, and religious revolutionaries could gain an audience and following.[5] Jesus appeared to be like one of these revolutionary leaders. He was greeted by the people in his "triumphal" procession into Jerusalem, where he may have been viewed as mocking the empire through his use of a donkey, a lowly animal associated with common labor and the poor. His actions in the Temple, where he disrupted the buying and selling taking place, also drew attention from those who were in power.[6]

Within a few days, the high priest and religious leaders of Jerusalem will be able to turn the crowd against Jesus. Although Jesus enters Jerusalem celebrated by the people, the people of Jerusalem will be manipulated into calling for his crucifixion in Matt 27:20. Even after his death, the chief priests and elders continue to plot against Jesus and organize against his potential followers, as seen in Matt 28:11–15.[7] When we take seriously Jesus's critiques of money, power, and wealth as well as the full significance of Jesus's anointing, it becomes clear why those in power found it necessary to plot against him and have him killed.

After they meet to plan their entrapment of Jesus in 26:3–5, we do not hear about Caiaphas and the chief priests until Matt 26:57–67 where, after Judas betrays him, Jesus is before the Sanhedrin, and they are looking for a legal argument to have him executed.[8] Then, although they had feared

5. This concept of crowd control is described in Marcus Borg and John Dominic Crossan, *The Last Week: What the Gospels Really Teach about Jesus's Final Days in Jerusalem* (San Francisco: HarperSanFrancisco, 2007), 2–5, 19–20.

6. Borg and Crossan, *The Last Week*, 3–4.

7. "While the women were on their way, some of the guards went into the city and reported to the chief priests everything that had happened. When the chief priests had met with the elders and devised a plan, they gave the soldiers a large sum of money, telling them, 'You are to say, "His disciples came during the night and stole him away while we were asleep." If this report gets to the governor, we will satisfy him and keep you out of trouble.' So the soldiers took the money and did as they were instructed. And this story has been widely circulated among the Jews to this very day" (Matt 28:11–15).

8. "Those who had arrested Jesus took him to Caiaphas the high priest, where the teachers of the law and the elders had assembled. But Peter followed him at a distance, right

that arresting Jesus during the Passover would lead to a riot, they turn on him and have him executed in public, perhaps deciding that it is necessary to move quickly and instill fear in his followers, even at the risk of public protest. In fact, perhaps they realize that the potential for an uprising is greater with Jesus alive. The only thing that happens in Matthew between the plotting by Caiaphas and the chief priests to move against Jesus in vv. 4–5 and Judas's betrayal of Jesus in vv. 14–16 is the anointing scene, to which we now turn. My exploration of these nine verses is an effort to understand what transpires there and whether it may have provoked Judas to betray Jesus and contributed to the decision of the chief priests and ruling elites to move publicly against this popular-movement leader.

Anointing a Christ to End Poverty

In Matt 26:6–13, the unnamed woman pours the ointment (*myron*) on Jesus's head. By doing this, she "anoints" Jesus. The word for "anointing" or "the anointed one" in Greek is *ho christos* or "the Christ." In Hebrew, the word is *mashiach* or "messiah."[9] The historical Jesus never claims himself to be a "messiah." Nevertheless, he is labeled a messiah by the early Jesus movements and generations of people to this day. This is true of the communities involved in the compilation of the Gospels, including the Gospel of Matthew, and it is even more prevalent in the letters of Paul, which contain over half the uses of *christos* in the New Testament. Even in the

---

up to the courtyard of the high priest. He entered and sat down with the guards to see the outcome. The chief priests and the whole Sanhedrin were looking for false evidence against Jesus so that they could put him to death. But they did not find any, though many false witnesses came forward. Finally two came forward and declared, 'This fellow said, "I am able to destroy the Temple of God and rebuild it in three days."' Then the high priest stood up and said to Jesus, 'Are you not going to answer? What is this testimony that these men are bringing against you?' But Jesus remained silent. The high priest said to him, 'I charge you under oath by the living God: Tell us if you are the Messiah, the Son of God.' 'You have said so,' Jesus replied. 'But I say to all of you: From now on you will see the Son of Man sitting at the right hand of the Mighty One and coming on the clouds of heaven.' Then the high priest tore his clothes and said, 'He has spoken blasphemy! Why do we need any more witnesses? Look, now you have heard the blasphemy. What do you think?' 'He is worthy of death,' they answered. Then they spit in his face and struck him with their fists. Others slapped him and said, 'Prophesy to us, Messiah. Who hit you?'" (Matt 26:57–67).

9. De Jonge, "Christ," *Anchor Bible Dictionary* 1:914–21.

first generations after the crucifixion and resurrection, Jesus is understood as Messiah,[10] and this term has both theological and political significance.

Jesus as an anointed popular king or prophet is in line with other revolutionary popular leaders contemporary with him. Richard Horsley reminds readers of the hopeful promise and violent repression of other popular-movement leaders at the time of Jesus:

> There were several mass movements composed of Jewish peasants from villages or towns such as Emmaus, Bethlehem, Sepphoris— people rallying around the leadership of charismatic figures viewed as anointed kings of the Jews. These movements occurred in all three principal areas of Jewish settlement in Palestine (Galilee, Perea, Judea), and just at the time when Jesus was presumably born. It is perhaps also worth noting that the city of Sepphoris, which was burned and its inhabitants sold into slavery in 4 B.C.E., was just a few miles north of the village of Nazareth, Jesus' home. Furthermore, the town of Emmaus, the location of one of the resurrection appearances according to the gospel tradition (Lk. 24:13–32), had been destroyed by the Romans in retaliation for another mass movement little more than a generation earlier. The memory of these popular messianic movements would no doubt have been fresh in the minds of most of the Jewish peasants who witnessed Jesus' activities.[11]

It is in relation to the hopes and dangers of popular movements that references to Jesus's kingship appear in Matthew. He is called the "king of the Jews" four times: in the infancy narrative, in which the wise men go to visit the newly born "king of the Jews" and bring myrrh and other luxury items (2:2) that are used in making *myron*; at his trial, when Pilate the Roman governor asks Jesus if he is the "king of the Jews" (27:11); by the soldiers who mock Jesus (27:29); and on the *titulus* when he is crucified (27:39). He is called "king of Israel" in Matt 27:42. In fact, the word "king," *basileus*, occurs twenty-two times in Matthew, referencing King David once, King Herod twice, and in parables about kings and the Kingdom of God/Heaven numerous times, including in Matt 25:34 as the judge of/for

10. Merrill Miller, "The Anointed Jesus," in *Redescribing Christian Origins*, ed. Ron Cameron and Merrill P. Miller, Society of Biblical Literature Symposium Series 28 (Leiden: Brill, 2004), 310.

11. Richard Horsley and John S. Hanson, *Bandits, Prophets, and Messiahs: Popular Movements in the Time of Jesus* (Harrisburg: Trinity Press International, 1999), 117.

the poor. Furthermore, in Matthew there are thirty mentions of *basileia* for "Kingdom of Heaven" and one reference to "Kingdom of Earth" (king of the world in Matt 17:25). In addition to a king, messiah, and descendent of King David, Jesus is a "Son of God" who will "save his people"—a salvation that targets poverty and oppression specifically, as I am arguing (1:21, 2:15, 3:17, 4:3–6, 8:29, 14:33, 16:16, and 26:63).

When Matthew applies the title *christos* to Jesus, suggesting that he is the (poor) anointed messiah, prophet, or king, he concisely summarizes the centrality of liberation, equality, and prosperity in the gospel and among the followers of Jesus.[12] In the Passion Narrative and other stories that came to make up the Gospels, Jesus is understood as a threat, an alternative "King of the Jews" by the ruling authorities and elites. Richard Horsley and John Hanson confirm an overtly political meaning to Jesus as "Christ/Messiah." They suggest that contemporary with Jesus there existed popularly acclaimed kings who challenged the ruling literate elites.[13]

> Before and after Jesus of Nazareth . . . there were several popular Jewish leaders, almost all of them from the peasantry, who, in the words of Josephus "laid claim to the kingdom," "donned the diadem," or were "proclaimed king" by their followers. It thus appears that one of the concrete forms which social unrest took in the late second temple period was that of a group of followers gathered around a leader they had acclaimed as king.[14]

After the defeat in the Jewish Wars of 66–70 CE (which Jews living in the ancient Near East considered another failed messianic movement), there was great need for Jesus's followers and the Matthean community

---

12. "Another presupposition for election as popular king is an organized following, indeed, a fighting force" (Horsley and Hanson, *Bandits, Prophets, and Messiahs*, 95).

13. It is questionable how connected to justice-making and popular movements the "anointed of Yahweh" were. Hanson and Horsley write that those in power in ancient Israelite society co-opted popular traditions of kingship and connected them to the Davidic king: "In sharp contrast to popular kingship, there emerged an official royal ideology, probably during the regimes of David and Solomon. The understanding of the king as 'the anointed of Yahweh' in all likelihood originated in popular traditions of kingship. However, in the royal psalms, liturgical expressions of the official royal ideology, 'the anointed of Yahweh' became identical with the Davidic king" (Horsley and Hanson, *Bandits, Prophets, and Messiahs*, 96–97).

14. Horsley and Hanson, *Bandits, Prophets, and Messiahs*, 88.

to locate leaders who would intervene on behalf of the majority poor and dispossessed.[15] Jesus is such a leader and so much more: he is a popularly acclaimed king who comes to address the social-economic crises of the late Second Temple period; he is crucified by the ruling elite but still resurrected by the God of Israel, becoming the founder of a social movement of the poor to right the wrongs of society; he is a Savior, 2,000 years later, whose redemptive love and prophetic witness still hold great power for millions worldwide.

Anointed Ones

In understanding the significance of the anointing of Jesus, we ought to look at the use of the language of anointing and anointed one(s) in the Hebrew Bible. There are thirty-eight or thirty-nine occurrences of *mashiach*, the Hebrew term for "messiah" or "anointed one,"[16] in Leviticus, 1 and 2 Kings, 1 and 2 Chronicles, Psalms, and the Latter Prophets, most often in describing patriarchs, high priests, and kings.[17] The Hebrew Bible refers

15. Richard Horsley asserts that numerous messiahs arose to this challenge: "Although Judean ruling and literate circles had no interest in the messiah, it was clear from the accounts of the Judean historian Josephus and other sources that the Judean and Galilean peasants produced several concrete movements led by a popularly acclaimed king or prophet. These concrete movements that assumed social forms distinctive to Israelite tradition, moreover, proved to be the driving forces of Judean history during the crises of late second-temple times" (Horsley and Hanson, *Bandits, Prophets, and Messiahs*, xiii).

16. There are scholarly debates about the meaning of "messiah." In the nineteenth–twentieth century, there was a messianic idea propagated by the likes of Emil Schürer and Joseph Klausner that included a cluster of attributes pertinent to the messiah which, according to Klausner, were: "the signs of the Messiah, the ingathering of the exiles, the reception of proselytes, the war with Gog and Magog, the Days of the Messiah, the renovation of the world, the Day of Judgment, the resurrection of the dead, the World to Come" (Klausner, *The Messianic Idea in Israel*, trans. W. F. Stinespring [New York: Macmillan, 1955], 385). What the "minimalist school" including van der Woude, Smith, De Jonge, Neusner, and Charlesworth countered with is not that messianic language does not have meaning but that it does not manifest in a reified messianic idea, where there is one messiah or a series of messiahs who are to reign in a new era; see Matthew Novenson, *Christ among the Messiahs: Christ Language in Paul and Messiah Language in Ancient Judaism* (New York: Oxford University Press, 2012), 34–40.

17. In *Judaism and Their Messiahs at the Turn of the Christian Era*, Jacob Neusner, an American academic scholar of Judaism, writes, "The term [*mashiach*] denotes one invested, usually by God, with power and leadership, but never an eschatological figure. Ironically,

to the virtues and promises of messiahs, which are referred to in modern churches and popular culture and cited in eschatological ways, including: evil and tyranny will not be able to stand before a messiah's leadership (Isa 11:4); he will attract people from all nations (Isa 11:10); there will be no more hunger or illness, and death will cease (Isa 25:8 and quoted in 1 Cor 15:5, mentioned below); the dead will rise again (Isa 26:19); he will be a messenger of peace (Isa 52:7); the ruined cities of Israel will be restored (Ezek 16:55); and weapons of war will be destroyed (Ezek 39:9).[18]

The Greek verb *chriō*, "to anoint," is used in a variety of places in the New Testament. The term is most often used in association with Jesus, including the important reference in Luke 4:18, where the Spirit of the Lord has anointed (*echrisen*) him to bring good news to the poor.[19] Paul uses the term to refer to the anointing by God of those who follow Jesus Christ (2 Cor 1:21). Matthew has the clearest focus on messiah and the most references to an "anointed one" of all the Gospels. There are sixteen references to the Christ, *ho christos*, "the anointed one," in Matthew. These include four times in the genealogy and birth story (1:1, 16, 17, 18; and 2:4), where "Matthew, having shown how Jesus becomes the child of Joseph, son of David, virtually creates the Davidic Messiah in the image of Jesus."[20] The term is then used eight times in the Passion Narrative (22:42; 23:10; 24:5, 23; 26:63, 68; 27:17; and 27:22). In one of the other four uses of "Christ" in Matthew, Peter says, "You are the Christ, the Son of the living God" in Matt 16:16; and Matt 12:18 proclaims that "here is the servant that [God] has chosen—[God] will

---

in the apocalyptic book of Daniel (9:25f), where an eschatological messiah would be appropriate, the term refers to a murdered high priest" (Jacob Neusner, William Green, and Ernest Frerichs, *Judaisms and Their Messiahs at the Turn of the Christian Era* [Cambridge: Cambridge University Press, 1987], 2).

18. Several occurrences of the term are cited in the New Testament in association with Jesus, giving them Christological significance in the later history of interpretation, including Acts 4:26 and Heb 1:9. The cited passages include Ps 2:2 (where it is announced that God's son is coming to straighten out the rulers of the earth); Ps 45:7 (which asserts that God has anointed this leader with an oil of gladness, and his robes are fragranced with myrrh); and Dan 9:25 (which says that the anointed one will be persecuted and killed by the rulers of the earth).

19. Herod and Pontius Pilate conspired to have the anointed (*echrisas*) Jesus crucified (Acts 4:27); Peter teaches about the anointed (*echrisen*) Jesus of Nazareth who healed and exorcised those under the control of the devil (Acts 10:38); and quoting Psalm 45, Hebrews tells us that God's son, Jesus, was anointed (*echrisen*) with the oil of joy (Heb 1:9).

20. Miller, "The Anointed Jesus," 321.

put [his] Spirit upon him and he will proclaim justice to all the nations" (quoting Isa 42:1).[21]

Anointed Kings and Prophets in the Hebrew Bible

The significance of anointing in the Hebrew Bible is particularly relevant to developing an understanding of the unnamed woman's actions and the response by Jesus and his disciples in Matthew 26. Who is this Messiah, and what does he stand for? What is a Messiah in that context? Anointing was used in the care of the body, in preparation of the dead for burial, and in caring for and honoring the poor and rich; in each of these cases, the person is only anointed once. Most of the acts of anointing in Israel were acts of consecration that bestowed divine authority on kings and prophets, introducing them to office. This is why so many of the occurrences of *mashiach* are in relationship to patriarchs, high priests, and kings. The specific anointing of rulers in the Hebrew Bible that grounds the anointing in Matt 26:7, which I will highlight with more detail, appears in Exodus 30; 1 Samuel 10, 16; 1 Kings 19:16; Ps 105:15; and 1 Chr 16:22. I have chosen these references because they depict kings and prophets being anointed (perhaps following the popular traditions' renditions of those anointings) and may have been familiar to the audience of Jesus's anointing.

Exodus 30 focuses on the oil that Moses is instructed to prepare to be the holy anointing oil (*myron*), which includes myrrh (*smyrna*) and other luxury items—reminding us that the wise men brought myrrh to Bethlehem because of its royal connotations. Additionally, Moses hears from God in Exodus 30 that he is to anoint Aaron and his sons as priests for God.

In 1 Sam 10:1 (LXX), Samuel is asked by God to anoint Saul as king. Samuel takes a vial of oil, pours it over Saul's head, kisses him, and states: "Has not the LORD anointed you ruler over his inheritance? You will reign over the LORD's people and save them from the power of their enemies round about. And this will be the sign to you that the LORD has anointed you ruler over his inheritance." This pericope is important because the details of the process of anointing are described (taking a vial of oil and pouring it on the king's head) and because the significance of the anointing is articulated (God's setting the king to rule over the people, protect

---

21. "Here is my servant, whom I uphold, my chosen one in whom I delight; I will put my Spirit on him, and he will bring justice to the nations" (Isa 42:1).

them from their enemies, and watch over God's blessings). First Samuel 16 also shows how anointing takes place when Samuel anoints David, an unlikely candidate to be king compared with his brothers, with a horn of oil poured over David's head. This passage reminds us that the anointing and an "anointed one" can come from unlikely places.

There are, in addition, three references to anointed prophets in the Hebrew Bible that are of note here. In 1 Kgs 19:16, God tells Elijah to anoint Jehu as king over Israel and Elisha as his successor prophet. And in both Ps 105:15 and 1 Chr 16:22, God warns kings not to harm God's anointed prophets. Attention to both anointed kings and anointed prophets brings Jesus's critique of earthly rulers and economic domination into perspective.

An Ointment for Prophets and Kings

The substance that the unnamed woman uses to anoint Jesus's head in Matt 26:7 is *myron*.[22] In the ancient world *myron* was a special commodity that connoted empire/royalty, burial, and wealth. A few of the specific Septuagint references to *myron*/anointing are of major interest to this study. Isaiah 25:7 (where the poor are lifted up and anointed with *myron*) perhaps parallels what is going on in Matthew 26, with Jesus as the poor person. Isaiah 25:7 is about anointing the poor (rather than reserving this honor for only the rich), and Jesus associates with the poor in Matthew 26. Furthermore, the following facts may parallel the economic critique in Matthew 26 that we explored in Chapter 5 above: (1) Isa 39:2 includes *myron* in the list of luxury items, (2) Prov 27:9 lists it as something very expensive and special, and (3) Jer 25:10 announces that it is something that God will take away because of the disobedience of the people. As I mentioned in the

22. There are sixteen uses of the Greek *myron* in the Septuagint: in Exod 30:25 (where it is the name for the holy anointing oil and contains myrrh, cassia, and other luxury spices), 1 Chr 9:30 (which also refers to the special ointment made by priests for anointing), 2 Chr 16:14 (where it is the perfume with which Asa the king is buried), Ps 133:2 (which refers to an ointment on Aaron's head), Prov 27:9 (which refers to the heart delighting in wine and nice ointments), Amos 6:6 (which is an indictment against those who live luxuriously, drink strained wine, and use the finest ointments), Isa 25:7 (a song about the justness of God, who will make the ungodly fall, lift up the poor, and anoint his people), Isa 39:2 (where *myron* is included in a list of the finest spices and other items including myrrh and gold), Jer 25:10 (which refers to the Lord taking everything away from the people who did not follow him, including the scent of perfume and other nice things), and Ezek 27:17 (where Judah and Israel are said to be merchants of ointment and corn).

previous chapter, *myron* is included in the list of commodities bought and sold in Revelation 18, where it appears near the selling of the bodies and souls of slaves as well as luxury items.

Pliny the Elder discusses *myron* in *Natural Histories*, where he calls it a royal unguent that is made in Syria (where Antioch is located) and prepared for kings of Parthia.[23] Josephus mentions *myron* in relation to kingship and as a critique of luxury. In *Jewish Antiquities*, he recalls the "celebrations" at the death of King Agrippa, where the people mockingly wore garlands, were anointed with unguents (*myron*), and were accused of being disrespectful regarding the benefactions and generosity of the king.[24] Elaine Wainwright points out that Josephus uses the Greek words *myron* and *katacheō* together[25] when he writes, "after crowning and anointing him with unguents."[26] Luzia Sutter Rehmann discusses the oil used in the anointing scene as well and suggests that, since olive oil,[27] which is oil used for cooking and other daily practices, is the base of any ointment (*myron*) used to anoint Jesus (including in the other Gospel stories), it brings real-life issues, including food and hunger, wealth and money, and economy into the story.[28] In fact, Ze'ev Safrai documents that oil was one of the main crops and therefore a main source of income in Roman Palestine and central to agricultural production, trade, and commerce; oil is thereby another way to explore the economy in more detail.[29]

23. Pliny, *Nat.* 13.2:17–19 (Rackham, LCL).

24. Josephus, *Ant.* 19:358 (Feldman, LCL).

25. This is most likely done in a symbolic reference to Plato's treatment of Homer.

26. Elaine Wainwright, *Towards a Feminist Critical Reading of the Gospel according to Matthew* (Berlin: de Gruyter, 1991), 128.

27. Martin Goodman also discusses the economic significance of oil. Oil was one of three staples produced from the land; it was important for Jews and all those living in the Roman world. In fact, Josephus documents a controversy regarding Jews buying foreign/ Gentile oil. See Martin Goodman, *Judaism in the Roman World: Collected Essays*, Ancient Judaism and Early Christianity 66 (Boston: Brill Academic, 2006), 187–200.

28. "The questions about tithing of perfumed oil can be taken as a starting point for a new reading of the anointing accounts. Whether in the pharisaic household, or in the house of the sisters Martha and Mary, or in the house of Simon the Leper—the olive oil arouses questions of belonging and solidarity, which are found in some accounts of Josephus (*Vita*, *BJ*) as well as in debates of the rabbis (Mishna)" (Luzia Sutter Rehmann, "Olivenöl als Zündstoff: Die vier Salbungsgeschichten der Evangelien im Kontext des Judentums des Zweiten Tempels," *Lectio Difficilior* 1 [2013]: 1).

29. Ze'ev Safrai, *The Economy of Roman Palestine* (New York: Routledge, 1994).

Jesus the Christ in Matthew 26

Based on historical study as well as the biblical text, we find three levels to the anointing in Matt 26:7 that can inform its significance: anointing as hospitality for rich and poor, anointing for burial, and anointing as the proclaiming of a popular king/prophet/religious leader.[30] Indeed, the anointing by the unnamed woman follows the formula for anointing kings and prophets in the Hebrew Bible.[31] The specific practice of anointing by pouring oil on the head was used as a symbolic act for the official designation and setting apart of a person for a particular public leadership function in the community. Indeed, the only act needed for choosing and establishing a new king or prophet was for oil (usually with the Greek *elaion*) to be poured on the head of the person being anointed.[32] The anointing of priests followed a similar pattern: Exodus 30 (discussed above) explains that Aaron and other priests should be anointed with *myron* and gives the "recipe" for the ointment that consecrates holy things. Kings and important people were anointed (with *myron*) for burial as well.

On a basic level, Jesus is anointed in Simon's house in Bethany as an act of care and love for a poor person. We know from Matthew—especially Matt 25:40 referred to above and the historical context laid out in Chapter 4—that Jesus is poor himself. In three places in Matthew, he is portrayed as vulnerable and needing care. Each of these should alert the reader to the poverty and political repression of empire and why it is significant that the unnamed woman cares for Jesus in Matthew 26. First, Joseph takes the baby Jesus to Egypt so that he will escape the murderous wrath of Herod. Second, at the beginning of Jesus's ministry, he is baptized by John the Baptist; even Jesus had to be baptized and announced as the Son of God by forces other than himself. Then third, the unnamed woman ministers to and anoints him. She is able to see that Jesus is in need rather than being someone who himself is always helping the needy. So, this act of anointing by the unnamed woman is an act of care and love for a poor person.

30. De Jonge, "Christ," *Anchor Bible Dictionary* 1:914–21.
31. *Myron* is the word used for the ointment/oil with which the woman anointed Jesus. *Myron* was used to anoint kings and priests, to anoint for burial, and as a luxury.
32. Daniel Fleming, "The Biblical Tradition of Anointing Priests," *Journal of Biblical Literature* 117 (1998): 401–14; and Wainwright, *Towards a Feminist Critical Reading of the Gospel according to Matthew*, 126–29.

The anointing of Jesus as a poor person echoes the eschatological feast in Isa 25:4–8, where Isaiah presents a song about the justness of God, who will make the ungodly fall and lift up the poor. This song includes anointing God's people with *myron* (25:7) and vanquishing death (25:8).[33] In this use of anointing with *myron*, the poor are anointed and honored; they are under the special care of God. Jesus frequently associates with the poor in Matthew, and this association echoes God's banquet and refuge for the poor in Isa 25:4, where God is the stronghold of the poor. This signals that God's messiahs are charged with caring for the poor. To organize society around the needs of the vulnerable is the responsibility of anointed ones—specifically, to lead movements aimed at saving the people from poverty and oppression and to protect God's creation from mistreatment, devastation, and further exile.

Elisabeth Schüssler Fiorenza writes about Jesus's anointing: "Since the prophet in the Old Testament anointed the head of the Jewish king, the anointing of Jesus' head must have been understood immediately as the prophetic recognition of Jesus, the Anointed, the Messiah, the Christ. According to the tradition it was a woman who named Jesus by and through her prophetic sign-action."[34] Elaine Wainwright acknowledges that Jesus's anointing may not exactly follow the pattern of anointing kings in the Old Testament, pointing out that when kings are anointed in the Hebrew Scriptures it is usually the Greek word *elaion* rather than *myron* being used. She notes, however:

> As Jesus enters into his passion, a woman pours oil over his head, an action which, in itself, could be construed as further messianic acclaim, the language which differs from expected language for sacred anointings being an indication that a different type of kingship is un-

---

33. "You have been a refuge for the poor, a refuge for the needy in their distress, a shelter from the storm and a shade from the heat. For the breath of the ruthless is like a storm driving against a wall and like the heat of the desert. You silence the uproar of foreigners; as heat is reduced by the shadow of a cloud, so the song of the ruthless is stilled. On this mountain the LORD Almighty will prepare a feast of rich food for all peoples, a banquet of aged wine—the best of meats and the finest of wines. On this mountain he will destroy the shroud that enfolds all peoples, the sheet that covers all nations; he will swallow up death forever. The Sovereign LORD will wipe away the tears from all faces; he will remove his people's disgrace from all the earth. The LORD has spoken" (Isa 25:4–8). The vanquishing of death is referred to in 1 Cor 15:5 as well.

34. Elisabeth Schüssler Fiorenza, *In Memory of Her: A Feminist Theological Reconstruction of Christian Origins* (New York: Crossroad, 1983), xiv.

derstood here. The use of language other than the typical language of messianic anointing may also result from an androcentric perspective which will not allow a woman to assume the role of anointing which was reserved for men.[35]

As Wainwright indicates, the unnamed woman is demonstrating that Jesus is a special ruler and king, even prophet, a poor "messiah" chosen by God to protect the poor and bring instruction to/judgment on wealth and money, in line with other popularly acclaimed revolutionary prophets contemporary with Jesus. Nowhere else in the Gospel of Matthew is Jesus anointed, not even at his burial.[36] Therefore, when the unnamed woman pours the *myron* on Jesus's head in Matt 26:7, she anoints him "Christ."[37] Indeed, the fact that the woman anoints Jesus with *myron* may be evidence enough that Jesus is king and prophet, and this word choice introjects into this passage both Jesus's death and a critique on wealth.[38]

If we combine the messianic anointing and prophetic critique in the Hebrew Scriptures with the social and economic contextualization of *myron* from Josephus and Pliny, the anointing scene is understood as an alternative crowning of Jesus and a simultaneous judgment on economic

35. Wainwright, *Towards a Feminist Critical Reading of the Gospel According to Matthew*, 129.

36. Mary Magdalene and the women do not bring spices to the tomb in Matt 28:1 because he has already been prepared for burial by the unnamed woman in Matt 26:7. In Mark's Gospel, Mary Magdalene and the other women do bring spices to anoint Jesus for burial but, since he is resurrected, they do not anoint in this scene (Mark 16:1–3). Therefore, in Mark and Matthew, the unnamed woman performs the burial rite of anointing. In John's Gospel, Joseph of Arimathea and Nicodemus prepare the dead body for a Jewish burial (John 19:39–40). It is possible that Mark and Matthew used the story of the anointing before burial because there was no anointing afterward.

37. Ulrich Luz concludes that Jesus is not anointed as a king/messiah in this scene, but Elisabeth Schüssler Fiorenza insists that he is (Schüssler Fiorenza, *In Memory of Her*, 152–53). Luz uses the Septuagint translation *myron* for the Hebrew word *masal* to point out that kings are not anointed with *myron* but with *elaion* (Ulrich Luz, *Matthew 21–28*, trans. James E. Crouch, Hermeneia [Minneapolis: Fortress, 2007], 334). However, King Asa's burial with *myron* and the general custom/practice of anointing a king as laid out in 1 Samuel 10 and 16 (where kings are anointed by pouring oil on their heads) still parallel the anointing in Matt 26:7. Additionally, there is clearly an emphasis on kingship and messiah in Matthew, and nowhere else in the entire Gospel is Jesus anointed to become "Christ."

38. The third use of *myron*, by the prophets in a critique on wealth, is of importance to this biblical study. In other places in this book, I have shown that Jesus criticizes wealth, especially the use of wealth to exploit and oppress the poor.

exploitation. It alludes to the festivities at the death of Agrippa and the prophetic cry of Amos (e.g., Amos 6:6)[39] and Jeremiah (e.g., Jer 25:10)[40] against rulers who exploit and exclude—instead of the rich and powerful being anointed with luxury and wealth, in this episode Jesus, a poor man, is anointed. It puts us in mind of the messianic banquet in Isaiah 25 where God is preparing a banquet of decadent food for all people, especially the poor. One can also imagine that the act of "crowning" is in contradistinction to the mock crowning of the soldiers later in the Passion Narrative (Matt 27:28–31). It is in this tradition that the unnamed woman anoints Jesus to become the ruler of God's empire, and it is because of this that he is crucified as king.

Thus it becomes clear that the anointing story itself is the turning point for the Gospel of Matthew and the crucifixion/resurrection narrative of Jesus as a whole. In Matt 26:1–10, Jesus is anointed as a poor person and as a Christ/Messiah who is a prophet and popularly acclaimed king, responsible for bringing God's reign of economic justice on earth. His anointing happens at the same time as the high priest and other Jerusalem elites are plotting to crucify Jesus as a threat to their own power, which is linked to the power of the empire. In fact, his anointing makes him even more of a threat and alternative to Caesar. By focusing on the action of anointing Jesus and the use of the term *myron* within the scriptural context of anointed prophets and kings, we can see that an economic critique is central to Matthew's Gospel. Although there has been less emphasis on the economic dimensions of the Messiah in traditional Christology, Matthew's references to the anointed one encouraged readers of his time to understand the Hebrew Scriptures' inclusion of protection for the poor, and the end of exploitation, death, and war as essential to identifying an anointed one.

The Six *M*s of Jesus's Messianic Leadership

In exploring Jesus's practices and teachings in the Gospel of Matthew, we see that he condemned the Roman Empire and promoted communities

---

39. "You drink wine by the bowlful and use the finest lotions [*myron*], but you do not grieve over the ruin of Joseph" (Amos 6:6).

40. "I will banish from them the sounds of joy and gladness, the voices of bride and bridegroom, the sound of millstones and the light of the lamp" (Jer 25:10).

of resistance and renewal across the Mediterranean. Building on the evidence presented in Chapters 1 and 4 of this book, we can use the language of anointing in its scriptural context to provide additional support for the interpretation of Jesus as the leader of a social movement in first-century Palestine. In Matthew, Jesus and his community of followers dealt with the politics of food and healthcare, practiced a new form of counterimperial community, and developed a mission that has lasted two millennia. This is the very definition of "Messiah/Christ." Following developments in the study of social history which posit that social transformation is fueled by the poor and dispossessed (also argued in Chapter 4 above), I contend that Jesus's teachings and actions with regard to poverty, wealth, and power, especially in Matthew's Gospel, lend further support to a portrayal of him as a social-movement leader. Exploring the teachings and actions of the Messiah Jesus in Matthew, I want to propose six *M*-words that highlight the focus on justice and movement-building in the Gospel: message, martyrdom, miracles, media, mentoring, and missionary work.

Message: Jesus proclaimed the "good news" that everyone was created in the image of God and has worth. Jesus and his disciples demonstrated this "good news" through shared meals, conversation, and healing. Jesus told stories and used metaphors whereby the "least and the last" become the "greatest and the first" (Matt 25:40; 18:1–4; 23:11); and the poor are proclaimed "blessed" (Matt 5:1).

Martyrdom: Jesus and the disciples revealed the inequities of Roman society, which excluded the sick and the poor (Matt 11:5). By turning over the tables in the Temple, Jesus disrupted commerce and drew attention to the system of economic and ritual exchange that impoverished and excluded so many poor people (Matt 21:12). Jesus was accused of sedition and crucified by Rome as an enemy of the state and alternative "king of the Jews" (Matt 26:63–68; 27:24–44).

Miracles: As a poor man working among the poor of his society, Jesus performed miracles that were about providing the survival needs of the people—food, healthcare, and other human rights denied them by the society and economic system of that time. In story after story, Jesus heals the sick, raises the dead, and casts out demons (Matt 8:1–34; 9:1–38; 14:34–36; 20:28–34). Faced with a hungry crowd of more than five thousand, who were eager but too hungry to learn, Jesus turned to his disciples and said, "You give them something to eat" (Matt 14:13–21; 16:9).

Media: Jesus and his disciples used various means of communication. He preached sermons and handed down instruction as in the Sermon on

142

the Mount (Matthew 5–7). He traveled throughout the area, connecting up with more communities and people. Indeed, theirs was a peripatetic movement: the Roman roads served as a medium through which Jesus and his followers carried their message.

Mentoring: Political education and leadership development were at the heart of the early Christian movement. Jesus unveiled the ways in which the Roman Empire produced this misery throughout his ministry, in particular to his disciples: in his responsiveness to lepers (Matt 8:2; 10:8; 26:6), through his exposure of the Temple system's regularized defrauding of the poor (21:12), and in his teachings in parables (13:1–53; 18:10–14, 23–34; 22:1–14; 25:1–30). Jesus developed leadership by trusting his followers to carry out healing and preaching and then return together to reflect on their experiences. When Jesus was doing miracles himself, he was developing other leaders. Jesus also focused on self-doubt and self-hatred, exorcising spirits and demons (Matt 4:24; 8:16; 8:28–34)—a major obstacle that poor people must confront and conquer if they are to be successful leaders.

Missionary Work: In his own life and ministry, Jesus represented the coming together of the other five Ms of movement-building. Each of these inseparable things raised the consciousness of and built a movement among the people who were called the "least of these" (Matt 25:40). The finale of the Gospel of Matthew (Matt 28:16–20), called the "Great Commission," is about charging Jesus's disciples to follow him in carrying forward their seditious mission. Focusing on this mission reminds us that all individuals are crucial contributors to the movement's success or failure—that it is about them and their own choices—not solely about Jesus and his charismatic personality.

Jesus's Revolutionary Economic Program

Indeed, Jesus demonstrates he is a different kind of king, with an alternative system of governance to Rome's system. In Matthew, Jesus, the "son" of David—the long-awaited, future ideal king, called the Messiah/Christ (see 1:1–16)—is charged with leading the people in a new exodus, ruling God's Kingdom, and protecting the poor as a poor person himself.

Based on close exegetical work of Matthew, historical-critical scholarship of Galilee, Antioch, and the larger Roman Empire, and my contextual Bible-study commitments as experienced through "Reading the Bible with the Poor," especially described in the Leadership School Bible study from Chapter 2, I suggest that Jesus was a teacher, leader, prophet, and ruler of a budding, revolutionary social movement of the poor that practiced and preached about God's coming reign of abundance, dignity, and prosperity for all. This role was understood theologically and politically as a messianic position in Matthew's Gospel through the use of the language of anointing and the actions of the unnamed woman. This religious and political movement was accurately understood by the ruling elite of the Roman Empire to be in stark opposition to Rome, especially with respect to its economic, political, and religious structure. Indeed, a focus on economic justice and covenantal community in the Gospel of Matthew is the starting point for any rereading of the passage "the poor you will always have with you" in Matt 26:11, and for understanding Jesus's condemnation of the practices and people that exploit and exclude the common people.

Conclusion

In the main, the repression of the struggles of the poor has been met with silence and indifference. . . . We must repent. We must commit ourselves to taking a stand with the poor. We must commit ourselves to insisting that democracy is for everyone. . . . It is not a question of bussing poor people in to NGO meetings where they are exhibits rather than full and equal participants. It is not a question of experts speaking for the poor. Taking a stand with the poor is a matter of walking the path of suffering and struggle with the poor. It requires a presence within the struggles of the poor.[1]

—South African Bishop Rubin Phillip

The intensity of poverty and dispossession in contemporary America and the urgency of efforts by the poor to build a movement to end poverty have instigated and shaped this book. It is informed by decades of poor people organizing a movement to end poverty, by the hard-fought lessons and theologies learned in and developed out of communities in struggle. In my experience, the text "the poor you will always have with you" in Matthew 26 is the major biblical roadblock to people coming forward with solutions to end poverty. The supposed inevitability of poverty and biblical justification for it, common to most interpretations of the story, make it a

---

1. Bishop Rubin Phillip, "Remembering Steve Biko: A Bright and Guiding Light in Dark Times," http://abahlali.org/node/9189. At this web site is more of Bishop Rubin Phillip's statement delivered at St Philip's Anglican Church, Fingo Village in Grahamstown, on September 19, 2012.

popular proof text used by rich and poor people alike. I argue that rather than interpreting this line to justify poverty's existence, one should read it as a reminder that poverty is not God's will but is the result of people's disobedience to God's commandments and Jesus's teachings. It ought to be understood as saying that a plan to overcome poverty—with the Sabbath and Jubilee prescriptions at the core—is central to the gospel message, mission of Jesus, and realization of God's Kingdom. It must be interpreted to support the idea that Jesus Christ, the Messiah of the poor, our Lord and Savior, was a spiritual- and social-movement leader who urged his followers to commit themselves to movements for social transformation and highlighted the moral, political, and epistemological agency of the poor. This Messiah Jesus provided a deep economic critique suggesting that adherence to charity and dominant economic systems and structures just made the problem of poverty worse.

In order to build this argument, I have undertaken a thorough exegetical analysis of the anointing of Jesus by the unnamed woman in Matt 26:1–26, as well as its intertextuality with Deuteronomy 15. This has included a focus on both how the anointing signifies Jesus's role as ruler of God's Kingdom and how Jesus assesses the dominant economic system—including buying and selling, money, patronage, and charity—as being sources of poverty rather than eliminators of it. At the core of my argument is the fact that the anointing story itself is the turning point for the Gospel of Matthew and the crucifixion/resurrection narrative of Jesus as a whole. This contrasts with other interpretations, in which Matt 26:1–16 is a secondary and transitory story, with the main emphasis being placed on the following events of the Last Supper. Far from God's Kingdom condoning poverty, exploitation, or dispossession, this story puts poverty and economic justice at the center of Jesus's mission.

This telling of the story is consistent with other biblical teachings on poverty; it is more consistent, in fact, than an interpretation in which Jesus cannot or will not end poverty. There are passages such as Matthew 25 in which Jesus reminds us that what we do to the least of these, we do to him. There is the story in Exodus 16 of the manna that God sends from heaven when the Israelites are living in the wilderness after escaping from slavery; the manna is enough for everyone but too much for no one. The prophets all emphasize our duty to care for the widow, the orphan, those in need. The story of the community of goods in Acts 2 and 4 reveals that the early Christians had no needy people among them because they shared and cared for each other. In Luke 4 Jesus reads from the scroll of the prophet

Isaiah and announces that he has come to fulfill this passage: to proclaim release to the captives, to bring good news to the poor, to let the oppressed go free. And even the Apostle Paul discusses collecting for the poor more than any other theological issue in his original letters, including Romans, Galatians, Philippians, 1 Corinthians, and 2 Corinthians.

This exegesis has been informed by a methodology and hermeneutic of "Reading the Bible with the Poor" in which I have investigated historical issues by placing them in conversation with contemporary issues (including taxation, debt, infrastructure and development, charity and patronage, poverty, wealth, and political power) and drawn parallels between contemporary stories of poor people surviving and organizing today, and New Testament stories. The application of this hermeneutic to contemporary reinterpretations of Matthew 26 reveals a biblical hermeneutic of solidarity and liberation that is important, not only for the lives of faithful followers of Jesus, but for the breaking out of a movement to end poverty around the world.

Reading the Bible with the Poor[2]

The method of contextual biblical study that I have used in this book draws on the methods used in South Africa with the Academy of the Poor, and in Latin American with liberation theology and Christian base communities. What is distinctive about my reinterpretation of "the poor you will always have with you" and the methodology of "Reading the Bible with the Poor" in general is its US context: a large population of impoverished Christians who are already familiar with the Bible, a population already steeped in a rights-based framework, and a heterogeneous group of poor people that is growing every day.

As I discussed in the Introduction and Chapters 1 and 2, one of the main purposes of this book and "Reading the Bible with the Poor" is to allow poor people the opportunity to make their own interpretations of and draw parallels to biblical texts, thereby affecting popular conceptions of poverty, religiosity, and modes of social transformation. Since biblical

2. I discuss the use of the Bible in a human rights framework elsewhere in Liz Theoharis and Willie Baptist, "Teach as We Fight, Learn as We Lead: Lessons in Pedagogy and the Poverty Initiative Model," in *Pedagogy for the Poor*, ed. Willie Baptist and Jan Rehmann (New York: Teachers College, 2011), 160-78.

interpretation has been in the hands of scholars and preachers who are predominantly trained in institutions of higher education, offering the space for poor people to interpret biblical stories and apply these interpretations to their life situations motivates a significant contribution to the field of biblical studies.

Previously, when poor people gathered to do Bible study, it was typically in the context of a Sunday School class, oftentimes under the direction and leadership of a pastor or another established leader, and often only addressing texts that the established leaders deemed relevant. "Reading the Bible with the Poor" provides a more far-ranging approach by giving the poor people agency and placing their analysis at the center of the discussion. This includes a broad range of texts, including difficult biblical texts on poverty, along with insisting that leaders of the Bible study be organized poor people themselves. Indeed, it is particularly important to return to and reinterpret religious texts that have been used to justify poverty by defining obedience to God in individualistic terms, between a human on earth and God in heaven.

Some assert that the theological condoning of poverty is because many American churches have lost a connection to the poor.[3] But mere awareness of poverty issues does not transform interpretations of "the poor you will always have with you" or of other texts used in justifying poverty. Many poor people believe the same ideas about who is to blame for poverty that middle-income or wealthy people believe.[4] This is why I have found it important to base new interpretations of the text, not just on ideas from the poor, but on ideas from the organized poor. Just as not having a connection to the poor can justify middle-income ideas on why people are poor, not having a connection to organized poor people can justify a charity approach—an approach that teaches that what the fortunate, especially Christians, need to do is save the poor, rather than seeing that the poor have the potential "to save the soul of America" as Rev. Dr. King asserted.

The form of leadership-development and consciousness-raising employed in our method of "Reading the Bible with the Poor" combines rigorous study and applied practice. Churches, classrooms, antipoverty cam-

3. Jim Wallis, *God's Politics: Why the Right Gets It Wrong and the Left Doesn't Get It* (San Francisco: HarperCollins, 2005), 211.
4. Throughout my two decades of antipoverty organizing, I have found that many poor people blame themselves for their poverty and are therefore ashamed of being poor.

paigns, and organized protests all become locations for contextual Bible study and political education. This has been effective in helping promote a transformation of values, including new theoretical interpretations and new leadership practices alongside the organized poor.

The approach to choosing particular biblical texts themselves merits some attention. Rather than isolating a biblical text particularly focused on poverty, which potentially leads to proof-texting, "Reading the Bible with the Poor" uses an arc of biblical texts that extends from Genesis to Revelation and is representative of an authentic (textually faithful, unmanipulated) biblical theology focused on poverty and liberation. In many cases, biblical interpretation focuses on individual and isolated texts rather than bringing disparate texts together and seeing the connections and intertextuality. I am interested in larger biblical themes of justice and the connections or incongruities between texts. This does not mean that I find liberation in every text or biblical book. Instead, I acknowledge the various and competing strands in the Bible and reflect on ways in which they may be influenced by power, inequality, and domination.[5]

Overall, "Reading the Bible with the Poor" uses a poverty lens to look at the Bible. With any biblical text, beginning with the creation story, we ask the question: are the texts relevant to situations of low-wage work, hunger, homelessness, and the work of social and economic transformation? Beginning with the hypothesis that many of our biblical texts record stories of poor people coming together with God's support to make meaning of their lives and improve their living conditions, we find numerous parallels in the biblical stories to poor people organizing today.

A Modern Parable

I view the anointing at Bethany as a modern parable. It is the story of a poor leader of a transformative movement for social and economic equality who comes to power and is betrayed, criticized, and executed for it; he subsequently rises from his grave and passes the responsibility

---

5. For more information on biblical theology see: Wes Howard-Brook, *"Come Out My People!": God's Call Out of Empire in the Bible and Beyond* (Maryknoll, NY: Orbis, 2010), and Walter Brueggemann, *Old Testament Theology: An Introduction*, Library of Biblical Theology (Nashville: Abingdon, 2008).

for building and sustaining this movement on to others. The scene looks like this:

An unnamed woman, perhaps a prostitute or other oppressed character, comes into the house of a sick and marginalized person and pours a very expensive substance onto the head of a poor man who has committed his life to being a grassroots community teacher and leader. The special anointing ointment she uses signifies that he has fulfilled the requirements for becoming an official prophetic ruler; he is part of a long line of freedom fighters in the oppressed people's tradition, into which he was born. He is set up as an alternative leader to the oppressive sovereign of the prevailing society. That established, powerful sovereign has also been anointed with expensive ointment but to a role that is responsible for taking people's land and livelihood, allows people to be paid too little to survive, and forces them to live in slavery and dispossession. When the unnamed woman pours the ointment on the alternative leader, she also anoints him for his burial. Realizing that the state will execute him for his prophetic and revolutionary-movement leadership, the woman wants to ensure that his body is prepared for his burial rather than being left for the wolves, rats, vultures, or imperial guards to devour.

When the woman anoints him, she is chided by the followers of this newly anointed prophetic leader for her actions. They accuse her of destroying a very expensive and valuable item. They say that if they (not she) had sold that ointment instead, they could have earned a lot of money and made a very big donation to the poor. In reality, in some iterations of the story, these followers use poor people as an excuse to make money for themselves. They are what could be called "poverty pimps"—individuals and institutions who line their pockets as they "help the poor." They have no interest in ending poverty, because poverty and homelessness are big businesses.

But the movement leader doesn't praise his followers for their idea of addressing poverty, and he stops them from being able to add money to their own pockets. Instead, he holds up the woman for her alleged waste of the ointment. He criticizes his followers for adhering to the status quo, for following the will of the ruler of the existing oppressive society. His response—"the poor you will always have with you"—quotes a story in an ancient tradition of liberation and freedom fighting; it comes from a text held sacred by the people. The quoted story explains that if people follow God's commandments there will be no poverty, and it lays out what the people of God must do to follow God's will and ensure that God's bounty is to be enjoyed by all. It concludes that, because people may not follow what God has arranged, it is everyone's duty to God to "open your hand to the poor and needy neighbor." This story suggests that if the followers and other concerned people continue to offer charity and Band-Aids instead of social transformation, with the poor at the helm, poverty will not cease (in disregard of and disobedience to God). It reminds the prophetic leader's followers that their plan to address poverty actually benefits and props up the status quo.

This prophetic leader does not pit the poor against himself. Instead, he suggests that the ending of everyone's poverty is his significant role and the role of other poor movement-leaders. The foundation of the movement to materialize God's reign on earth is not the rich, not the big social-service providers, not the sovereign who executes those who seek to transform society, but God's children, the poor who are working to transform society and improve their own and everyone's life. God is not only aligned with the poor but is, in fact, present in (and of) these leaders and the movement of the poor.

Throughout these biblical stories and the anointing, in particular, this anointed movement leader, through his words and deeds, is a challenge to the Powers That Be, rather than a conformer to a world that dehumanizes and impoverishes. He is betrayed and executed by the state because of his relationship to the poor and his stance that God's reign should be here on earth and should prioritize the poor; it is a reign in which debts are forgiven, mouths are fed, and community is built. This story doesn't end with death, however. Although given the death penalty, this prophetic leader and alternative ruler is raised from the dead. And his resurrection is coupled with the resurrection of many others—the tombs break open, and many of the past and present prophets and leaders of the earlier liberation movements are brought back to life alongside him.

The Movement to End Poverty Today

The last part of the above parable, drawn from Matthew 27, is often called the resurrection of the saints. It emphasizes that many are needed to bring about God's reign of abundance here on earth. It connects Jesus to the prophets who came before him and to those who will follow him. It suggests that when prophetic leaders are willing to be executed, defamed, humiliated in public, those who have been asleep or waiting or dead to the hope of a different world can also be resurrected.

It also reminds me of the stories of Tent City and St. Edward's Church takeover in the opening chapter above. Just a few blocks from St. Edward's Church, on a rundown block of row houses that demonstrate the economic deprivation of the neighborhood, is a Keith Harring mural. The painting is a memorial to Kathleen Sullivan, a 23-year-old woman who was killed by a drunk driver when biking home from a Kensington Welfare Rights Union (KWRU) meeting late one night. This graffiti memorial wall was painted by a number of the teenagers from KWRU, who wanted to remember Kathleen and the contribution she made to building a movement to end poverty. And although most other walls in this part of town were painted over immediately either by the city or by other graffiti artists, Kathleen's Wall lasted for years because of what she stood for in the community.

Kathleen and her wall have been added to the antipoverty movement's list of "Fallen Fighters." She is one of the people who came before and announced the coming of another. She showed the way to a new world. In fact, she is really important to me because she's the person who introduced me to the movement to end poverty in 1994. She has been resurrected by means of that wall and through the memory of the example that she manifested for the rest of us. For me, she is one of the resurrected saints from Matthew 27 who is teaching us to follow God's commandments in Deuteronomy 15—to end poverty to the ends of the earth—and Jesus's critique of an economic system that exploits and excludes in Matthew 26.

This interpretation of Matthew's passion and the story of the unnamed woman anointing Jesus Christ therefore becomes the paradigm or key with which to interpret the rest of the Bible.

This reinterpretation of "the poor you will always have with you" also reminds me of a scene from Toni Morrison's book, *Beloved*. Near the end, when slavery has ended and the community has come together, Morrison writes:

> She did not tell them to clean up their lives or to go and sin no more. She did not tell them they were the blessed of the earth, its inheriting meek or its glorybound pure. She told them that the only grace they could have was the grace they could imagine. That if they could not see it, they would not have it.[6]

This quote resonates with some slogans from KWRU and its predecessor, the National Union of the Homeless. Slogans like "no housing, no peace," "you only get what you're organized to take," "each one, teach one so we

6. Toni Morrison, *Beloved* (New York: Plume, 1994), 130.

can reach one more" insist that the poor have power and agency and can wake up this democracy and nation.

Preacher, professor, and Poverty Initiative leader Barbara Lundblad suggests that faith and vision are key to any endeavor to bring about freedom and liberation: a belief that ending poverty is possible, an understanding that this is what God requires, and a conviction that this is how Christians must act out their commitment to Jesus.

> Do we need more statistics? More courage? More time to volunteer? Perhaps most of all we need more faith. Jesus' parable [on the rich man and Lazarus] ends with these ironic words: "Abraham said to the rich man, 'If they do not listen to Moses and the prophets, neither will they be convinced even if someone rises from the dead.'" Someone has risen from the dead. What more do we need?[7]

Indeed, our Lord Jesus Christ has risen from the dead! In Matthew 27, his resurrection happens alongside the resurrection of the saints. In my experience at Kensington, this resurrection of KWRU and a budding movement of the poor also took place after the death of Kathleen Sullivan. But too often we forsake the belief that ending poverty is possible. Instead of realizing the resurrection of Jesus and all of his disciples who stand for justice, we ignore the controversial, revolutionary nature of a poor, resurrected Jesus as Lord and Savior, who challenges the wealthy, immortalized Caesar. We forget that Jesus's Kingdom is about economic and social rights in the here and now and that the Messiah Jesus came to usher in this reign. The good news of the Bible has been reduced to an individualized acceptance of Jesus Christ as a Lord and Savior, severed from his mission to the world. We deny that the poor are at the center of God's concern, ignoring that Jesus was a leader of a revolutionary movement of the poor, who— rather than mitigating the unfortunate inevitability of poverty—called for a movement to transform heaven and earth.

A social movement to end poverty is developing in the United States. Many of us see and imagine a world without hunger, homelessness, and misery. With the commitment and determination of those whom Rev. Dr. Martin Luther King Jr. called a "'freedom church' of the poor," this vision is being made manifest on earth. Will you heed God's call to end poverty?

7. Barbara Lundblad, "Closing the Great Chasm: Faith & Global Hunger Part 2," http://day1.org/2036-closing_the_great_chasm_faith__global_hunger_part_2.

Bibliography

Websites

"Bible FAQs: How Many Different Languages Has the Bible Been Translated Into? Statistical Summary Provided by UBS World Report." *Biblica* (March 2002). http://www.biblica.com/bible/bible-faqs/how-many-different-languages -has-the-bible-been-translated-into/.

"Bible FAQs: What Is the Main Message of the Bible?" *Biblica.* http://www.biblica .com/bible/bible-faqs/what-is-the-main-message-of-the-bible/.

Coalition for the Homeless. http://www.coalitionforthehomeless.org/.

Coalition of Immokalee Workers. http://ciw-online.org/.

"The Declaration of Independence: A Transcription, July 4, 1776." http://www.archives .gov/exhibits/charters/declaration_transcript.html.

Kairos: The Center for Religions, Rights and Social Justice. http://kairoscenter.org/.

Media Mobilizing Project in Philadelphia. http://mediamobilizing.org/.

Michigan Welfare Rights Organization. http://mwro.org/.

National Coalition for the Homeless. http://www.nationalhomeless.org/.

Poverty Initiative. http://povertyinitiative.org/.

United Workers. http://unitedworkers.org/.

Vermont Workers' Center. http://www.workerscenter.org/.

Published Works

Adam, A. K. M. *What Is Postmodern Biblical Criticism?* Minneapolis: Augsburg Fortress, 1995.

———, ed. *Postmodern Interpretations of the Bible: A Reader.* New York: Chalice, 2001.

Adamo, David Tuesday. *Biblical Interpretation in African Perspective.* Lanham, MD: University Press of America, 2006.

Aichele, George, Jr. "Poverty and the Hermeneutics of Repentance." *Cross Currents* 38 (1988–89): 458–67.

Albertz, Rainer. *A History of Israelite Religion in the Old Testament Period.* 2 vols. Translated by John Bowden. Louisville: Westminster John Knox, 1994. Translation of *Religionsgeschichte Israels in alttestamentlicher Zeit.* Göttingen: Vandenhoeck & Ruprecht, 1992.

Alexander, T. Desmond, and Simon Gathercole, eds. *Heaven on Earth: The Temple in Biblical Theology.* Carlisle: Paternoster, 2004.

Allen, Isaac. *Is Slavery Sanctioned by the Bible?* Boston: American Tract Society, 1860. Reprint, CreateSpace Independent Publishing Platform, 2013.

Anderson, Carol. *Eyes off the Prize: The United Nations and the African American Struggle for Human Rights, 1944–1955.* Cambridge: Cambridge University Press, 2003.

Appian. *Roman History.* 4 vols. Loeb Classical Library. Cambridge: Harvard University Press, 1912–13.

Arias, Mortimer. "The Jubilee: A Paradigm for Mission Today." *International Review of Mission* 73.289 (January 1984): 33–48.

Aristotle. *Art of Rhetoric.* Loeb Classical Library. Cambridge: Harvard University Press, 1926.

———. *Nicomachean Ethics.* Translated by H. Rackham. Loeb Classical Library. Cambridge: Harvard University Press, 1926.

Aslan, Reza. *Zealot: The Life and Times of Jesus of Nazareth.* New York: Random House, 2013.

Atkins, Margaret, and Robin Osbourne. *Poverty in the Roman World.* Cambridge: Cambridge University Press, 2003.

Aune, David. *The New Testament in Its Literary Environment.* Library of Early Christianity. Louisville: Westminster John Knox, 1985.

———, ed. *The Gospel of Matthew in Current Study: Studies in Memory of William G. Thompson, S.J.* Grand Rapids: Eerdmans, 2001.

Aus, Roger D. "Paul's Travel Plans to Spain and the 'Full Number of the Gentiles' of Rom. XI 25." *Novum Testamentum* 21 (1979): 232–62.

Avalos, Hector. *Slavery, Abolitionism, and the Ethics of Biblical Scholarship.* Sheffield: Sheffield Phoenix, 2013.

Bacon, Benjamin. "Jesus and the Law: A Study of the First 'Book' of Matthew (MT. 3–7)." *Journal of Biblical Literature* 47 (1928): 203–31.

Bageant, Joe. *Deer Hunting with Jesus: Dispatches from America's Class War.* New York: Crown, 2007.

Baker, David. *The Coming of the Messiah.* Philadelphia: Spenba, 1961.

Baptist, Willie, and Mary Bricker-Jenkins. "The Movement to End Poverty in the United States." Pages 103–20 in *Economic Rights in Canada and the United States.* Edited by Rhoda E. Howard-Hassmann and Claude E. Welch Jr. Philadelphia: University of Pennsylvania Press, 2006.

———, Mary Bricker-Jenkins, and Monica Dillon. "Taking the Struggle on the Road:

The New Freedom Bus—Freedom from Unemployment, Hunger and Homelessness." *Journal of Progressive Human Services* 10, no. 2 (1999): 7–29.

———, and Cheri Honkala. "A New and Unsettling Force." *The Other Side Magazine* (Winter 2003): 38–39.

———, and Jan Rehmann. *Pedagogy of the Poor: Building the Movement to End Poverty*. New York: Teachers College Press, 2011.

———, and Noelle Damico. "Building the New Freedom Church of the Poor." *Cross Currents* 55 (2005): 352–63.

Bartchy, Scott S. *First-Century Slavery and the Interpretation of 1 Corinthians 7:21*. Eugene, OR: Wipf & Stock, 2003.

Bauday, John. "Poverty in Pauline Studies: A Response to Steven Friesen." *Journal for the Study of the New Testament* 26 (2004): 363–66.

Beavis, Mary Ann. "'Expect Nothing in Return': Luke's Picture of the Marginalized." *Interpretation* 48 (1994): 357–68. Reprinted, pp. 142–54 in *Gospel Interpretation: Narrative-Critical and Social-Scientific Approaches*. Edited by Jack Dean Kingsbury. Harrisburg, PA: Trinity Press International, 1997.

Berryman, Phillip. *Liberation Theology*. Philadelphia: Temple University Press, 1987.

Betz, Hans Dieter. *The Sermon on the Mount: A Commentary on the Sermon on the Mount, Including the Sermon on the Plain (Matthew 5:3–7:27 and Luke 6:20–49)*. Hermeneia. Minneapolis: Augsburg Fortress, 1995.

Bible & Culture Collective. *The Postmodern Bible*. New Haven, CT: Yale University Press, 1997.

Birch, Bruce C. "The First and Second Books of Samuel." Pages 947–1383 in *Numbers to Samuel*. Vol. 2 of *The New Interpreter's Bible*. Nashville: Abingdon, 1998.

———. "Hunger, Poverty and Biblical Religion." *Christian Century* 92 (1975): 593–99.

Blasi, Anthony J., Paul-Andre Turcotte, and Jean Duhaime. *Handbook of Early Christianity: Social Science Approaches*. Walnut Creek, CA: AltaMira, 2002.

Bloom, Joshua, and Waldo E. Martin Jr. *Black against Empire: The History and Politics of the Black Panther Party*. Berkeley: University of California Press, 2013.

Borg, Marcus J. *Meeting Jesus again for the First Time: The Historical Jesus and the Heart of Contemporary Faith*. San Francisco: HarperOne, 1995.

———, and John Dominic Crossan. *The Last Week: What the Gospels Really Teach about Jesus's Final Days in Jerusalem*. San Francisco: HarperSanFrancisco, 2007.

Boring, M. Eugene. *An Introduction to the New Testament: History, Literature, Theology*. Louisville: Westminster John Knox, 2012.

Branch, Taylor. *Parting the Waters: America in the King Years 1954–63*. New York: Simon & Schuster, 1989.

Brooks, Oscar Stephen. *The Sermon on the Mount: Authentic Human Values*. Lanham, MD: University Press of America, 1985.

Brown, Francis, with S. R. Driver and Charles A. Briggs. *The New Brown-Driver-Briggs-Gesenius Hebrew and English Lexicon: With an Appendix Containing the Biblical Aramaic*. Peabody, MA : Hendrickson, 1979.

Bibliography

Brown, Raymond E. *The Birth of the Messiah.* New York: Doubleday, 1993.

———. "Review of William Klassen, *Judas: Betrayer or Friend of Jesus?*" *Journal of Biblical Literature* 117 (1998): 134–36.

Brueggemann, Walter. "Conversations among Exiles." *The Christian Century* 114, no. 20 (1997): 630–32.

———. *An Introduction to the Old Testament: The Canon and Christian Imagination.* Minneapolis: Augsburg Fortress, 1991.

———. *Old Testament Theology: An Introduction.* Library of Biblical Theology. Nashville: Abingdon, 2008.

———. *Sabbath as Resistance: Say No to a Culture of Now.* Louisville: Westminster John Knox, 2014.

———. "The Secret of Survival: Jeremiah 20:7–13; Matthew 6:1–8." *Journal for Preachers* 26, no. 2 (2003): 42–47.

———. *A Social Reading of the Old Testament.* Minneapolis: Fortress, 1994.

Bultmann, Rudolf. *The Gospel of John: A Commentary.* Oxford: Blackwell, 1971.

Burridge, Richard A. *Four Gospels, One Jesus? A Symbolic Reading.* 2nd ed. Grand Rapids: Eerdmans, 2005.

———. *What Are the Gospels? A Comparison with Graeco-Roman Biography.* 2nd ed. Biblical Resource Series. Grand Rapids: Eerdmans, 2004.

Byron, John. "Living in the Shadow of Cain: Echoes of a Developing Tradition in James 5:1–6." *Novum Testamentum* 48 (2006): 261–74.

Cameron, Ron, and Merrill P. Miller, eds. *Redescribing Christian Origins.* Society of Biblical Literature Symposium Series 28. Leiden: Brill, 2004.

Capper, Brian. "Essene Community Houses and Jesus' Early Community." Pages 472–502 in *Jesus and Archaeology.* Edited by James H. Charlesworth. Grand Rapids: Eerdmans, 2006.

Cardenal, Ernesto. *The Gospel in Solentiname.* Revised, one-volume edition, Maryknoll, NY: Orbis, 2010. Reprint of *The Gospel in Solentiname.* Translated by Donald D. Walsh. 4 vols. Maryknoll, NY: Orbis, 1976–82. Translation of *El Evangelio en Solentiname.* Salamanca, Spain: Ediciones Sígueme, 1975–77.

Carter, Edward J. "Toll and Tribute: A Political Reading of Matthew 17.24–27." *Journal for the Study of the New Testament* 25 (2003): 413–31.

Carter, Warren. *Matthew and the Margins: A Sociopolitical and Religious Reading.* Maryknoll, NY: Orbis, 2000.

———. "Paying the Tax to Rome as Subversive Praxis: Matthew 17.24–27." *Journal for the Study of the New Testament* 76 (1999): 3–31.

Carvalho, Corrine L. *Primer on Biblical Methods.* Winona, MN: Anselm Academic, 2009.

Casanova, Ron, and Stephen Blackburn. *Each One Teach One: Up and Out of Poverty, Memoirs of a Street Activist.* New York: Curbstone, 1996.

Charlesworth, James, ed. *The Messiah: Developments in Earliest Judaism and Christian-

ity. The First Princeton Symposium on Judaism and Christian Origins. Minneapolis: Fortress, 1992.

Charron, Katherine. *Freedom's Teacher: The Life of Septima Clark.* Chapel Hill: University of North Carolina Press, 2009.

Chase, Robert T. "Class Resurrection: The Poor People's Campaign of 1968 and Resurrection City." *Essays in History* 40 (1998): n.p.

Chowder, Ken. "John Brown's Holy War: PBS Documentary Transcript." http://www.pbs.org/wgbh/amex/brown/filmmore/transcript/transcript1.html.

Christensen, Duane. *Deuteronomy.* 2 vols. Word Biblical Commentary 6a–b. Nashville: Thomas Nelson, 2001–2.

Cicero, Marcus Tullius. *Cicero.* Translated by H. M. Hubbel et al. 32 vols. Loeb Classical Library. Cambridge: Harvard University Press, 1913–2010.

Clark, Howard. *The Gospel of Matthew and Its Readers: A Historical Introduction to the First Gospel.* Bloomington: Indiana University Press, 2003.

Clements, Ronald. "The Book of Deuteronomy: Introduction, Commentary and Reflections." Pages 269–538 in *Numbers–Samuel.* Vol. 2 of *The New Interpreter's Bible.* Nashville: Abingdon, 1998.

Coakley, J. F. "The Anointing at Bethany and the Priority of John." *Journal of Biblical Literature* 107 (1988): 241–56.

Coffin, William Sloane. *The Collected Sermons of William Sloane Coffin: The Riverside Years.* 2 vols. Louisville: Westminster John Knox, 2008.

Coleman, Thomas. "Binding Obligations in Romans 13:7: A Semantic Field and Social Context." *Tyndale Bulletin* 48 (1997): 307–27.

Collins, John. *The Scepter and the Star: The Messiahs of the Dead Sea Scrolls and Other Ancient Literature.* Anchor Bible Reference Library. New York: Doubleday, 1995.

Combrink, H. J. B. "The Structure of the Gospel of Matthew as Narrative." *Tyndale Bulletin* 34 (1983): 61–90.

Cone, James. *God of the Oppressed.* Maryknoll, NY: Orbis, 1997.

Consalvo, Mia, Nancy Baym, Jeremy Hunsinger, Klaus Bruhn Jensen, John Logie, Monica Murero, and Leslie Regan Shade, eds. *Internet Research Annual: Selected Papers from the Association of Internet Researchers Conferences 2000–2002.* Vol. 1. New York: Peter Lang, 2004.

Conway, Colleen. *Behold the Man: Jesus and Greco-Roman Masculinity.* New York: Oxford University Press, 2008.

Coogan, Michael. *A Brief Introduction to the Old Testament: The Hebrew Bible in Its Context.* Oxford: Oxford University Press, 2009.

Cotton, Roger. "Anointing in the Old Testament." http://www.agts.edu/faculty/faculty_publications/articles/cotton_anointing.pdf.

Crehan, Kate. *Gramsci, Culture, and Anthropology.* Berkeley: University of California Press, 2002.

Crossan, John Dominic. *The Historical Jesus: The Life of a Mediterranean Jewish Peasant.* San Francisco: HarperOne, 1993.

————. *Jesus: A Revolutionary Biography*. San Francisco: HarperOne, 2009.

————, and Jonathan Reed. *In Search of Paul: How Jesus's Apostle Opposed Rome's Empire with God's Kingdom*. San Francisco: HarperSanFrancisco, 2004.

Damico, Noelle. *Living Micah's Call, Doing Justice, Loving Kindness, Walking Humbly with God: A Guide for Congregations*. New York: National Council of Churches, 2001.

Danker, Frederick W. *The Concise Greek-English Lexicon of the New Testament*. Chicago: University of Chicago Press, 2009.

————. "The Literary Unity of Mark 14:1–25." *Journal of Biblical Literature* 85 (1966): 468.

Davids, Peter. "Theological Perspectives on the Epistle of James." *Journal of the Evangelical Theological Society* 23 (1980): 97–103.

Davies, Stevan L. *Jesus the Healer: Possession, Trance, and the Origins of Christianity*. New York: Continuum, 1995.

Davies, W. D. "The Jewish Sources of Matthew's Messianism." Pages 494–511 in *The Messiah: Developments in Earliest Judaism and Christianity*. Edited by James Charlesworth. Minneapolis: Fortress, 1992.

Davis, Mike. *City of Quartz: Excavating the Future in Los Angeles*. London: Verso, 1990.

————. *Planet of Slums*. London: Verso, 2006.

De Jonge, Marinus. "Christ." Pages 914–21 in vol. 1 of *Anchor Bible Dictionary*. Edited by David Noel Freedman. 6 vols. New York: Doubleday, 1992.

DiFazio, William. *Ordinary Poverty. A Little Food and Cold Storage*. Philadelphia: Temple University Press, 2006.

Dio Chrysostom. *Dio Chrysostom*. Translated by J. W. Cohoon et al. 5 vols. Loeb Classical Library. Cambridge: Harvard University Press, 1932–51.

Dittmer, John. *Local People: The Struggle for Civil Rights in Mississippi*. Champaign, IL: University of Illinois Press, 1995.

Dodd, C. H. *Historical Tradition in the Fourth Gospel*. Cambridge: Cambridge University Press, 1963.

————. *Parables of the Kingdom*. New York: Scribner, 1961.

Douglass, Frederick. *Narrative of the Life of Frederick Douglass: An American Slave, Written by Himself*. London: St. Martin's Press, 2002.

————. "Speech on the Dred Scott Decision, May 1857." http://teachingamerican history.org/library/document/speech-on-the-dred-scott-decision-2/.

————. "West India Emancipation: Speech Delivered at Canandaigua, New York, August 3, 1857." http://www.lib.rochester.edu/index.cfm?PAGE=4398.

Dube, Musa. *Postcolonial Feminist Interpretation of the Bible*. St. Louis: Christian Board of Publication, 2000.

————, ed. *Other Ways of Reading: African Women and the Bible*. Global Perspectives on Biblical Scholarship 2. Atlanta: Society of Biblical Literature, 2001.

————, and Musimbi Kanyoro, eds. *Grant Me Justice! HIV/Aids & Gender Readings of the Bible*. Maryknoll, NY: Orbis, 2005.

Bibliography

Dubois, W. E. B. *Black Reconstruction in America 1860–1880*. New York: Harcourt, Brace, 1935. Reprinted, New York: Free Press, 1999.

Duchrow, Ulrich. *Alternatives to Global Capitalism: Drawn from Biblical History, Designed for Political Action*. Heidelberg: Kairos Europa with International Books, 1995.

————. *Global Economy: A Confessional Issue for the Churches?* Geneva: WCC, 1987.

Dumenil, Gérard, and Dominique Lévy. *Capital Resurgent: Roots of the Neoliberal Revolution*. Cambridge: Harvard University Press, 2004.

Dyson, Michael Eric. *I May Not Get There with You: The True Martin Luther King, Jr.* New York: Free Press, 2001.

Ekblad, Bob. *Reading the Bible with the Damned*. Lexington, KY: Westminster John Knox, 2005.

Elgin, Duane. *Voluntary Simplicity: Toward a Way of Life That Is Outwardly Simple, Inwardly Rich*. New York: Morrow, 1981. Reprinted, San Francisco: Harper, 2010.

Elliot, Neil. *The Arrogance of Nations: Reading Romans in the Shadow of Empire*. Paul in Critical Contexts. Minneapolis: Fortress, 2008.

Emerson, Ralph Waldo. "Remarks at a Meeting for the Relief of the Family of John Brown, at Tremont Temple, Boston, November 18, 1859." http://www.rwe.org/x -john-brown-speech-at-boston/.

Evans, Craig. *Matthew*. New Cambridge Biblical Commentary. Cambridge: Cambridge University Press, 2012.

Ewherido, Anthony O. *Matthew's Gospel and Judaism in the Late First Century C.E.: The Evidence from Matthew's Chapter on Parables (Matthew 13:1–52)*. Studies in Biblical Literature 91. New York: Peter Lang, 2006.

Fee, Gordon. *New Testament Exegesis: A Handbook for Students and Pastors*. 3rd ed. Louisville: Westminster John Knox, 2002.

Felder, Cain Hope. *Stony the Road We Trod: African American Biblical Interpretation*. Minneapolis: Augsburg Fortress, 1991.

Fiensy, David A. *The Social History of Palestine in the Herodian Period: The Land Is Mine*. Studies in the Bible and Early Christianity. Lewiston, NY: Edwin Mellen, 1991.

————, and Ralph K. Hawkins, eds. *The Galilean Economy in the Time of Jesus*. Atlanta: Society of Biblical Literature, 2013.

Fleming, Daniel. "The Biblical Tradition of Anointing Priests." *Journal of Biblical Literature* 117 (1998): 401–14.

Ford, Elizabeth. "Matthew 26:6–13." *Interpretation* 59 (2005): 400–402.

Fowler, Robert, Edith Blumhofer, and Fernando Segovia, eds. *New Paradigms for Bible Study: The Bible in the Third Millennium*. New York: T&T Clark International, 2004.

Francis (Pope). "On the Proclamation of the Gospel in Today's World (*Evangelii Gaudium*)." http://w2.vatican.va/content/francesco/en/apost_exhortations/ documents/papa-francesco_esortazione-ap_20131124_evangelii-gaudium.html.

Freedman, David Noel. "Deuteronomy." Pages 168–83 in vol. 2 of *Anchor Bible Dictionary*. Edited by David Noel Freedman. 6 vols. New York: Doubleday, 1992.

———. "Poor/Poverty." Page 402 in vol. 4 of *Anchor Bible Dictionary*. Edited by David Noel Freedman. 6 vols. New York: Doubleday, 1992.

Freire, Paolo. *Pedagogy of the Oppressed*. New York: Bloomsbury Academic, 2000.

Freyne, Sean. *Galilee from Alexander the Great to Hadrian: A Study of Second Temple Judaism*. Wilmington, DE: Michael Glazier, 1980.

Friesen, Steven. "Poverty in Pauline Studies: Beyond the So-Called New Consensus." *Journal for the Study of the New Testament* 26 (2004): 323–61.

Fuglseth, Kare Sigvald. *Johannine Sectarianism in Perspective: A Sociological, Historical, and Comparative Analysis of Temple and Social Relationships in the Gospel of John, Philo, and Qumran*. Leiden: Brill, 2005.

Funicello, Teresa. *Tyranny of Kindness: Dismantling the Welfare System to End Poverty in America*. New York: Atlantic Monthly Press, 1994.

Funk, Robert. *The Five Gospels: What Did Jesus Really Say? The Search for the Authentic Words of Jesus*. San Francisco: HarperOne, 1996.

Gale, Aaron M. "God, Galilee, and the Gospels Revisited: Was Matthew Written from Bethsaida?" *Proceedings: Eastern Great Lakes and Midwest Biblical Societies* 28 (2008): 15–24.

Garrow, David. *Bearing the Cross: Martin Luther King Jr. and the Southern Christian Leadership Conference*. San Francisco: William Morrow, 2004.

Georgi, Dieter. *Remembering the Poor: The History of Paul's Collection for Jerusalem*. Nashville: Abingdon, 1992.

Glancy, Jennifer. *Slavery in Early Christianity*. New York: Oxford University Press, 2002.

Goldsmith, William W., and Edward J. Blakely. *Separate Societies: Poverty and Inequality in U.S. Cities*. Philadelphia: Temple University Press, 1992.

Goode, Judith, and Jeff Maskovsky, eds. *The New Poverty Studies: The Ethnography of Power, Politics, and Impoverished People in the United States*. New York: New York University Press, 2001.

Goodman, Martin. *Judaism in the Roman World: Collected Essays*. Ancient Judaism and Early Christianity 66. Boston: Brill Academic, 2006.

Gopp, Amy. "Ritualizing with the Poor: The Potter's Field Memorial Service." M.A. thesis, Union Theological Seminary in the City of New York, 2005.

Gottwald, Norman. *The Tribes of Yahweh: A Sociology of the Religion of Liberated Israel, 1250–1050 B.C.E.* Sheffield: Sheffield Academic Press, 1999.

Gowler, David. "'At His Gate Lay a Poor Man': A Dialogic Reading of Luke 16:19–31." *Perspectives in Religion Studies* 32 (2005): 249–65.

Gramsci, Antonio. *The Antonio Gramsci Reader: Selected Writings 1916–1935*. Edited by David Forgacs. New York: New York University Press, 2000.

———. *Selections from the Prison Notebooks*. Edited and translated by Quintin Hoare and Geoffrey Nowell Smith. New York: International Publishers, 1971.

Bibliography

Green, Joel. *Hearing the New Testament: Strategies for Interpretation*. Grand Rapids: Eerdmans, 1995.

Gruen, Erich S. "The Expansion of the Empire under Augustus." Pages 147–97 in *The Augustan Empire, 43 B.C– A.D. 69*. Edited by Alan Bowman, Edward Champlin, and Andrew Lintott. Cambridge Ancient History 10. Cambridge: Cambridge University Press, 1996.

Gutierrez, Gustavo. *On Job: God-Talk and the Suffering of the Innocent*. Translated by Matthew O'Connell. Maryknoll, NY: Orbis Books, 1987.

———. *A Theology of Liberation: History, Politics, and Salvation*. Translated by Caridad Inda and John Eagleson. Maryknoll, NY: Orbis, 1988.

Hagner, Donald. *Matthew*. 2 vols. Word Biblical Commentary 33A–33B. Dallas: Word, 1995.

Hallo, William. "New Moons and Sabbaths: A Case-Study in the Contrastive Approach." *Hebrew Union College Annual* 48 (1977): 1–18.

Hamerton–Kelly, R. G. "Attitudes to the Law in Matthew's Gospel: A Discussion of Matthew 5:18." *Bulletin for Biblical Research* (1972): 19–32.

Hamilton, Jeffries. "Ha'areṣ in the Shemitta Law." *Vetus Testamentum* 42 (1992): 214–22.

Hamilton, Mark. "Sabbatical Year." Pages 11–13 in vol. 5 of *The New Interpreter's Dictionary of the Bible*. Edited by Katherine Doob Sakenfeld. 5 vols. Nashville: Abingdon, 2009.

Hanson, K. C., and Douglas Oakman. *Palestine in the Time of Jesus: Social Structures and Social Conflicts*. Minneapolis: Augsburg Fortress, 2002.

Harding, Vincent. *Martin Luther King: The Inconvenient Hero*. Maryknoll, NY: Orbis, 2008.

Hare, Douglas R. A. "How Jewish Is the Gospel of Matthew?" *Catholic Biblical Quarterly* 62 (2000): 275.

Harrill, J. Albert. *Slaves in the New Testament: Literary, Social, and Moral Dimensions*. Minneapolis: Augsburg Fortress, 2005.

Harrington, Daniel. *The Gospel of Matthew*. Sacra Pagina 1. Collegeville, MN: Liturgical Press, 1991.

Harvey, David. *A Brief History of Neoliberalism*. Oxford: Oxford University Press, 2005.

———. *The Condition of Postmodernity*. Oxford: Blackwell, 1990.

Hatina, Thomas R., ed. *The Gospel of Matthew*. Vol. 2 of *Biblical Interpretation in Early Christian Gospel*s. Library of New Testament Studies. New York: T&T Clark, 2008.

Haynes, Stephen R. *Noah's Curse: The Biblical Justification of American Slavery*. Religion in America Series. New York: Oxford University Press, 2002.

Hays, Richard B. *Echoes of Scripture in the Letters of Paul*. New Haven, CT: Yale University Press, 1993.

Heen, Erik. "Radical Patronage in Luke–Acts." *Currents in Theology and Mission* 33 (2006): 445–58.

Hendrickx, Herman. *Studies in the Synoptic Gospels: The Infancy Narratives, The Passion*

Narratives of the Synoptic Gospels, The Resurrection Narratives of the Synoptic Gospels, The Sermon on the Mount. London: Geoffrey Chapman, 1984.

Hengel, Martin. *Crucifixion*. Translated by John Bowden. Facets. Minneapolis: Fortress, 1977.

———. *The Zealots: Investigations into the Jewish Freedom Movement in the Period from Herod I until A.D. 70*. Translated by John Bowden. Edinburgh: T&T Clark, 1989. Translation of *Die Zeloten*. Tübingen: Mohr Siebeck, 1976.

Hertig, Paul. "The Jubilee Mission of Jesus in the Gospel of Luke: Reversals of Fortune." *Missiology* 26 (1998): 167–79.

Herzog, William. *Parables as Subversive Speech: Jesus as Pedagogue of the Oppressed*. Louisville: Westminster John Knox, 1994.

———. *Prophet and Teacher: An Introduction to the Historical Jesus*. Louisville: Westminster John Knox, 2005.

Hezser, Catherine, ed. *The Oxford Handbook of Jewish Daily Life in Roman Palestine*. New York: Oxford University Press, 2010.

Hoover, Roy W., ed. *Profiles of Jesus*. Santa Rosa, CA: Polebridge, 2002.

Hoppe, Leslie. *There Shall Be No Poor among You: Poverty in the Bible*. Nashville: Abingdon, 2004.

Horsley, Richard. *Covenant Economics: A Biblical Vision of Justice for All*. Louisville: Westminster John Knox, 2009.

———. *Jesus and Empire: The Kingdom of God and the New World Disorder*. Minneapolis: Augsburg Fortress, 2002.

———. *Jesus and the Politics of Roman Palestine*. Columbia: University of South Carolina Press, 2013.

———. *Jesus and the Powers: Conflict, Covenant, and the Hope of the Poor*. Minneapolis: Fortress, 2010.

———. *Jesus and the Spiral of Violence: Popular Jewish Resistance in Roman Palestine*. Facets. Minneapolis: Augsburg Fortress, 1993.

———. *Paul and Empire: Religion and Power in Roman Imperial Society*. Harrisburg, PA: Trinity Press International, 1997.

———. *The Prophet Jesus and the Renewal of Israel: Moving beyond a Diversionary Debate*. Grand Rapids: Eerdmans, 2012.

———, with Jonathan A. Draper. *Whoever Hears You Hears Me: Prophets, Performance, and Tradition in Q*. New York: Bloomsbury T&T Clark, 1999.

———, with John S. Hanson. *Bandits, Prophets, and Messiahs: Popular Movements in the Time of Jesus*. Harrisburg: Trinity Press International, 1999.

———, and Neil A. Silberman. *The Message and the Kingdom: How Jesus and Paul Ignited a Revolution and Transformed the Ancient World*. Minneapolis: Augsburg Fortress, 2002.

———, and James Tracy, eds. *Christmas Unwrapped: Consumerism, Celluloid, Christ, and Culture*. New York: Bloomsbury T&T Clark, 2001.

Bibliography

Horton, Myles. *The Long Haul: An Autobiography*. New York: Teachers College Press, 2003.

Howard-Brook, Wes. *"Come Out My People!": God's Call Out of Empire in the Bible and Beyond*. Maryknoll, NY: Orbis, 2010.

Hoyt, Thomas. "The Poor/Rich Theme in the Beatitudes." *Journal of Religious Thought* 37.1 (1980): 31–41.

Hughes, Dewi. *Power and Poverty: Divine and Human Rule in a World of Need*. Downers Grove, IL: IVP Academic, 2008.

Hurtado, Larry W. "The Jerusalem Collection and the Book of Galatians." *Journal for the Study of the New Testament* 5 (1979): 46–62.

Ipsen, Avaren. *Sex Working and the Bible*. Sheffield: Equinox, 2009.

Jenkins, Philip. *The New Faces of Christianity: Believing the Bible in the Global South*. New York: Oxford University Press, 2002.

Jones, Gareth Stedman. *An End to Poverty? A Historical Debate*. New York: Columbia University Press, 2008.

Josephus, Flavius. *Josephus*. Translated by H. St. J. Thackeray et al. 10 vols. Loeb Classical Library. Cambridge: Harvard University Press, 1926–65.

Juel, Donald. *Messianic Exegesis: Christological Interpretation of the Old Testament in Early Christianity*. Philadelphia: Fortress, 1988.

Kahl, Brigitte. "And She Called His Name Seth . . . (Gen 4:25): The Birth of Critical Knowledge and the Unread End of Eve's Story." *Union Seminary Quarterly Review* (1999): 19–28.

———. *Armenevangelium und Heidenevangelium: "Sola Scriptura" und die Ökumenische Traditionsproblematik im Lichte von Väterkonflikt und Väterkonsens bei Lukas*. Berlin: Evangelische Verlag, 1987.

———. "Arme wird es immer geben?" *Neue Stimme*, Mainz. 2 (1986), 21–25.

———. *Galatians Re-Imagined: Reading with the Eyes of the Vanquished*. Paul in Critical Contexts Series. Minneapolis: Augsburg Fortress, 2010.

———. "Peter's Antiochene Apostasy: Re-Judaizing or Imperial Conformism? An Intertextual Exploration." *Forum* 3.1 (2014): 27–38.

———. "Toward a Materialist-Feminist Reading." Pages 225–40 in *A Feminist Introduction*. Vol. 1 of *Searching the Scriptures*. Edited by Elisabeth Schüssler Fiorenza. New York: Crossroad, 1993.

———, Davina Lopez, and Hal Taussig, eds. "New Testament and Roman Empire." *Union Seminary Quarterly Review* 59.3–4 (2005).

Kaplan, Jonathan. "1 Samuel 8:11–18 as a Mirror for Princes." *Journal of Biblical Literature* 131 (2012): 625–42.

King, Martin Luther, Jr. *A Testament of Hope: The Essential Writings and Speeches of Martin Luther King, Jr.* Edited by James M. Washington. San Francisco: HarperOne, 2003.

———. *The Trumpet of Conscience*. New York: Harper & Row, 1968. Reprinted, Boston: Beacon, 2011.

164

————. *Where Do We Go from Here: Chaos or Community?* New York: Harper & Row, 1967. Reprinted, Boston: Beacon, 2010.

Klassen, William. *Judas: Betrayer or Friend of Jesus?* Minneapolis: Fortress, 1996.

Klausner, Joseph. *The Messianic Idea in Israel, From Its Beginning to the Completion of the Mishnah.* Translated by W. F. Stinespring. New York: Macmillan, 1955.

Klein, Naomi. *The Shock Doctrine: The Rise of Disaster Capitalism.* New York: Metropolitan, 2007.

Knight, Douglas A. *Law, Power, and Justice in Ancient Israel.* Library of Ancient Israel. Louisville: Westminster John Knox, 2011.

Koehler, Ludwig, Walter Baumgartner, and Johann J. Stamm. *The Hebrew and Aramaic Lexicon of the Old Testament.* Leiden: Brill, 1994–2000.

Kohlenberger, John, Edward Goodrick, and James Swanson. *The Greek-English Concordance to the New Testament with the New International Version.* Grand Rapids: Zondervan, 1997.

Krugman, Paul. *The Return of Depression Economics and the Crisis of 2008.* New York: Norton, 2009.

Kupp, David. *Matthew's Emmanuel: Divine Presence and God's People in the First Gospel.* Cambridge: Cambridge University Press, 1996.

Lange, Harry de. "The Jubilee Principle: Is It Relevant for Today?" *Ecumenical Review* 38 (1986): 437–43.

Larson, Kate Clifford. *Bound for the Promised Land: Harriet Tubman—Portrait of an American Hero.* New York: Ballantine, 2004.

Leacock, Eleanor. *The Culture of Poverty: A Critique.* New York: Touchstone, 1971.

Léon-Dufour, Xavier. "Sabbath." Pages 335–40 in *Dictionary of Biblical Theology.* Edited by X. Léon-Dufour. Boston: Word Among Us Press, 1988.

Levine, Amy-Jill, and Marc Zvi Brettler. *The Jewish Annotated New Testament: New Revised Standard Version.* New York: Oxford University Press, 2011.

Levine, Amy-Jill, ed. *A Feminist Companion to Luke.* Feminist Companion to the New Testament and Early Christian Writings. Cleveland: Pilgrim Press, 2004.

Levinson, David. "Food Programs." Page 164 in vol. 1 of *Encyclopedia of Homelessness.* Edited by David Levinson. 2 vols. New York: SAGE, 2004.

Lewis, Oscar. "The Culture of Poverty." *Scientific American* 215, no. 4 (1966): 3–9.

————. *Five Families: Mexican Case Studies in the Culture of Poverty.* San Francisco: HarperCollins, 1975.

————. *La Vida: A Puerto Rican Family in the Culture of Poverty.* New York: Random House, 1966.

Licona, Michael. *The Resurrection of Jesus: A New Historiographical Approach.* Downers Grove, IL: InterVarsity, 2010.

Loader, W. R. G. "Son of David, Blindness, Possession, and Duality in Matthew." *Catholic Biblical Quarterly* 44 (1982): 570–85.

Longenecker, Bruce. *Remember the Poor: Paul, Poverty, and the Greco-Roman World.* Grand Rapids: Eerdmans, 2010.

———, and Kelly Liebengood, eds. *Engaging Economics: New Testament Scenarios and Early Christian Reception.* Grand Rapids: Eerdmans, 2009.

Love, Stuart L. *Jesus and Marginal Women.* Cambridge: James Clarke, 2010.

Lundblad, Barbara. "Closing the Great Chasm: Faith & Global Hunger Part 2." http://day1.org/2036-closing_the_great_chasm_faith__global_hunger_part_2.

Luz, Ulrich. *Matthew.* Translated by James E. Crouch. 3 vols. Hermeneia. Minneapolis: Fortress, 2001–7.

Mack, Burton. *Who Wrote the New Testament? The Making of the Christian Myth.* San Francisco: HarperOne, 1996.

Malina, Bruce, and Richard Rohrbaugh. *Social-Science Commentary on the Gospel of John.* Minneapolis: Fortress, 1998.

Marable, Manning. *Malcolm X: A Life of Reinvention.* New York: Penguin, 2011.

Martin, Dale. "Review Essay: Justin J. Meggitt, *Paul, Poverty and Survival.*" *Journal for the Study of the New Testament* 24 (2001): 51–64.

McBride, Dean. "Book of Deuteronomy." Pages 108–17 in vol. 2 of *The New Interpreter's Dictionary of the Bible.* Edited by Katherine Doob Sakenfeld. 5 vols. Nashville: Abingdon, 2009.

McConnell, Richard S. *Law and Prophecy in Matthew's Gospel: The Authority and Use of the Old Testament in the Gospel of St. Matthew.* Basel: Friedrich Reinhardt Komm., 1969.

McDonald, L. M. "Antioch (Syria)." Pages 34–36 in *Dictionary of New Testament Background.* Edited by Craig A. Evans and Stanley E. Porter. Downers Grove, IL: InterVarsity, 2000.

McEleney, Neil J. "Matthew 17:24–27: Who Paid the Temple Tax? A Lesson in Avoidance of Scandal." *Catholic Biblical Quarterly* 38 (1976): 178–92.

McGovern, Arthur F. *Liberation Theology and Its Critics.* Maryknoll, NY: Orbis, 1989.

McKenzie, Steven, and Stephen Haynes, eds. *To Each Its Own Meaning: An Introduction to Biblical Criticisms and Their Application.* 2nd ed. Louisville: Westminster John Knox, 1999.

McLeod, Edward. "Between Text and Sermon: Deuteronomy 15:1–11." *Interpretation* 65 (2011): 180–82.

McNally, David. *Another World Is Possible: Globalization & Anticapitalism.* Winnipeg: Arbeiter Ring, 2006.

McNeile, Alan Hugh. *The Gospel according to St. Matthew: The Greek Text with Introduction, Notes, and Indices.* London: Macmillan, 1915.

Mdlalose, Bandile. "God in My Struggle." http://abahlali.org/node/8911.

Meggitt, Justin. *Paul, Poverty, and Survival.* Edinburgh: T&T Clark, 1998.

Melick, Richard R., Jr. "The Collection for the Saints: 2 Corinthians 8–9." *Criswell Theological Review* 4 (1989): 97–117.

Migne, J.-P., ed. *Patrologia graeca.* 162 vols. Paris, 1857–86.

Milgrom, Jacob. *Leviticus: A Book of Ritual and Ethics.* Continental Commentary. Minneapolis: Fortress, 2004.

Miller, Patrick. *Deuteronomy*. Interpretation. Louisville: Westminster John Knox, 1990.

Miller, Susan. "The Woman Who Anoints Jesus (Mark 14:3–9)." *Feminist Theology* 14 (2006): 221–36.

Morgen, Sandra. "The Agency of Welfare Workers: Negotiating Devolution, Privatization, and the Meaning of Self-Sufficiency." *American Anthropologist* 103 (2001): 747–61.

Morris, Aldon. *The Origins of the Civil Rights Movement*. New York: Free Press, 1986.

Morrish, George. *A Concordance of the Septuagint*. Grand Rapids: Zondervan, 1976.

Murch, Donna. *Living for the City: Migration, Immigration, and the Rise of the Black Panther Party in Oakland, California*. Chapel Hill: University of North Carolina Press, 2010.

Myers, Bryant. "Will the Poor Always Be with Us?" http://www.evangelicalsforsocial action.org/holistic-ministry/will-the-poor-always-be-with-us/.

Myers, Ched. *The Biblical Vision of Sabbath Economics*. Washington, DC: Church of the Saviour Publishing, 2001.

—————, Joseph Nangle, Cynthia Moe-Lobeda, Stuart Taylor, Marie Dennis, and Karen Lattea. *"Say to This Mountain": Stories of Mark's Discipleship*. Maryknoll, NY: Orbis, 1996.

Nash, June. *From Tank Town to High Tech: The Clash of Community and Industrial Cycles*. New York: State University of New York Press, 1989.

Nessan, Craig. "The Gospel of Luke and Liberation Theology: On Not Domesticating the Dangerous Memory of Jesus." *Currents in Theology and Mission* 22 (1995): 130–38.

Neusner, Jacob, William Green, and Ernest Frerichs. *Judaisms and Their Messiahs at the Turn of the Christian Era*. Cambridge: Cambridge University Press, 1987.

Newsom, Carol, and Sharon H. Ringe, eds. *Women's Bible Commentary: Expanded Edition with Apocrypha*. Louisville: Westminster John Knox, 1998.

Noll, Mark A. *The Civil War as a Theological Crisis*. Chapel Hill: The University of North Carolina Press, 2006.

Novakovic, Lidija. *Messiah, the Healer of the Sick: A Study of Jesus as the Son of David in the Gospel of Matthew*. Wissenschaftliche Untersuchungen zum Neuen Testament 2.170. Tübingen: Mohr Siebeck, 2003.

Novenson, Matthew. *Christ among the Messiahs: Christ Language in Paul and Messiah Language in Ancient Judaism*. New York: Oxford University Press, 2012.

Now on PBS. "Facts and Figures: The Homeless." http://www.pbs.org/now/ shows/526/homeless-facts.html.

Oakman, Douglas. *Jesus and the Economic Questions of His Day*. Lewiston, NY: Edwin Mellen, 1986.

—————. *Jesus and the Peasants*. Matrix: The Bible in Mediterranean Context. Eugene, OR: Wipf & Stock, 2008.

Oates, Stephen. *To Purge This Land of Blood: A Biography of John Brown*. Amherst: University of Massachusetts Press, 1984.

Bibliography

O'Connor, Alice. *Poverty Knowledge: Social Science, Social Policy, and the Poor in Twentieth-Century U.S. History.* Princeton, NJ: Princeton University Press, 2001.

Oden, Robert A., Jr. "Taxation in Biblical Israel." *Journal of Religious Ethics* 12 (1984): 162–81.

Osbourne, Grant R. *Matthew.* Zondervan Exegetical Commentary on the New Testament. Grand Rapids: Zondervan, 2010.

Overman, Andrew. *Matthew's Gospel and Formative Judaism: The Social World of the Matthean Community.* Minneapolis: Fortress, 1990.

Pastor, Jack. *Land and Economy in Ancient Palestine.* London: Routledge, 1997.

Payne, Charles. *I've Got the Light of Freedom: The Organizing Tradition and the Mississippi Freedom Struggle.* Berkeley: University of California Press, 2007.

Peppard, Michael. *The Son of God in the Roman World: Divine Sonship in Its Social and Political Context.* London: Oxford University Press, 2012.

Pepper, William F. *An Act of State: The Execution of Martin Luther King.* New York: Verso, 2008.

———. *Orders to Kill: The Truth behind the Murder of Martin Luther King.* New York: Carroll & Graf, 1995.

Perkins, Pheme. "Taxes in the New Testament." *Journal of Religious Ethics* 12 (1984): 182–200.

Petit, Paul. *Pax Romana.* Translated by J. Willis. London: Batsford, 1976.

Phillip, Rubin. "Remembering Steve Biko: A Bright & Guiding Light in Dark Times." http://abahlali.org/node/9189.

Pilgrim, Walter E. *Good News to the Poor: Wealth and Poverty in Luke–Acts.* Minneapolis: Augsburg, 1981.

Piven, Frances Fox, and Richard Cloward. *Poor People's Movements: Why They Succeed, How They Fail.* New York: Vintage, 1978.

Pixley, Jorge, and Clodovis Boff. *The Bible, the Church, and the Poor: Biblical, Theological, and Pastoral Aspects of the Option for the Poor.* Maryknoll, NY: Orbis, 1987.

Pliny. *Natural History.* Translated by H. Rackham. 10 vols. Loeb Classical Library. Cambridge: Harvard University Press, 1938–63.

Plutarch. *Plutarch.* 28 vols. Loeb Classical Library. Cambridge: Harvard University Press, 1914–2004.

Poppendieck, Janet. *Sweet Charity: Emergency Food and the End of Entitlement.* New York: Penguin, 1998.

Portes, Alejandro, Manuel Castells, and Lauren A. Benton, eds. *The Informal Economy: Studies in Advanced and Less Developed Countries.* Baltimore: Johns Hopkins University Press, 1989.

Poverty Initiative. *A New and Unsettling Force: Re-igniting Rev. Dr. Martin Luther King's Poor People's Campaign.* New York: Poverty Initiative, 2009.

Price, Randall. "The Concept of the Messiah in the Old Testament." http://www.worldofthebible.com/Bible%20Studies/The%20Concept%20of%20the%20Messiah%20in%20the%20Old%20Testament.pdf.

Price, S. R. F. "Rituals and Power." Pages 47–71 in *Paul and Empire: Religion and Power in Roman Imperial Society.* Edited by Richard Horsley. Harrisburg, PA: Trinity Press International, 1997.

Pruitt, Brad. "The Sabbatical Year of Release: The Social Location and Practice of Shemittah in Deuteronomy 15:1–18." *Restoration Quarterly* 52 (2010): 81–92.

Pui-lan, Kwok. *Postcolonial Imagination and Feminist Theology.* Louisville: Westminster John Knox, 2005.

Putnam, Robert D. *Bowling Alone: The Collapse and Revival of American Community.* New York: Simon & Schuster, 2000.

Ransby, Barbara. *Ella Baker and the Black Freedom Movement: A Radical Democratic Vision.* Chapel Hill: University of North Carolina Press, 2002.

Reed, Adolph. *Class Notes: Posing as Politics and Other Thoughts on the American Scene.* New York: New Press, 2000.

Rehmann, Luzia Sutter. "Olivenöl als Zündstoff: Die vier Salbungsgeschichten der Evangelien im Kontext des Judentums des Zweiten Tempels." *Lectio Difficilior* 1 (2013): 1–25.

Rhoads, David. "The Gospel of Matthew. The Two Ways: Hypocrisy or Righteousness." *Currents in Theology and Mission* 19 (1992): 453–61.

Ricoeur, Paul. *Essays on Biblical Interpretation.* Philadelphia: Fortress, 1980.

Roberts, J. J. M. "The Old Testament's Contribution to Messianic Expectations." Pages 39–51 in *The Messiah: Developments in Earliest Judaism and Christianity.* Edited by James Charlesworth. Minneapolis: Fortress, 1992.

Robertson, Jesse. *The Death of Judas: The Characterization of Judas Iscariot in Three Early Christian Accounts of His Death.* Sheffield: Sheffield Phoenix, 2012.

Robinson, William. *A Theory of Global Capitalism: Production, Class, and State in a Transnational World.* Baltimore: Johns Hopkins University Press, 2004.

Roelofs, Joan. *Foundations and Public Policy: The Mask of Pluralism.* Binghamton, NY: State University of New York Press, 2003.

Rowland, Christopher, and Mark Comer. *Liberating Exegesis: The Challenge of Liberation Theology to Biblical Studies.* Louisville: Westminster John Knox, 1990.

Sachs, Jeffrey. *The End of Poverty: Economic Possibilities for Our Time.* New York: Penguin, 2005.

Safrai, Ze'ev. *The Economy of Roman Palestine.* New York: Routledge, 1994.

Sanders, E. P. *The Historical Figure of Jesus.* New York: Penguin, 1996.

Sawyer, John. *The Fifth Gospel: Isaiah in the History of Christianity.* Cambridge: Cambridge University Press, 1996.

Schmidt, Thomas. *Hostility to Wealth in the Synoptic Gospels.* Sheffield: JSOT Press, 1987.

Schnider, Franz. "Prophets." Pages 183–86 in vol. 3 of the *Exegetical Dictionary of the New Testament.* Edited by Horst Balz and Gerhard Schneider. 3 vols. Grand Rapids: Eerdmans, 1990–93.

Bibliography

Schüssler Fiorenza, Elisabeth. *In Memory of Her: A Feminist Theological Reconstruction of Christian Origins*. New York: Crossroad, 1983.

———. *Jesus and the Politics of Interpretation*. New York: Bloomsbury Academic, 2001.

———, ed. *Searching the Scriptures: A Feminist Commentary*. 2 vols. New York: Crossroad, 1993–94.

Scott, James C. *Domination and the Arts of Resistance: Hidden Transcripts*. New Haven, CT: Yale University Press, 1990.

———. *Weapons of the Weak: Everyday Forms of Peasant Resistance*. New Haven, CT: Yale University Press, 1987.

Seccombe, David Peter. *Possessions and the Poor in Luke–Acts*. Linz: Studien zum Neuen Testament und seiner Umwelt, 1982.

Segovia, Fernando. *Decolonizing Biblical Studies: A View from the Margins*. New York: Orbis, 2000.

———. "Methods for Studying the New Testament." Pages 1–9 in *New Testament Today*. Edited by Mark Allan Powell. Louisville: Westminster John Knox, 1999.

———, and R. S. Sugirtharajah, eds. *Postcolonial Commentary on the New Testament Writings*. New York: T&T Clark, 2007.

Seneca. *Seneca*. 11 vols. Loeb Classical Library. Cambridge: Harvard University Press, 1913–2004.

Smith, Christian. *The Emergence of Liberation Theology*. Chicago: The University of Chicago Press, 1991.

Smith, Dennis. *From Symposium to Eucharist: The Banquet in the Early Christian World*. Minneapolis: Fortress, 2003.

Sorek, Susan. *Remembered for Good: A Jewish Benefaction System in Ancient Palestine*. Sheffield: Sheffield Phoenix, 2010.

Soulen, Richard, and R. Kendall Soulen. *Handbook of Biblical Criticism*. 3rd rev. ed. Louisville: Westminster John Knox, 2001.

Stegemann, Ekkehard W., and Wolfgang Stegemann. *The Jesus Movement: A Social History of Its First Century*. Translated by O. C. Dean Jr. Minneapolis: Fortress, 1999.

Stock, Brian. *After Augustine: The Meditative Reader and the Text*. Philadelphia: University of Pennsylvania Press, 2001.

Stoops, R. F. "Jewish Coinage." Pages 222–25 in *Dictionary of New Testament Background*. Edited by Craig A. Evans and Stanley E. Porter. Downers Grove, IL: InterVarsity, 2000.

Suetonius. *The Lives of the Caesars*. 2 vols. Loeb Classical Library. Cambridge: Harvard University Press, 1914.

Sugirtharajah, R. S. *Troublesome Texts: The Bible in Colonial and Contemporary Culture*. The Bible in the Modern World 17. Sheffield: Sheffield Phoenix, 2008.

———, ed. *Voices from the Margin: Interpreting the Bible in the Third World*. Maryknoll, NY: Orbis Books, 2006.

Tacitus. *The Histories and The Annals*. 4 vols. Loeb Classical Library. Cambridge: Harvard University Press, 1937.

Bibliography

Takeover: Heroes of the New American Depression. Directed by Peter Kinoy and Pamela Yates. 1990. New York: Skylight Pictures, 1994. DVD.

Talbert, Charles H. *Matthew*. Paideia: Commentaries on the New Testament. Ada, MI: Baker Academic, 2010.

————. *Reading the Sermon on the Mount: Character Formation and Decision Making in Matthew 5–7*. Ada, MI: Baker Academic, 2006.

Taussig, Hal. *In the Beginning Was the Meal: Social Experimentation and Early Christian Identity*. Minneapolis: Fortress, 2009.

————, ed. *A New New Testament: A Bible for the 21st Century Combining Traditional and Newly Discovered Texts*. New York: Houghton Mifflin Harcourt, 2013.

Tcherikover, Victor. *Hellenistic Civilization and the Jews*. Peabody, MA: Hendrickson, 1999.

Theissen, Gerd. "The Social Structure of Pauline Communities: Some Critical Remarks on J. J. Meggitt, *Paul, Poverty and Survival.*" *Journal for the Study of the New Testament* 24 (2001): 65–84.

Theoharis, Jeanne. *The Rebellious Life of Mrs. Rosa Parks*. New York: Beacon, 2013.

————, and Komozi Woodard. *Groundwork: Local Black Freedom Movements in America*. New York: New York University Press, 2005.

Theoharis, Liz. Review of *Paul and Empire: Religion and Power in Roman Imperial Society*, ed. Richard Horsley (Harrisburg: Trinity Press International, 1997), *Jesus: A Revolutionary Biography*, by John Dominic Crossan (San Francisco: HarperSanFrancisco, 1994), and *Jesus and the Politics of Interpretation*, by Elisabeth Schüssler Fiorenza (New York: Continuum, 2001). *Union Seminary Quarterly Review* 59 (2005): 203–8.

————, Noelle Damico, and Willie Baptist. "Responses of the Poor to Empire, Then and Now." *Union Seminary Quarterly Review* 59 (2005): 162–71.

————, and Willie Baptist. "Reading the Bible with the Poor." Pages 21–52 in *Reading the Bible in an Age of Crisis: Political Exegesis for a New Day*. Edited by Bruce Worthington. Minneapolis: Fortress, 2014.

————, and Willie Baptist. "Teach as We Fight, Learn as We Lead: Lessons in Pedagogy and the Poverty Initiative Model." Pages 160–78 in *Pedagogy for the Poor*. Edited by Willie Baptist and Jan Rehmann. New York: Teachers College, 2011.

Thiemann, Ronald. "The Unnamed Woman at Bethany." *Theology Today* 44 (1987): 179–88.

Thomas-Jones, Angela. *The Host in the Machine: Examining the Digital in the Social*. Oxford: Chandos, 2010.

Tigay, Jeffrey. *Deuteronomy: The JPS Torah Commentary*. New York: Jewish Publication Society, 2003.

Torre, Miguel de la. *Reading the Bible from the Margins*. Maryknoll, NY: Orbis, 2002.

Ukpong, Justin, Musa W. Dube, Gerald O. West, Alpheus Masoga, Norman K. Gottwald, Jeremy Punt, Tinyiko S. Maluleke, and Vincent L. Wimbush, eds. *Reading the Bible in the Global Village: Cape Town.* Global Perspectives on Biblical Scholarship. Cape Town: Society of Biblical Literature, 2002.

Velleius Paterculus. *Velleius Paterculus and Res Gestae Divi Augusti.* Loeb Classical Library. Cambridge: Harvard University Press, 1924.

Vermes, Geza. *Christian Beginnings: From Nazareth to Nicaea.* New Haven, CT: Yale University Press, 2013.

Wafawanaka, Robert. *Am I Still My Brother's Keeper? Biblical Perspectives on Poverty.* Lanham, MD: University Press of America, 2012.

Wagner, David. *What's Love Got to Do with It? A Critical Look at American Charity.* New York: New Press, 2000.

Wainwright, Elaine. *Towards a Feminist Critical Reading of the Gospel according to Matthew.* Berlin: de Gruyter, 1991.

Wallis, Jim. *Faith Works: Lessons from the Life of an Activist Preacher.* New York: Random House, 2000.

———. *God's Politics: Why the Right Gets It Wrong and the Left Doesn't Get It.* San Francisco: HarperCollins, 2005.

Wells, Harry K. *Pragmatism: Philosophy of Imperialism.* New York: International Publishers, 1954.

Wengst, Klaus. *Pax Romana and the Peace of Jesus Christ.* Philadelphia: Fortress, 1987.

West, Gerald. *The Academy of the Poor: Towards a Dialogical Reading of the Bible.* Interventions. Sheffield: Sheffield Academic Press, 1999.

———. *Biblical Hermeneutics of Liberation: Modes of Reading the Bible in the South African Context.* Pietermaritzburg: Cluster, 1991.

West, Guida. *The National Welfare Rights Movement: The Social Protest of Poor Women.* Westport, CT: Praeger, 1981.

White, Leland. "Grid and Group in Matthew's Community: The Righteousness/Honor Code in the Sermon on the Mount." *Semeia* 35 (1986): 61–90.

Williams, Delores. *Sisters in the Wilderness: The Challenge of Womanist God-Talk.* Maryknoll, NY: Orbis, 2000.

Wimbush, Vincent. *African Americans and the Bible: Sacred Text and Social Texture.* New York: Continuum, 2001.

———. *The Bible and African Americans: A Brief History.* Minneapolis: Fortress, 2003.

Winget, Larry. *You're Broke Because You Want to Be: How to Stop Getting By and Start Getting Ahead.* New York: Gotham, 2009.

Wright, N. T. *Who Was Jesus?* Grand Rapids: Eerdmans, 1993.

Zanker, Paul. *The Power of Images in the Age of Augustus.* Ann Arbor: University of Michigan Press, 1990.

Zinn, Howard. *SNCC [Student Nonviolent Coordinating Committee]: The New Abolitionists.* Boston: Beacon, 1964.

Zucchino, David. *Myth of the Welfare Queen.* New York: Scribner, 1997.

Subject Index

Adams, Glenda, 23
Alan, Russ J., 19n
Almirón, Erika, 42, 45, 48, 49
almsgiving. *See* charity and almsgiving in the Roman Empire (euergetism)
Alston, Onleilove, 30, 32, 35, 41–43, 45, 48
anointed ones (biblical language of), 133–37; Matthew's term *ho christos*, 130–31, 132, 134–35; and "messiah" in the Hebrew Bible, 133–34; *myron* (ointment for prophets and kings), 102n, 104, 130, 135–40, 140n; pattern of anointing kings and prophets in the Hebrew Bible, 135–37, 139–40, 140n
anointing at Bethany (Matthew 26:6–13), 34–52, 100–124, 149–51; as act of care and love for Jesus as poor person, 138–39; anointing as king/Christ/messiah, 41–42, 50, 116, 130–33, 138, 139–41; Bethany: house of Simon the Leper, 36, 40–41, 95–97; biblical scholars' debate over whether poverty is the subject, 23–26, 97; in context of Jesus's actions in the Temple, 40, 96–97, 119n, 129; in context of Last Judgment and Jesus's identification with the poor, 39, 46, 52, 80, 99, 127–28, 146; in context of Roman Empire's social and economic inequality, 40, 95–99; disciples' chiding of the unnamed woman for wasting the ointment and destroying the vial, 24, 42–43, 101–6, 112; disciples' suggestion that the ointment could have been sold for charity, 24, 42–44, 101–3, 106, 112; intertextuality with Deuteronomy's Jubilee codes, 44, 45, 51, 60; Jesus on the disciples' misunderstanding of the unnamed woman's gift, 43, 101–6, 112–13, 118–20; Jesus's announcement of his impending death, 44–46, 98–99, 115–17, 119–20, 127–30; Jesus's economic critique of charity, 31, 43–44, 48–49, 101–3, 112–20; Jesus's economic critique of poverty, 50–51, 73–74, 95–99, 100–124, 140–41; Jesus's passing his mission on to his disciples, 98–99, 119–20; Jesus's praise of the unnamed woman, 112–15, 118–20; John's Gospel, 16, 50, 95n, 102; Luke's Gospel, 50, 95n, 104, 134; Mark's Gospel, 16, 95n, 98–99, 106n, 140n; as modern parable, 149–51; Poverty Scholars' reanalysis of, 34–52; as preparation of Jesus's body for burial, 45, 49, 115–17, 140n; the shared meal and open commensality, 96; transla-

173

Subject Index

Jubilee. *See* Deuteronomy 15's Jubilee passages; *shemittah* (debt forgiveness/remission and sabbatical year)

Judas: betrayal of Jesus, 120–24, 129–30; blood money and the chief priests, 121–22; John's Gospel on money for the poor, 42–43, 120; and money transactions in Matthew's Passion Narrative, 120–24; potter's field burial, 121–22

JUNTOS (Philadelphia), 42

Kahl, Brigitte, 54n

Kairos Center for Religions, Rights, and Social Justice, xvii, 100; Poverty Initiative/Kairos Center at Union Theological Seminary, xvi–xvii, 23, 30, 100

Kensington Welfare Rights Union (KWRU) (Philadelphia), xvii, 1–12, 151–53; community support for, 2, 3–4, 7; homeless families and Tent City project, xvi, 2–4, 9, 151–52; homeless takeover of St. Edward's Catholic Church, 1–12, 151–52; identification with Jesus as poor and homeless, 4–5; and the "New Underground Railroad," 4; and poverty of the Kensington neighborhood, 9–10, 152

Keyes, Charlotte, 38–39, 41–44, 46, 51

King, Martin Luther, Jr., 59, 75–76, 125; call for end of the "three evils of society," xviii; and a "freedom church of the poor," 2, 153; Poor People's Campaign, xvii, xviii, 38, 75n; on true compassion vs charity (as "more than flinging a coin at a beggar"), 44, 49, 100–101, 124

"King of the Jews," 77–78, 131–33, 142

Kireopoulos, Antonios, 14–15

Klausner, Joseph, 133n

Kris, Mary Ellen, 45–46, 51–52

Landless Workers' Movement of Brazil, xvii

Last Judgment and Jesus's identification with the poor ("the least of these"), 39, 46, 52, 80, 99, 127–28, 146

The Last Week of Jesus (Borg and Crossan), 45, 59

Levine, Amy-Jill, 24–25

liberation theology, 53, 147

Lindsay, Phil, 44–45

Longenecker, Bruce, 84n

Luke's Gospel: anointing at Bethany in, 50, 95n, 104, 134; communion formula, 117; Jesus's inaugural speech on the poor, xi, 87, 146–47; Jesus's poverty and homelessness, 5

Lundblad, Barbara, 153

Luz, Ulrich, 25–26, 140n

Macon, Isaac, 23

Mailman School of Public Health at Columbia University, ix

Mark's Gospel: on almsgiving, 106n; the anointing at Bethany in, 16, 95n, 98–99, 106n, 140n; on Judas's betrayal, 120n; the women bringing spices to the tomb, 140n

Mary Magdalene, 140n

Matthew 26:11 ("the poor you will always have with you"): grammatical structure, 98; intertextuality with Deuteronomy 15's Jubilee codes, 31, 44, 45, 51, 60, 63–64, 73–74, 146; Jesus as poor person making the statement, 35–36, 51–52, 76–80, 97–99; and Jesus's critique of poverty/inequality in the Roman Empire, 50–51, 73–74, 95–99, 100–124, 140–41; Jesus's economic critique of charity, 31, 43–44, 48–49, 101–3, 112–20; and King's quote on true compassion and charity, 44, 49, 100–101, 124. *See also* anointing at Bethany (Matthew 26:6–13); biblical response to poverty (popular and academic treatments of); Jesus's economic critique of poverty

Matthew's Gospel: the adoption of Je-

Scripture Index